ON THE ACCURACY OF
ECONOMIC OBSERVATIONS

ON THE
ACCURACY OF
ECONOMIC
OBSERVATIONS

SECOND EDITION, COMPLETELY REVISED

❖ ❖

BY OSKAR MORGENSTERN

PRINCETON, NEW JERSEY
PRINCETON UNIVERSITY PRESS

PREFACE TO THE FIRST EDITION

This study is the preliminary result of a prolonged concern with the properties of economic data. Most recently the problem of accuracy arose again in connection with an investigation into the structure of the American economy by means of input-output tables. These are arrangements of the sales and purchases of industries which show the interconnectedness of the entire economy. They are attempts to provide information Quesnay intended to give in the ancient "Tableau Economique"; they were first used by W. W. Leontief.[1]

Investigations by various authors will be published subsequently. It is hoped that they will initiate a Princeton series of Econometric Studies dealing with the manifold problems of economic models and their quantitative application. One of these applications, "linear programming," is at present under consideration by various groups.

The subsequent pages were presented in only slightly different form at the Conference on Linear Programming called by the Cowles Commission at the University of Chicago in June 1949. The *Proceedings* of that conference, which will be published in the near future (by J. Wiley & Sons, New York) under the title "Activity Analysis of Production and Allocation," will contain a two-page summary of this monograph. The Symposium will provide the most comprehensive picture of the purposes, methods and accomplishments of linear programming in the economic domain so far available. Except for various references to this field and to input-output tables, the text of this study is, however, entirely self-contained. An abstract of the original paper was also presented on behalf of the author

---

[1] *The Structure of the American Economy*, Cambridge, (1941). Compare also "Input-Output Analysis and Its Use in Peace and War Economies" (paper by Leontief and discussion by S. Fabricant and others), *American Economic Review, Proceedings*, Vol. XXXIX, 1949, pp. 211–240.

by Professor S. Kuznets to the Congress of the International Statistical Institute at Bern in September 1949.

This work was undertaken with the support of the Office of Naval Research under contract N6onr-27009 and grateful acknowledgment is made.

Many experts were consulted at various stages. I wish to express particular thanks to Professor H. Hotelling and Professor F. F. Stephan, who have helped me to clear up some particular points, informed me of some special literature and encouraged me to publish the study.

My greatest indebtedness is to Mrs. Judith B. Balderston, Research Assistant at Princeton University, for her untiring efforts in preparing much of the material and for actually drafting several sections from which the following text finally arose.

The responsibility for errors, however, rests alone with me.

OSKAR MORGENSTERN

February 1950
Princeton University

PREFACE TO SECOND EDITION

THIS BOOK addresses itself to both the general reader and the professional economist. The former will see that decisions made in business and in public service are based on data that are known with much less certainty than generally assumed by the public or the government. The second will discover that even most widely accepted figures frequently have error components of unexpected magnitude, and consequently cast doubt on many currently accepted analyses in economics. We all shall have to go through a long and painful process of adjusting to the fact of error. Although the natural sciences—sometimes called the "exact" sciences—have been concerned with the accuracy of measurements and observations from their earliest beginnings, a great crisis was nevertheless suffered by them when it became clear that absolute precision and certainty of important kinds of observations were impossible to achieve in principle. The situation in the social sciences may not be simpler, but even if it should be, there exists no comparable tradition of exploring errors and evaluating their influence upon economic science and its application. However, when the true conditions are realized, there will evolve a more powerful and realistic theory. We must carefully distinguish between what we think we know and what we really do and can know.

The second edition of this work has been almost completely rewritten. The first edition, published in 1950, went out of print in 1952 but the republication was postponed time and again until now. Other work has been responsible for the delay, notwithstanding the fact that the problems treated in the present work have always occupied a central role in my life. The temptation to let the book grow was therefore very strong and, despite efforts to resist, this volume is now more than twice as large as its predecessor. I hope it still strikes a good balance between readability and thoroughness. Indeed, completeness is out of the question, since the number of economic data is limitless; and the task of scientific enquiry being an unending one, the problems of knowledge can never be resolved to our full satisfaction.

Over the years many friends and associates, too numerous to mention, have been good enough to discuss the issues raised by the first edition of this book. I want to thank in particular, however, Karl Borch, Clive W. J. Granger, Michio Hatanaka, Herman F. Karreman, Johann Pfanzagl, Frederick F. Stephan, George Stolnitz, and Mitsuo Suzuki. For all later phases of the preparation of the manuscript I owe a great debt to Nevins D. Baxter, John G. Cragg, Morton Davis, and Dorothy Green with whom almost all points were discussed in detail, and who gave valuable suggestions and support which sprang from their genuine interest in this venture. The manuscript was typed by Lois Crooks and Helen Perna with their usual competence.

This work was done at the Econometric Research Program of Princeton University, which is variously supported by the Office of Naval Research, The National Science Foundation, the Rockefeller Foundation, the Carnegie Corporation, and industry. Grateful acknowledgement is made to all of them. In the preface to the first edition, the hope was expressed that a series of econometric studies would be initiated. Several books in this general area have since been sponsored by and are attributable to the program, and other works are in the publisher's hands or in preparation. In addition, a series in Mathematical Economics, edited by Harold Kuhn and myself, is being initiated at Princeton University Press. The publisher is owed a great debt for the patience with which he has waited for the manuscript of this revised edition to become available.

OSKAR MORGENSTERN

Econometric Research Program
Princeton University
April 1963

❖ CONTENTS ❖

ix

CONTENTS

❧ TABLES ☙

xi

⟿ FIGURES ⟾

CONTENTS

PART ONE

ACCURACY AND ERROR

Qui numerare incipit errare incipit

❖ CHAPTER I ❖

THE NATURE OF ECONOMIC DATA

1. Social and Physical Statistics

THIS STUDY aims at examining the conditions governing the accuracy of planned quantitative economic observations and, more widely, of economic statistics. Though this may seem to be a very simple matter, it will appear, on the contrary, that it is involved and difficult. Furthermore, the question of accuracy necessarily has ramifications in many fields, notably in that of economic and statistical theory.

We shall not deal to any particular extent with the accuracy of economic information not available in statistical, i.e., numerical, form. There is a vast body of important material currently used by economists which is non-numerical. It is either historical-descriptive in nature, or it consists of direct qualitative empirical observations by a given investigator who lives in a certain economic milieu or who participates in economic activities and business decisions. Some further information is derived from introspection, and this too has played a considerable role in the development of various branches of economic theory. All of these sources of information have, of course, various kinds of error for which allowance should be made, if only the source and extent of the error were known. This is of especial importance when this type of evidence is brought into contact with that which appears in numerical form. Such combinations are inevitable and are therefore highly characteristic of economics.

All economic decisions, whether private or business, as well as those involving economic policy, have the characteristic that quantitative and non-quantitative information must be combined into one act of decision. It would be desirable to understand how these two classes of information can best be combined. Obviously, there must exist a point at which it is no longer meaningful to sharpen the numerically available information when the other, wholly qualitative, part is important,

3

though a notion of its "accuracy" or "reliability" has not been developed.

We shall not be much concerned with qualitative forms of information or evidence. In particular, we are not dealing with the deep-lying problems of combining quantitative and non-quantitative evidence as it enters economic analysis. Such a discussion would require a more profound methodological study than is attempted here. However, it will be useful if the reader will remind himself of the existence of this problem in evaluating the whole of our present subject matter.

There are many reasons why one should be deeply concerned with the "accuracy" of quantitative economic data and observations. Clearly, anyone making use of *measurements* and *data* wishes them to be accurate and significant in a sense still to be defined specifically. For that reason a level of accuracy has to be established. It will depend first of all on the particular purpose for which the measurement is made. Generally, an economic description consists of simultaneous or successive observations from various fields, combined with deductive analysis. It will be seen later (Chapter V) that the value of an observation depends not only on its own immediately recognizable level of accuracy but also upon the particular way the observation has been combined with others (many of them non-numerical), the nature and number of computational steps involved in order to arrive at a desired form, e.g., an index, etc. The very notion of accuracy and the acceptability of a measurement, observation, description, count—whatever the concrete case might be—is inseparably tied to the use to which it is to be put. In other words, there is always a theory or model, however roughly formulated it may be, a purpose or use to which the statistic has to refer, in order to talk meaningfully about accuracy. In this manner the topic soon stops being primitive; on the contrary, very deep-lying problems are encountered, some of which have only recently been recognized.

The second part of this investigation of economic data is only a sample and illustration for a large-scale empirical study which ought to be undertaken cooperatively by many institutions. It arose originally from the needs of a specific situation: Economists are interested in the collection and use of data giving information about production and the volume of sales and receipts by industry arranged in so-called "input-output" tables. These are to be studied by means of suitable models and should become amenable to numerical evaluation (prediction). This involves an exceedingly large number of computations, and at least for purely mathematical reasons alone, quantitative information about the quality of the data is indispensable.[1]

To give an idea of the magnitude of the tasks involved in input-output studies it is sufficient to visualize that the representation of a highly complex modern economy by 100 industries or activities is in fact not very detailed. But if the sales of each industry to each other industry are arranged in rows and the purchases of each from all others in columns, we obtain a table $100 \times 100 = 10,000$ fields. In this there will be many zeros, because some industries or activities have no direct or only negligible dealings or connections with other industries or activities. (While every industry will buy soap, only a few will buy jet engines.) If we were to represent the American economy by 200 different activities, there would be 40,000 fields, a truly formidable number of possible interconnections. To interpret these a system of equations has to be written. Even on a much smaller scale, say 10 industries, "direct" and "intuitive" interpretation is impossible, as anyone will confirm who has ever guessed at the solution of a system of only three linear equations in three unknowns. Any result which by necessity must be numerical can be obtained only by extensive computations. The nature of these computations depends on the economic model that is supposed to describe the form of the interdependence. Clearly, it would not be advisable, indeed it would be outright foolish, to deal with these exceedingly complex problems in a practical-numerical manner unless the data are really satisfactory, where "satisfactory" must be given a specific meaning. And when we have 10,000, 40,000, or even 250,000 fields to fill with information about the sales and purchases of individual

---

[1] For an exposition of the input-output approach and for the most penetrating examination of its contributions and limitations, cf. M. Hatanaka, *The Workability of Input-Output Analysis* (Ludwigshafen am Rhein, 1960). This book can serve as a model for combining economic and statistical techniques of investigation.

industries, the problems of accuracy immediately assume formidable proportions. Also, unless the quality of the information warranted it, it would be unjustified to feed so many numbers into expensive electronic computers for which there are always important alternative uses, for example in other sciences. But without specific investigations, no one can know what the quality is, or ought to be, so that the undertaking of millions of computations could be justified. Whether the data are "satisfactory" depends on their use and on the fundamental mathematical problems that are involved in making such decisions.

What was said here about input-output tables serves only as an illustration. Wherever an economic argument is being made, or an inference is derived from comparing statistics of different economic activities, the matter of the accuracy of these data arises. This may involve questions of comparability on grounds of definitions and concepts used. It may concern numerical operations of various kinds. For the latter the big problem is to what extent the methods of analysis are sensitive to errors that the data inevitably must contain. Proper attention will be paid to this issue in Chapter VI.

A study of the entire complex of the accuracy of existing statistics or observations is not only helpful but also indispensable in designing programs for the collection of new, improved data. Since the process of producing statistics is for the most part continuous, i.e., an unending one, the practical significance of such studies is immediate. In many offices in which statistics are gathered special efforts are being made to improve the quality of the data; nevertheless a systematic approach is frequently lacking. Some scientific organizations have taken up the issue from time to time without registering decisive progress. We mention, for example, the International Statistical Institute. The Committee of Statistical Experts of the League of Nations, of which the author was a member, was concerned with similar questions, but had to limit itself either to theoretical problems (e.g., designing a logically satisfactory scheme for the making of statistics on capital formation or on balances of payments[2]) or to the problems of statistical policy (e.g., im-

---

[2] Cf. "Statistics Relating to Capital Formation," by the Committee of Statistical Experts, League of Nations, Geneva, 1938.

plementing international agreements directed toward the uniform classification of goods entering foreign trade). Such work, however necessary and successful, now being continued on a much larger scale by the United Nations, can only be preliminary to an investigation of the value of the observations, because, as will be seen, this value depends on the particular theoretical framework into which they are to be fitted and upon the kind and number of the calculations involved.

So far everything that has been said applies *mutatis mutandis* also to the natural, i.e., physical and biological, sciences. There, too, the "accuracy" of observations depends upon the uses to which the data are to be put, and consequently the mathematical problems arising from the extent of calculation and numerical application are identical. Even if economic statistics did not possess their own peculiar properties, the fact that examination of accuracy has been more neglected by economists than by natural scientists (to whom this is now a routine matter) provides an excuse for investigating the situation here. However, economic and social statistics do have their own additional peculiarities, as the following discussion will demonstrate.

Fundamentally, we observe that *at least all sources of error that occur in the natural sciences also occur in the social sciences:* or, in other words, the statistical problems of the social sciences cannot possibly be less serious than those of the natural sciences. Indeed, the situation is far more complicated and therefore requires the most detailed scrutiny. Consequently, the treatment of errors of observation in the social sciences has to be at least as extensive and the standards have to be at least as severe as those used in the natural sciences. In fact, however, there is much less occupation with errors than in the other fields. This is undoubtedly one of the reasons why the social sciences have had a rather uncertain development.

In examining the nature and possibilities of errors in economic data, we use only a common sense approach—or what we believe to be common sense. The errors in these data cannot always be formulated according to strict statistical theory for the simple reason that no such exhaustive theory is available for many social phenomena. The opportunity will arise subsequently to point out some of the most important gaps. They will turn out to be serious enough to deserve the attention of many minds.

2. THE REPORTING OF ECONOMIC STATISTICS

In the *physical sciences* it is customary to report data together with their carefully determined errors of observation and use them correspondingly. When the error is not mentioned explicitly, it is because it can generally be assumed to be well-known, or because the values reported have already entered into physical theories which determine an admissible error level, and their limitations are then those of the respective theory. To give an illustration, it may not be necessary to state every time the error in the measurement of the velocity of light because this value is indissolubly tied up with the theory of relativity. The situation is similar for other constants (cf. Chapter II, Section 9). When new measurements are made the error must always be stated. Thus exaggeration of the significance of the new results is avoided, and they assume their proper place in physical theory. Some measurements are good, others are poor, but the effort is constantly being made to reduce the error as far as possible. This depends on new ideas, new instruments, and new materials; and so the knowledge of physical data is forever being improved.

In the *social sciences* such habits have not been developed. This is no doubt partly due to the extreme difficulty of estimating errors of observation quantitatively, as will be seen in the subsequent pages. Furthermore, experimental-empirical work is still only in its infancy in economics (and even more so in sociology)—in spite of the impressive masses of statistics that pour out daily. Also, the specific connection between the reporting of data and their use for purposes of economic theory is weak and uncertain.

Yet, it ought to be clear *a priori* that most economic statistics should not be stated in the manner in which they are commonly reported, pretending an accuracy that may be completely out of reach and for the most part is not demanded. Changes in consumers' total spending power are reported and taken seriously, down to the last billion or less (i.e., *variations* of less than one-half of one percent!), price indices for wholesale and retail prices are shown to second decimals, even though there have been so many computing steps that the rounding-off errors alone may obliterate such a degree of precision. Unemployment figures of several millions are given down to the last 1,000's (i.e., one-hundredths of one percent "accuracy"!), when certainly the 100,000's or in some cases perhaps even the millions are in doubt.[3] All this is stated without any reference whatsoever to the error of observation. It will be seen later that national income and consumers' spending power probably cannot be known now in part without an error of ± 10 to ± 15 percent.[4]

Even though the public is not informed about comparative detail and is fundamentally in no position to judge, it is sometimes extremely suspicious of economic and social statistics. False opinions prevail—which the statistician rightly tries to destroy—according to which anything and everything can be "proved" by statistics, that statistics are only another, more sophisticated form of lying, etc. While fundamentally untrue, such opinions persist. It would be difficult to show that they are also directed towards the wide use of statistics in the natural sciences. This is, indeed, a devastating popular criticism[5] of the state of economic information. The public is further confused by the fact that for one and the same phenomenon, often widely different measurements are offered at the same time, e.g., for the number of unemployed, the national income, or the total amount of some agricultural product. The expert insider may be able to account for such differences and know, for example, that the harvest estimates of the Department of Agriculture have as a rule been better than those of the Bureau of the Census, but even he will usually find it difficult to follow up all references in order to arrive at this judgment, provided the references are even given at the place where he encounters the

[3] But a probable error of 2 or 3 percent is considered small enough in some new and decisive measurements of the stability of planetary motions in investigating the validity of relativity theory! Cf. G. M. Clemence (U.S. Naval Observatory), "Relativity Effects in Planetary Motion," *Proc. Amer. Phil. Soc.*, Vol. 93, p. 532.

[4] See Chapter XIV below.

[5] A good and popular account exposing frequent deliberate and involuntary misuses of statistics by choosing "suitable" bases for indexes, poor averages, misleading graphs, etc., appears in D. Huff, *How to Lie With Statistics* (New York, 1954).

statistics. But the expert who knows about agricultural statistics may be quite helpless (or at least be confronted with a task of major proportions) when it comes to appraising the statistics of savings, foreign trade, or employment. How can the ordinary user of statistics know about such things?

This list could be continued almost endlessly. We prefer, however, to take up the issue systematically and to come back to the matter of presentation of economic statistics after a more complete discussion of error. Concrete examples will then be shown in Part II.

The omission of any reference to error also has an important bearing on policy-making. Since decisions for far-reaching measures are often based upon information about alleged, minute changes in phenomena, investigations of the present type should have high practical significance. Business also must be deeply concerned about these matters since its decisions are dependent upon information about markets, prices, profits, national income, and many other factors. For example, wage agreements involving millions of workers are sometimes based on price indices which record alleged changes of price levels up to one-tenth of one percent! Common price and cost of living indices are reported in this form. They are splashed across the front pages of newspapers together with the most important political news of the day. These price changes are then interpreted as a measure of the success or failure of government policy and the existence or absence of inflation. In fact these minute changes show nothing at all.

The selection of a particular index out of several, or even the question of which prices to include and which formula to use assumes immediate practical significance and is part of the political power struggle. This will become an increasingly important issue when new methods, which are now being developed for the solution of problems of business logistics and business strategy, are used in practical life. At present, "business surveys" and "market researches" are sometimes suspect (quite aside from their interpretations), especially when they are based on questionnaires, canvassing, polling by salesmen, and are not handled with the statistical acumen these methods demand.[6] Similarly, the value of the logistics programs and related studies in the Armed Forces rests on the quality of the data.

Finally, we mention a serious organizational difficulty in discussing and criticizing statistics. These are virtually always produced by large organizations, government or private; and these organizations are frequently mutually dependent upon each other in order to function normally. Often one office cannot publicly raise questions about the work of another, even when it suspects the quality of the work, since this might adversely affect bureaucratic-diplomatic relations between the two and the flow of information from one office to another might be hampered. A marked *esprit de corps* prevails. All offices must try to impress the public with the quality of their work. Should too many doubts be raised, financial support from Congress or other sources may not be forthcoming. More than once has it happened that Congressional appropriations were endangered when it was suspected that government statistics might not be 100 percent accurate. It is natural, therefore, that various offices will defend the quality of their work even to an unreasonable degree.

Congress has repeatedly made unreasonable demands which are either impossible to fulfill or can be met only at fabulous cost. It appears natural to a congressman that the number of cows be counted right down to the last cow in each county of his district, though from a national point of view that number may be satisfactory if known to the first digit only. Similarly, businessmen often take the position that aggregative statistical projections, based on samples, be detailed to a degree which would exceed the power of any known statistical technique even in the absence of any sampling error. The notion that a statistic with a known error need not be useless or is incompetently made is not easily established. But if it is being made clear how enormously the costs of every improvement in detail rise, then it will be necessary to make a deliberate choice be-

---

[6] There exist, of course, excellent organizations in these fields which use the most modern statistical techniques; some are associated with universities, others are commercial enterprises.

tween the value of further information of a certain kind and its cost.

Only when an adequate scientific spirit prevails among those who produce and those who use the statistics, can one expect a substantial change in the general situation. Such a spirit must originate among the scientists and scholars using statistics. They must refrain first of all from applying statistics unless they fulfill exacting, clearly described standards. In this way, they will come to the aid of the statistics producing agencies and protect them against unreasonable demands. The public in general and Congress in particular must be made to understand that there cannot be absolute accuracy, that there must be error, and that the important thing to do is to try to uncover, remove, or at least limit the error. Everyone has to learn how to live with errors and incomplete information. What is more, the situation is never stable, making this a very difficult, continuing task. The physical world is not absolutely determined, and the social world is obviously only a part of it.

The professional users of economic and social statistics strangely enough often seem to be less skeptical than the public. The widespread, and undoubtedly exaggerated, distrust by the latter group is exceedingly important to the attempts to improve economic statistics in at least two ways. First, progress in this field cannot be accomplished without broad public support of the appropriations of funds. Second, the willingness of this group to provide information to the statistician depends on the public's confidence in the information previously published and on its approval or disapproval of these statistics. Distortions in the presentation of statistics may occur when the organizations using the data are completely different from those originally collecting the data. These interrelations are, however, of great practical significance.

⌁ CHAPTER II ⌁

SOURCES AND ERRORS OF
ECONOMIC STATISTICS

THE TERM "error" has in many contexts a precise statistical meaning. It can be expressed numerically as the probable error or standard error in comparing various samples of the same population or, as in our case, various measurements of the same economic quantity.

In the present study, a slightly broader notion of error will be used. It will not always be possible to apply current statistical theory to our treatment, for elements of bias and differences in definition are present which prevent normal distribution of the observations, creating circumstances which cannot be readily treated according to classical notions of probable error. Thus, we shall be forced to use a common sense approach and, at times, literary argument rather than exacting statistical measures.

An error is normally viewed to be an expression of imperfection and of incompleteness in description. It is on principle impossible to remove either of them fully, but work should be directed toward expressing numerically the range of the joint influence of both the incompleteness and imperfection. Such numerical expressions would guide the use of the observations and also provide a stimulus to reduce the errors. Philosophically speaking, the problem of error is much deeper, as particularly modern physical theory has demonstrated. But our concern is much more restricted and so we proceed to discuss the most important characteristics of economic (and many other social) statistics.

1. LACK OF DESIGNED EXPERIMENTS

Economic statistics are not, as a rule, the result of designed experiments,[1] although one of the earlier great economists, J.

[1] Exceptions are, e.g., the attempts by L. L. Thurstone to determine indifference curves, about which cf. "The Indifference Function," *Journal of*

H. von Thünen, conducted careful experiments in administering his estate, kept extensive records of his operations which he then analyzed, thereby anticipating much of the later marginal utility theory. But in general, economic statistics are merely by-products or results of business and government activities and have to be taken as these determine. Therefore, they often measure, describe, or simply record something that is not exactly the phenomenon in which the economist would be interested. They are often dependent on legal rather than economic definitions of processes.

A significant difference between the use of data in the natural and social sciences is that in the former the *producer* of the observations is usually also their *user*. If he does not exploit them fully himself, they are passed on to others who, in the tradition of the sciences, are precisely informed about the origin and the manner of obtaining these data. Furthermore, new data have to be fitted into a vast body of data which have been tested over and over again and into theories which have passed through the crucible of application. Also, the quality of the work of the observers is well-known, and this contributes to establishing a level of precision of and confidence in the information. In the natural sciences, even the most abstract theorists are exceedingly well informed about the precise nature, circumstances, and limitations of experiments and measurements. Indeed, without such knowledge their work would be entirely impossible or meaningless.

Social Psychology, Vol. II (1931), pp. 139–167; W. A. Wallis and M. Friedman, "The Empirical Derivation of Indifference Functions," in *Studies on Mathematical Economics and Econometrics* (Chicago, 1942). More recently we have the determination of utility functions by F. Mosteller and P. Nogee. Here real experiments under strict controls are involved. Cf. "An Experimental Measurement of Utility," *Journal of Political Economy,* Vol. 59 (1951), pp. 371–404, followed by much work by many authors. An extensive discussion of the role of experiments is given in my "Experiment and Large Scale Computation in Economics" in *Economic Activity Analysis* (New York, 1954), pp. 484–549. Since then much experimental work has been done, particularly in regard to n-person games. (Cf. *Recent Advances in Game Theory,* Proceedings of a Princeton University Conference, 1961, especially the survey by L. E. Fouraker.) This will not be discussed here since these activities lie on the edge of our present concern, which is with the more commonplace statistics of the economist.

In the social sciences the situation is quite different. It is not often feasible (because of the mass observations—cf. 5 below—or for reasons of general lack of information) to be aware of the detailed nature of the data. Summarization of data is often performed by widely separated statistical workers who are likewise far removed from the later users. And finally, the tradition has simply not yet fully established itself for the users to insist upon being fully informed about all steps of the gathering and computing of statistics. Anyone who has used economic statistics, even when prepared by the finest economic-statistical institutions, knows how exceedingly difficult it is to reestablish the conditions under which they were collected, their domain, the precise activity they define, etc., although it may be decisive to be fully informed about these various stages. One of the main reasons for this difficulty is that economic data as a rule have to cover long periods of time in order to be useful. It is rarely the case that single pieces of information, not concerned with processes that extend into the past and are likely to continue into an indefinite future, are of value for economic analysis. Thus economic data are normally time series, i.e., numbers of the same kind of event, say the price of bread, strung out over time. When the series are long, as they ought to be, it is often exceedingly difficult to know how the data were obtained in the past and to what extent temporal comparability is assured.

Many producers of primary statistics make a considerable effort to inform the reader of the details of composition, stages of classification, and all other characteristics of the statistics. There are too many cases, however, where this description is sketchy and where large gaps remain. Sometimes this is due to negligence and the belief that the authority of the reporting agency is great enough to inspire full confidence in the statistics. Such authority never exists for scientific purposes. On the other hand, the great detail involved in the collection of most economic information makes it virtually impossible physically to reproduce the entire background of the descriptive detail each time that some figures are given or used. Sometimes the official commentary to statistical tables is exceedingly lengthy and fills volumes, impossible to absorb in a manner which would lead to a correction of the given numbers by the user. By swamping the user with hosts of footnotes and explanations, the makers of statistics try to absolve themselves from the need to indicate numerical error estimates. Thus, a dilemma exists that could only be overcome by the development and indication of a quantitative measure expressing the error. As will be seen, such numerical expressions are lacking at the present time; in some cases they may never become available.

The deficiency of information on procedures of data gathering is usually less striking when *sampling* methods are used to obtain economic statistics. Although a sample may sometimes be bad and though there may be other objectionable features, their construction is subject to scientific scrutiny, and the problems that must be solved in setting up a good sample are very well known. The solutions are a function of the state of sampling theory and its application in the given case. Sampling statistics in economics—a technique which we do not discuss here any further—are fortunately gaining in importance. They suggest themselves in particular when great aggregates have to be measured, such as the determination of the volume of industrial output, share of market, sales, foreign trade, and so on. Sampling is also highly valuable in constructing price statistics. In general, it can be said that the possibilities of sampling procedures have not yet been fully utilized in economics. Wherever estimates are necessary, and often they are the only possible way to arrive at some aggregates, sampling is indispensable. This is true, for example, in estimating items in the balance of payments, such as travelers' expenditures abroad, etc., where a direct approach to totals is clearly out of the question. In addition, sampling statistics can be used as checks on complete counts in order to improve the latter. Unfortunately not enough use is made of this opportunity.

Sampling, however, is a possible additional source of error when mistakes are made in the application of the technique. Such mistakes are sometimes exceedingly difficult to avoid and some striking instances are known, as revealed by special investigations.[2] Furthermore, sampling statistics are susceptible to

[2] Social Science Research Council, *Committee Report on Pre-Election Polls and Forecasts*, 1949.

European countries with capital punishment threatened for disclosure! Even in the United States incomplete figures are released in the field of atomic energy, although the known total appropriations for the Atomic Energy Commission indicate that this is one of the largest American industrial undertakings.[8] The same applies in this field to all present (and will apply to all future) atomic powers. The budget for the Central Intelligence Agency, unquestionably running into hundreds of millions of dollars, is hidden in a multitude of other accounts in the Federal Budget, invalidating also those accounts. The Russian defense budget is only incompletely known. An example of government falsification of statistics is Nazi Germany's stating its gold reserves far below those actually available, as was revealed by later information. Or, more subtly, indexes of prices are computed and published from irrelevant prices in order to hide a true price movement.[9] Central banks in many countries, the venerable Bank of England not excepted, have for decades published deliberately misleading statistics, as, for example, when part of the gold in their possession is put under "other assets" and only part is shown as "gold." In democratic Great Britain before World War II, the Government's "Exchange Equalization Account" suppressed[10] for a considerable period all statistics about its gold holdings, although it became clear later that these exceeded the amount of gold shown to be held by the Bank of England at the time. This list could be greatly lengthened. If respectable governments falsify information for policy purposes, if the Bank of England lies and hides or falsifies data, then how can one expect minor operators in the financial world always to be truthful, especially when they know

[8] This is of great importance for the construction of reasonably specific economic models when numerical evaluation is desired.

[9] This, however, occurs at a higher level of statistics with which we are not concerned in this study. It is, of course, of the greatest importance. We are dealing in this book chiefly with *primitive* observations.

[10] Suppression *per se* is, of course, not an outright falsification. But the point is that by means of suppression other information of even high "accuracy" becomes invalidated, if not wholly worthless. The accompanying and inevitable misinterpretations of other statistics may be intended. Corrections are then not made by the suppressing agencies because these would permit conclusions referring back to the hidden information. Thus, we have at best specious accuracy (cf. Chapter III).

the other kinds of error derived from faulty classification, time discrepancies, poor recording, etc. These will be discussed below. Sampling errors, of course, can be estimated and are usually stated. Although they do not account for the entire error or provide a way to its numerical evaluation, the indication of this component is extremely valuable.

Even though sampling procedures are being more widely introduced, the largest masses of economic statistics simply accrue without any overall scientific design or plan. It would probably be impossible to make general plans for collecting statistics without violating some basic principles of the free exchange economy. Thus the development of economics is dependent to a very high degree upon an agglomeration of statistics which in the main is rather accidental from the point of view of economic theory.

The interplay between theory, measurement, and data collection should be as intimate in economics as it is in physics, but we are far from having reached this condition. However, the signs are multiplying that economics is moving in this direction.[3]

2. HIDING OF INFORMATION, LIES

There is overly often a deliberate attempt to hide information. In other words, economic and social statistics are frequently based on evasive answers and *deliberate lies* of various types. These lies arise, principally, from misunderstandings, from fear of tax authorities, from uncertainty about or dislike of government interference and plans, or from the desire to mislead competitors. Nothing of this sort occurs in nature. Nature may hold back information, is always difficult to understand, but it is believed that she does not lie deliberately.[4] Ein-

[3] A useful survey of the problem of measurement in the various sciences is found in *Measurement, Definitions and Theories*, C. W. Churchman and P. Ratoosh, eds. (New York, 1959). This book has contributions by Karl Menger, Patrick Suppes, R. Duncan Luce, and others. An important publication is J. Pfanzagl, *Die Axiomatischen Grundlagen einer allgemeinen Theorie des Messens* (Würzburg, 1959). Cf. also J. von Neumann and O. Morgenstern, *op. cit.*, pp. 16–24.

[4] Hence, the description of statistics as a two-person game has to take both of these classes separately into account. For the view that the fundamental problem of statistics is equivalent to that of a game of strategy, cf.

stein has aptly expressed this fact by saying: "Raffiniert ist der Herr Gott, aber boshaft ist er nicht."[5] In that he follows Descartes and Bacon and adheres to the classical idea of the "*veracitas dei.*" The difference between describing a statistical universe made up of physical events exclusively and one in which social events occur can be, and usually is, profound. We observe here a significant variation in the structure of the physical and social sciences, provided it is true that nature is merely indifferent and not hostile to man's efforts to finding out truth—it certainly not being friendly. We shall assume indifference, though proof is, I believe, lacking.

The fact, all too frequently occurring, that statistics are sloppily gathered and prepared at the source, for example, by the firms giving out the requested information, is a different matter altogether; it is less serious than the fact of evasion, which may or may not be present at the same time. It will be seen that the lie can also take the form of handing out literally "correct," but functionally and operationally meaningless or false statistics (cf. p. 65).

Deliberately untrue statistics offer a most serious problem with broad ramifications in the realm of statistical theory, where, however, the nature and consequences of such statistics do not seem to have been explored sufficiently. It is frequently to the advantage of business to *hide* at least some information. This is easily seen—if not directly evident—from the point of view of the theory of games of strategy. Indeed, the theory of games finds a very strong corroboration in the indisputable fact that there *are* carefully guarded business secrets. Law cannot always force correct information into the open; on the contrary, it often makes some information even more worth hiding (e.g., when taxes are imposed). The incentive to lie, or at

least to hide, is also strongly influenced by the competitive situation: the more prevalent are monopolies, quasi-monopolies, or oligopolies, the less trustworthy are many statistics deriving from those industries, especially information about prices because of secret rebates granted to different customers.[6] Consequently, statistics derived from this kind of basic data suffer greatly in reliability. For example, where national income or personal income distribution is computed on the basis of income tax returns, the results will be of widely different accuracy for different countries, tax rates, tax morale, price movements, etc. It is well known that income tax returns for France and Italy, and probably many other countries, have only a vague resemblance to the actual, underlying income patterns of those countries. Yet it is on the basis of tax returns that important and elusive problems, such as the validity of the "Pareto distribution" (cf. p. 50) explaining the inequality of personal incomes, are minutely studied. For sales—an item of primary importance in input-output studies—it must be remembered that sales prices constitute some of the most closely guarded secrets in many businesses. The same is often true for inventories. A prime example is the distilling industry.[7] There it is vital for one company not to let any other know what its stock is, lest it suffer in the inevitable price and market struggle.

Governments, too, are not free from falsifying statistics. This occurs, for example, when they are bargaining with other governments and wish to obtain strategic advantages or feel impelled to bluff. More often, information is simply blocked for reasons of military security or in order to hide the success or failure of plans. In Fascist and Communist totalitarian countries the suppression of statistics is often carried very far. For example, foreign trade data are considered secret in some eastern

A. Wald, "Statistical Decision Functions Which Minimize the Maximum Risk," *Annals of Mathematics,* Vol. 46 (1945), especially pp. 279–80. Cf., also below, footnote 12, p. 22. An excellent discussion of the basic aspects of this decision problem is in the paper by J. Milnor, "Games Against Nature," in Thrall, Coombs, and Davis, *Decision Processes* (New York, 1954). Cf. also R. Duncan Luce and H. Raiffa, *Games and Decisions,* Introduction and Critical Survey (New York, 1957).

[5] Inscription on the mantle of a fireplace in Fine Hall in Princeton University: "The Lord God is sophisticated, but not malicious."

[6] Cf. O. Morgenstern, "Free and Fixed Prices in the Depression," *Harvard Business Review,* Vol. x (October 1931), pp. 62–68, where a description is given of the secret and widely varying rebates granted customers during bad times and cancelled when business improves. During these times list prices usually remained unchanged, but these were the "prices" used in price indexes, while the true situation was entirely different! Nothing has changed in these practices since 1931.

[7] A good illustration is offered by John McDonald, "Seagram in the Chips," *Fortune,* Volume 38 (1948), pp. 96–101. This paper describes a very interesting game situation.

that the Bank of England and so many other central banks are not?

A special study of these falsified, suppressed, and misrepresented government statistics is greatly needed and should be made. The probably deliberate over and understatements of needs and resources in the negotiations concerned with the international food situation, the Marshall Plan, etc., offer vast opportunities for such investigations—if the truth can be found out.

When the Marshall Plan was being introduced, one of the chief European figures in its administration (who shall remain nameless) told me: "We shall produce any statistic that we think will help us to get as much money out of the United States as we possibly can. Statistics which we do not have, but which we need to justify our demands, we will simply fabricate." These statistics "proving" the need for certain kinds of help, will go into the historical records of the period as true descriptions of the economic conditions of those times. They may even be used in econometric work!

The true or imagined purpose of statistics often has a great influence upon the answers (especially in designed statistics). In undeveloped areas there is often an important element of "boasting," besides a general desire to give the questioner the kind of answer he would like to hear, however remote it might be from the truth.[11]

A very modern and unusually important instance of the problem of obtaining data is the problem of inspection in arms control. There, sampling would have to be used in order to discover possible evasions through secret production of arms, secret atomic tests, etc. An international inspection team would encounter great difficulties not yet resolved by modern statistics. A theory of "sampling in a hostile environment" is now under development; it would be applicable to many other situations of the social world.

---

[11] It is reported that in Russia in the early 1930's the central statistical authorities had worked out "lie-coefficients" with which to correct the statistical reports according to regions, industries, etc. Nothing definite is known, but quite recently Khrushchev has accused especially Russian agricultural circles of reporting grossly false statistics.

Where such conditions prevail, the designer may have to hide the purpose of the statistic and the nature of the statistical procedure from the subject, who, in his turn, tries to hide the truth. This is the precise setup of a non-strictly determined two-person game where both sides have to resort to mixed or "statistical" strategies.[12] It is an ironic circumstance that in order to get good statistics, "statistical strategies" may have to be used!

Proper techniques of questioning will have to be worked out to produce a minimum of error under these conditions.[13] These phenomena may also be viewed as disturbances of the subjects interrogated. They are familiar to anthropologists who find conditions in primitive societies to have changed after these have previously been visited by other anthropologists. Conditions of disturbances occur also in physical experiments where in some well-defined cases in quantum mechanics it has been shown impossible *on principle* to obtain certain types, or, rather, certain combinations, of information.

The undeniable existence of an unknown but undoubtedly substantial amount of deliberately falsified information presents a unique feature for the theoretical social sciences, totally absent in the natural sciences, whether historical or theoretical.

History too has to cope with this difficulty. Falsifications are notorious there and can be found everywhere. Therefore, source criticism is a highly developed technique which every student

[12] This requires modifications—for the social sciences only!—in the theory developed by Wald, mentioned in footnote 4, page 18. There it is assumed that only nature resorts to a mixed strategy, the statistician using a pure one.

[13] This was done, for example, by A. C. Kinsey, W. B. Pomeroy, and C. E. Martin, *Sexual Behavior in the Human Male* (1948), cf. especially Chapter IV, p. 120 ff. There, lying, boasting, etc., were naturally encountered and a great effort was made to uncover these attitudes, to break the individual down, e.g., by rapid fire questions, long periods of interrogation, etc. In written questionnaires the subject may, however, be successful in persisting in his lies, because even complicated questionnaires can be analyzed and made to reveal traps. Thus, the problem is more complicated where written answers are involved. This would be the case, as a rule, in the collection of economic information involving many figures. The above work has been carefully examined by W. C. Cochran, F. Mosteller, and J. W. Tukey, "Statistical Problems of the Kinsey Report," *Journal of the American Statistical Association*, Vol. 48 (1953), pp. 673–716. This study is a model for the examination of statistical investigations.

of history has to learn in detail. A large literature exists in this field and many eminent historians have contributed to it. Without this tradition, the writing of history would be entirely worthless. Clearly, it is not simple to establish a "historical fact" or else there would be little need to re-write history as often as this is done (quite apart, of course, from the ever changing evaluation of the past).

A good illustration of the difficulty in determining the true value of historical claims is given in the classical work of Hans Delbrück,[14] who has carefully examined most military battles fought over the centuries with a view of determining the strength of the opposing forces. It is clear that the victors have always stated the defeated to have been much stronger than they were in order to make victory impressive, and the losers *vice versa* in order to make defeat excusable; this often creates figures which are impossible for the same occasion. Delbrück has found, for example, that if the Greek claims regarding the strength of the Persians at Thermopylae were true, there would not even have been room for the Persian troops to occupy the battlefield. Or, given the roads of the time, the last Persian troops would have just crossed the Bosporus when the first already had arrived in Greece. In this manner it goes throughout history, even up to most recent times, and what really happened is very difficult to find out.

Other instances from fields of social statistics or fact-finding are suicide statistics. They are notoriously bad because lay coroners so frequently disagree with medical men, and because great efforts have always been made to keep the fact of suicide secret.[15] This applies also to medical statistics; for generations it was considered improper to die of cancer, hence little mention of this disease. This shows up in the very limited value of statistics of death (the records of insurance companies notwithstanding). Time series, in particular, suffer from the fact that

[14] *Geschichte der Kriegskunst in Rahmen der Politischen Geschichte* (Berlin, 1900). A brief extract is found in his (now very rare) *Numbers in History, How the Greeks Defeated the Persians* (London, 1913).

[15] Accidents are another case where often great doubts prevail as to cause and effect. Probably most murders go undetected. For example, a very large proportion of hunting accidents are apparently murders; an investigation showing this was suppressed, however.

many diseases in former years were entirely unknown to medical science although people died of them. Thus, the "growth" of certain diseases is perhaps simply their better identification. This is notorious for mental illness. For example, there are many more mental cases in Sweden per 100,000 of population than in Yugoslavia. But this is simply due to the fact that in the former country the patient is taken care of in a hospital whereas in the latter he vegetates as the village idiot and is not recorded as a mental case. Death certificates are very difficult to make out when death is due, as is often the case, to several causes, e.g., pneumonia following upon some other affliction. Only a few countries demand autopsies in every case; and even then death cannot always be uniquely attributed to a single cause.

The difficulties of finding out what "facts" are can clearly be seen in legal procedure. Evidence is placed before juries but the outcome of their fact-finding is notoriously uncertain. In general, the experience is that the chances of establishing a fact as such before a court of law are very small and that a prediction of the outcome of a law suit is hazardous.[16] Many witnesses lie; sometimes perjury is discovered. Even when witnesses are truthful, or trying to be truthful, their statements are subject to all the doubts and limitations that have been brought out in a vast literature on the psychology of witnesses and the reliability of memory. It would lead too far afield to deal further with these matters here, though they do illuminate some of the difficulties of fact-finding encountered also in economics.

Without knowing the extent of the falsifications that actually occur in economic statistics, it is impossible to estimate their influence upon economic theory. But the peculiar feature remains that if economic theory is based on observations of facts (as it ought to be) these are not only subject to ordinary errors, but in addition to the influences of deliberate falsifications. If for no other reasons, this is a severe restriction on the operational value of economics as long as the magnitude of this factor has not been fully investigated. Here is a field where thorough studies are required; they will be difficult to make, but they

[16] Cf. for example, W. Seagle, *Law, The Science of Inefficiency* (New York, 1952).

promise important results. The theory of games takes full cognizance of the phenomenon wherever it becomes relevant.[17]

Falsification is difficult when it is attempted in a system or organization that is well described and understood. It is virtually impossible in a small mechanical system, though for large systems there are already doubts as to its working beyond a certain degree of reliability. To introduce a false circuit in an electronic computer would be foolish, since it is bound to be discovered. But social organizations are not nearly as well described as physical systems. Hence their working behavior cannot be predicted as precisely. This means that there are degrees of freedom in behavior which are compatible with alternative, equally plausible descriptions of the system. They need not differ profoundly. In addition, it should be noted, it is possible to prove that *there can be no complete formalization of society*. Consequently, a lie or falsification relating to some part or component of the system is exceedingly hard to discover, except by chance. Yet the chance factor itself is a necessary, constituent element of every social system. Without it "bluffing," a perfectly sound move in strategic behavior by elements (persons or firms) of a social organization, would be impossible. But it is a daily occurrence. Bluffing is an essential feature of rational strategies.

So we see that a lie or falsification has to be related to the degree of our knowledge of the framework within which it is attempted.

To give an illustration: Our knowledge of the population of a country, as established by a series of population counts, to which is added our knowledge of human reproductive ability makes it difficult to introduce in the next census willful distortions that would go beyond a certain measure. Lies—or other, ordinary errors—can be discovered, though this may be laborious (cf. p. 40 for an illustration regarding errors). An economy is much less understood and when a government, for example, reports to be in the possession of x millions of gold instead of the true y millions, this is very hard, if not impossible, to con-

[17] J. von Neumann and O. Morgenstern, *Theory of Games and Economic Behavior* (Princeton University Press, 1944), 3rd ed., 1953.

tradict, since both x and y may be compatible with our understanding of the economy and its workings. Experiments with individual firms have shown that many falsifications of production records cannot be discovered even by means of the most minute money accounting controls. When it comes to the recording of prices, movement of goods (especially in international trade, inventories, etc.), the possibilities are substantially widened. Even in production the wide substitutability of one material for another makes great variations plausible. Of course, nobody would believe that a large country could have doubled its steel capacity within one year—but we do not consider such crude matters.

When an economy is in the throes of a great development, coupled with a rapidly changing technology, the scope for misrepresentation is correspondingly widened. Our knowledge of dynamic processes is necessarily inferior to our ability to describe stationary conditions. Yet the economies we deal with are now and have been for decades in a period of active, dynamic, development.

In summarizing, we see that there are three principal sources of false representation: *First,* the observer, by making a selection as to what and how much to observe, introduces a bias which it is impossible to avoid, because a complex phenomenon can never be exhaustively described. This bias, common to all science, is of no concern here. *Second,* the observer may deliberately hide information or falsify his findings to suit his hypotheses or his political purposes. This occurs in historical writings, even in physical science in exceptional cases of fraud, and more frequently when economic and social statistics are used or abused in the hands of unscrupulous persons or institutions. Reference to some cases has been made above. *Third,* the observed may deliberately lie to the investigator. This is the crucial distinction between social and physical observations; in the latter, this factor is absent no matter how difficult it may be to discover the facts. To account for this additional character of observations in the social field, new ideas concerning the foundations of statistics are necessary, as has been indicated above. The distinction applies to both measurable and (for the time being) non-measurable information or observations.

3. The Training of Observers

Economic statistics, even when planned in detail, are frequently not gathered by highly trained observers but by personnel collected *ad hoc*. This is a source of the most serious kind of mass errors. Even trained census-takers and many others engaged in field work are not "observers" in a strict scientific sense. A scientific observer is the astronomer at his telescope, the physicist recording the scatter of mesons, the biologist determining the hereditary behavior of some cells, etc.; all are themselves scientists; they do not operate through agents many times removed. Except where experiments are involved, the social sciences will never get into an equivalent position as far as the basic raw material of observations is concerned. Because of the masses of data needed this would be physically impossible. We cannot place technically trained economists or statisticians at the gates of factories in order to determine what has been produced and how much is being shipped to whom at what prices. We will have to rely on business records, kept by men and, increasingly, by machines, none of them part of the ideally needed scientific set-up as such. If properly engineered (and costs of processing are a minor consideration), these data can be useful. In the future we will be able to rely more on automatic recording devices and computers, thereby improving, but also modifying, the picture.

It is well known from sampling experience (where, if properly done, one deals with strictly, though not always *well* designed statistics!) that the response is very different depending upon the type of observer, even if the latter is trained,[18] and should be—miraculously—free of bias. Detailed knowledge of how much improvement in statistics could be obtained by

---

[18] E.g., population statistics often show concentrations at the rounded off ages of 20, 25, 30, etc., which are in clear contradiction to earlier information. In other words, people prefer to indicate these ages, rather than their true ones which lie in between. The response to questions about attendance at college depends to a high degree upon the social status of the questioned and that of the investigator. If he appears to belong to the college-educated class, he will more often than not hear that the questioned went to college too, and vice versa. Some of these answers are also motivated by the fact that the questioned wishes to please the interrogator.

training, or more training (at greater expense!) is difficult to come by. Hence, the phenomenon, well known from experimental physics and astronomy, of the "personal equation" assumes very much larger proportions with less definite controls and perhaps even fundamentally different characteristics.

It could perhaps be argued that it should be possible to explore the nature of lies and the influence of training and bias of the observer thoroughly in controlled experiments. In other words, a sample would be designed which would be studied to the utmost degree; from the information thus gained one could then arrive at an evaluation of these factors, even in cases where no thorough exploration would be possible. It is to be doubted, however, that such a program can be carried out at the present state of affairs; it may even encounter systematic difficulties of a nature too deep to be discussed here.[19]

4. Errors From Questionnaires

Designed economic and social statistics often require the use of questionnaires. Some are presented orally; others require written answers. Some of the latter may at times contain several hundred questions directed to the same firm or individual. Errors can and do derive from the setting up of the questionnaires and from the answers. The questions should always be so formulated that unique answers are possible. But this is often not the case, for, on the contrary, many questions are not stated unambiguously or they require more intelligence for correct answers than is possessed by the person questioned. When large numbers of questions are involved, the possibility that contradictions will occur in the answers may be great, while at the same time significant omissions may be made. Often words are used that have emotional or political connotations and prejudice the answer, depending on the individual to whom they are presented. Some questions invite evasion, lies, and, when very numerous, a summary response (sometimes capricious) in order to save time, money, and generally to avoid bother and trouble. It also makes a great deal of difference whether the same questions are presented orally, in writing, by mail, etc.

---

[19] Cf. footnote 11, p. 21, and footnote 12, p. 228.

As is well known, each form of interrogation produces its own kind of bias. The process of asking questions and getting answers is a delicate psychological one. Apart from lying and refusal to give information, there is forgetfulness, prompting by the questioner with its own consequent bias, lack of comprehension of the question, etc. These phenomena have been studied in the literature.[20] Certain investigations of business decisions by means of questionnaires have produced results contradictory to expectations. In these cases, however, it is difficult to arrive at a conclusion, largely because it need not be assumed that business men always are able to interpret their own actions. A human being, though a living organism, is not necessarily able to describe its own functioning; yet he has a formidable "experience" of living. It takes several sciences to describe the process of living and to tell how the human body functions, and these sciences clearly have not yet come to the end of their questions and the search for answers.

The field of questionnaires is comparatively new in statistics, and the theory covering it is far from completely developed. Indeed, it is doubtful that even the qualitative description and enumeration of its characteristics is complete. Here we merely point to its existence (as in many other cases treated in this book) and emphasize its enormous importance, especially for those large data collections connected with input-output studies of industry and business, determination of incomes, spending habits, etc.

The difficulties of preparing good questionnaires and using them properly are, indeed, formidable but not appreciated by the public. The simple fact is that it is not easy to ask good questions and to insure that intelligent, reliable, and honest answers will be given. Science is, after all, nothing but a con-

[20] Cf. F. F. Stephan, "Sampling Opinions, Attitudes and Wants," *Proceedings of the American Philosophical Society*, Vol. 92 (February 1948), pp. 387–98; and F. F. Stephan and P. J. McCarthy, *Sampling Opinions, An Analysis of Survey Procedures* (New York, 1958), which gives a comprehensive and up-to-date discussion of the difficulties and the current ways to overcome them.

A particularly interesting work is S. L. Payne, *The Art of Asking Questions* (Princeton, 1951; Rev. Ed., 1955) which shows the many ambiguities in questions asked, the different associations they evoke, and what dangerous manipulations are possible.

tinuing effort to find the right questions, followed by the search for answers. And the question is often more important than the answer. It is not different in drawing up questionnaires for economic matters. Progress in science has often been blocked by having asked the wrong question. When a field such as economics depends so largely on asking humans rather than inanimate nature, the problem of the right question assumes new importance.

There is one requirement that can and should be fulfilled, whatever the state of the theory that covers the problems arising from the design and use of questionnaires: whenever questionnaires are used (or questions are asked orally), their precise text, with instructions for use, should be published together with the final results and interpretation. A mere paraphrasing of the question is insufficient because it may involve subtle changes in the meaning and undertones. In that respect, however, many producers of primary statistics, including government agencies, fail to comply and give only the vaguest kind of information about the underlying questions. This circumstance deprives the user of the results of a great deal of their value. Publicly used statistics for which the user does not have access to this information should be rejected, no matter how interesting and important the particular field may be. On the other hand, the publication of the frequently very numerous and complicated questions does not make the use of the answers any easier, because the reader is supposed to accomplish a difficult task of interpretation and evaluation for which he may not always be prepared.

Countless examples could be given of poorly designed questionnaires and samples. But we are not looking for the inadequate in economic statistics. Rather we try to assess the presumably best and to find out how much confidence can be placed in the work of the most renowned institutions. When troublesome errors are found there we have to conclude that elsewhere they will not be much different.

An interesting example, pertaining to questionnaires but pointing toward wider problems, is the following:

In 1953, the British Ministry of Labour and National Service conducted an enquiry into household expenditure by questionnaire and by interview. A total of 20,000 households were asked to list all their expenditures over a period of 3 weeks. Of the returns, only 12,911 were usable. The figures were broken down in many ways, one way being expenditure on various items by household against income of head of household. We can extract from Table 9 of the "Report of an Enquiry into Household Expenditure in 1953–54," (H.M.S.O., London), the figures indicated in our Table 1. We note the huge figure for weekly expenditure on women's outer clothing for the richest group (over £50). However, a footnote gives the reason for this: "One member of a household in this group spent £1,903 on one item during the period"—the item presumably being a very expensive fur coat. This fur coat keeps reappearing throughout other tables and each time provides us with a ridiculous figure. There is nothing *wrong* with the data; and the statisticians who wrote the report have been perfectly honest, but their results would have been more useful if the coat had been left out.

This example shows, incidentally, with what great care certain statistical phenomena have to be treated. When they are encountered and recognized, they give rise to refinements in statistical methodology which constitute a progress of our understanding of such situations. They also make it clear that there always have existed errors of a more elusive kind which now can be avoided. But the approach to these problems puts ever increasing demands also on the user of statistics which cannot always be met.

Specifically, the above example shows that it is dangerous to break down results of surveys into many very small groups. The number of "subjects" lying in some of these will be small and the results will be inaccurate. These "outlyers" are rare events (in terms of the sample) and probably belong to a different statistical distribution than the one encountered. They can mislead badly and will do so unless there is an immediate, intuitive reason to recognize the circumstances, as in the case of the fur coat. Even if its value had only been one-tenth it would still have biased the statistics, but this would not have been as obvious.

TABLE 1

WEEKLY INCOME OF HEAD OF HOUSEHOLD

	£50 or more		£30 to £50		£20 to £30		£14 to £20		£10 to £14		£8 to £10		£6 to £8		£3 to £6		Under £3	
Number in sample falling in this group	58		111		291		1,003		2,765		2,779		2,472		1,589		1,843	
	s.	d.	s.	d.	s.	d.	s.	d.	s.	d.	s.	d.	s.	d.	s.	d.	s.	d.
Weekly expenditure on Women's outer clothing	225	6.3	11	4.9	13	9.3	9	8.2	6	2.0	4	9.6	4	11.7	4	8.9	3	5.7

(s = shillings, d = pence)

Techniques for the rejection of outlyers have been developed.[21] They show that outlyers appear in many statistics and can lead to important inaccuracies unless good methods for their rejection are used. Poor methods can produce other biases, hard to discover.

We have introduced this matter in order to show that one may sometimes spot an obvious or striking fact and recognize it as an error or distortion; but behind it there usually are many more of the same kind, yet hidden and elusive. They can be brought to light only by sophisticated statistical theory.

5. MASS OBSERVATIONS

The factor has already been mentioned that in economics one has to deal with large masses of data. If the data be aggregates, these are necessarily made up from such large masses that this assumes particular significance because, as is often the case, they are usually made by hundreds, thousands, and even tens of thousands of "observers." These, as a rule, have only a limited training in observing, taking counts, recording answers. Mass observations have their own problems, even when undertaken in the best known manner. There is, for example, a summation of errors by the successive processing of the data (observers at various stages not being able or trained to correct the errors of the lower stages). These errors frequently are cumulative. There is no guarantee that they will cancel. They are important from the point of view of statistical theory, but the problems they offer are far from exhaustively treated. They have, however, shown up in population statistics with the consequence that even in modern times and in advanced countries sometimes millions of people are omitted or counted double (for the case of the United States Population Census of 1950, cf. footnote 26 on p. 40). It is easy to envisage what this means for population forecasts and other analyses of population movements. But such errors are unquestionably also encountered in other social and economic fields, though less frequently brought to light.

---

[21] Cf. T. S. Ferguson, "Rules for Rejection of Outliers," *Revue de l'Institut International de Statistique,* Vol. 29 (1961), pp. 29–43. This is a very useful survey with bibliography; in the latter we note particularly the recent contributions by F. E. Anscombe and J. W. Tukey.

Another factor deserves mention here: economic statistics, especially those obtained from mass observers, are themselves great accumulations of figures. Thus, the volume of economic data (not necessarily observations) is very great and keeps on increasing at a great rate. This is important inasmuch as it makes checks and corrections exceedingly difficult. The masses of statistical data are seldom condensed into constants, etc., as is the case in the natural sciences. Furthermore, they continue to grow at a rapid pace, because more money is spent on obtaining data, electronic data processing is expanding rapidly, and the complexity of life increases. This calls for more information about more and more things. The mere accumulation of data in itself presents a new problem to economics.

The increase in data is to some extent also confusing due to the fact that the same economic activity is being recorded by different agencies. Though they purport to measure the same thing (without being strictly scientific observers, in which case simultaneous observations would be a good thing), the series differ from each other. This makes it difficult for the outsider to know which series of data to use. For example, in the field of banking and monetary statistics, data are collected for, say, loans of commercial banks, by the Federal Reserve Board, the Federal Deposit Insurance Corporation, and the Flow of Funds Division of the Federal Reserve System. These series differ from each other, because of different concepts, definitions, samples, etc., and the user is at a loss to assess their value. Below, in Part II, such duplications are used to test statistics of agriculture, mining, and employment for their reliability. These tests give some indication about errors due to the above underlying differences. However, it is not always possible to make such evaluations, because the description of the data and the definitions used are not precise enough to know what is being measured.

When duplicating statistics are offered, some checks can be introduced by fitting the respective series into a model, say a simple Flow of Funds type of system, so as to gauge their value from the manner in which they fit together.

It is, of course, our fate, in science and business, to be confronted with a mounting volume of figures, only small quantities of which can become information and be absorbed with understanding, thus leaving us with the nagging feeling that among those not canvassed or discarded there may have been the truly relevant data!

6. LACK OF DEFINITION OR CLASSIFICATION

There is often lack of definition or classification of the phenomenon to be measured or recorded, and in addition, there is the difficulty of applying correctly even a faultless system of classification. The theoretical characteristics of, say, an industry or simply of a "price," are less well established than those of a wave length. Almost everything turns around the question of classification. This is a well known difficulty and much effort has been directed towards the establishment of uniform classifications, for example, of employment categories and commodities in foreign trade. But there are large fields where very little has been done and where deep theoretical problems await solution before classification can be significantly improved.[22] The combination of doubtful classifications and untrained observers gives great scope to possibilities of lying—a very grave issue. For example, false declarations of shipments as to contents, value, and destination can become commonplace. Or, if the lie factor is absent, there is still room for errors of other kinds. An important source is that the persons questioned simply do not know the answers. This may have an effect like lying, though the intent is lacking.

Frequently, mistakes are made although the classification is unambiguous, because another classification is more familiar to the observer and just as plausible. This happens when units of measurement are mixed up, e.g., long tons are used instead of short tons, yards instead of feet, etc. Similarly, fiscal and calendar years are often interchanged even though they need not coincide. The number of working days in a month are often not noted. Industry sometimes operates for time periods other

[22] This refers, for example, to the difficulties well known in the theory of monopolistic competition of even defining a "product" or an "industry." A good illustration of great practical significance is offered by the debate in the British Parliament (May 1946) concerning the nationalization of the iron and steel industry, cf. Hansard, *Parliamentary Debates*, especially of May 27, 1946.

than the calendar year and often uses a calendar of 13 instead of 12 months. From all this conflicts arise with the efforts to obtain comparable data. Furthermore, double counting occurs often—a particularly troublesome phenomenon especially when large aggregations have to be made, such as in national income statistics, total production counts, gross sales, etc.

Double counting and difficulties of classification due to lack or impossibility of precision in definitions occur in particular when large companies are considered. We give only one illustration: General Motors Corporation is a conglomeration of companies active in many industries. This corporation produces motorcars, airplane engines, diesel locomotives, electrical appliances, heating equipment, etc. Each one of these places the corporation into a separate industry. How is it to be classified? As a motorcar producer only? Should parts of it be recorded in different industries? How can this be done? By capital invested in different subsidiaries, by volume of sales or by the number of workers? How are their shares in the total profits—only given in consolidated form—to be determined (the economist necessarily being interested in the profitability and growth of the separate industries)? One could argue in the same manner for most large enterprises in the world. The problem grows in magnitude as "diversification" becomes more prevalent and as the rapid technological progress produces totally unexpected connections between industries which are technologically quite separated—not to mention the rapid appearance of lines of activities which cannot be fitted into any scheme which becomes obsolete as quickly as it is finished. So we have today a tire manufacturer who is a prominent producer of rocket fuel; an airplane maker who also produces nuclear reactors, chemicals, gravel, building materials, and musical instruments; a whiskey distiller who also manufactures electronic equipment; a flour mill that also makes balloons for high altitude flights. This list could be extended over many pages.

Clearly it is difficult to decide how to classify these firms, unless one wants to view them simply as holding companies which would not be correct either. Yet classification must be made. In different countries, entirely different practices may be worked out, and unification efforts, always slow, have little prospect when there is no firm theoretical basis, which is definitely lacking here.

Even if we limit ourselves to financial aspects, we find difficulties. Consider again the General Motors Corporation: It has a certain "value," for example, given by the number of shares outstanding multiplied by the market price per share. So does E. I. Dupont. But, in 1959, the latter company owned 63 million shares of General Motors (22.2 percent of General Motors stock), a fact that certainly has a bearing on the price of Dupont shares. If we add up the "values" of these two companies we get a false figure, whatever may be the worth of the method of finding the "values" in the first place. Sooner or later aggregates will be formed into which these two companies enter, and a significantly false figure of their combined total worth is obtained. This kind of interlinking goes through the whole business community in a most complex manner. It appears to be impossible to disentangle these interrelationships and, as far as one can know, this has not been attempted. The aggregates, as well as other measures derived from the data, will be cheerfully used in all kinds of economic studies and combined with other data in which large problems of a similarly basic character reside.

In foreign trade statistics, classification problems are as troublesome as they are important. Commodities from distant countries are often unfamiliar to the customs authorities and classifications that do not agree with each other often occur in the two trading countries in respect to the same commodity. This is one factor that contributes to the great differences to be observed in the reporting of the same international trade transaction by the exporting and importing country (cf. Chapter IX). The great technological progress since the end of World War II compounds the classification problem, as already noted above. But it assumes special significance in international trade. There new countries arise which are technologically backward but import advanced new products. They have great difficulty even in recognizing what some of the goods are and how they are to be listed in their statistics.

Perhaps equally important is the often arbitrary, willful, and frequently politically determined procedure employed by customs officials. In spite of a perfectly definite classification scheme, commodities are sometimes put into a similar category carrying higher duties in order to impede their import (or, as the case may be, into one that will make the import cheaper). This plays havoc, of course, with statistical accuracy. The bias is not constant because the arbitrariness of the officials is subject to orders from above due to policy changes under quickly varying influences. The state assumes a large role in such practices, especially when trade wars are raging or other political considerations prevail.[23]

The problems of classification are so involved and manifold that they would require lengthy treatment. The literature about classification, often pointing out real difficulties, sometimes patent absurdities, is large and continues to increase. It suffices to mention classification in this enumeration of sources of errors. In Part II some illustrations are given which serve to elucidate the gravity of the issue.[24] The removal of doubt about classification has been a concern of many international statistical conferences. The task is clearly an unending one, if only because technical progress gives rise to new products, processes, and materials, with innumerable cross-relations among them. (More will be said regarding definitions in Section 8 in connection with the *time* factor.)

We note, finally, that difficulties in defining and classifying may not produce "errors" in the usual statistical sense. This is suggested by examples where the difficulties of definition loom large, as in foreign trade (cf. Chapter IX). But the fact remains that if definitions are uncertain, vary frequently, and classifica-

[23] The classical examples are the "Hog-wars" between Austria-Hungary and Serbia, where hogs imported by the former were differently labelled in order to prevent or impede importation, etc., falsifying thereby also all relevant statistics for the period.

[24] The making of catalogs and their subsequent condensation—similar to a problem of aggregation—is of great importance in military logistics when it is recalled that the military have to deal with upward of an estimated 3,000,000 different items. This figure gives an idea of the magnitude of the problem of proper classification. It is, of course, not certain that all 3,000,000 items are really different from each other. For example, the same electronic tube may appear a few dozens of times (always with a different name and number), but it is no trivial matter to decide that they are all identical in their function and therefore could safely be substituted for each other.

tions are subject to much doubt, the data must reflect these conditions even though the convenient, normal notion of "error" is not directly applicable.

7. ERRORS OF INSTRUMENTS

Errors of instruments also play a role in the making of economic statistics, but they are probably not as important as in the natural sciences. Fewer instruments are used and in a less crucial manner. The principal "instruments" are still masses of human beings: for recording, interpreting, classifying, counting, questioning. The human limitations and frailties outweigh the faults of the technical instruments used: desk computers, punch cards, sorting machines, coding devices, etc. These may occasionally slip, but controls are good in general, and, as a rule, mistakes inherent in the machinery are quickly discovered. The machines are constantly improving. At the level of the statistical raw material—which is our primary concern—machines so far play a minor role, although their influence will increase as automation in the production process gains in significance. They will more slowly become important in the field of distribution which, however, tends to outweigh the manufacturing sector of the economy, at least as far as the number of people employed is concerned. The instruments often require ordinary but frequent transcriptions during which errors occur. There are further habitual misreadings of numbers and elementary computing mistakes in operations carried out mentally. All this produces errors which can be lumped together as "errors of instruments." A separation of the share of each component would be interesting but only possible after a detailed study of each concrete case.

Anyone familiar with the actual handling of statistical data at the primary level must be aware of the great number of possible errors and mistakes and of the frequency with which they occur. These are so deeply rooted that it is impossible, on purely theoretical-probabilistic grounds, to eliminate all of them all of the time. The problem is to appraise them and to reduce them to the minimum. In general, these errors add what is called "white noise" to the variance which the data possess.

One might also add reference to misprints in printed material, which are likewise in principle impossible to eliminate completely. A book of, say, 500 pages, with text and tables and formulas, may easily contain a total of one and a half or two million signs (including their position). The statistical laws of nature make it virtually impossible that a first printing contain no misprints. Neither can the manuscript from which it is made be free from errors.[25] Astronomical tables, however, are said to be free from misprints from their fourth or fifth revised printings on; but even this is uncertain. A comparison, free of all error, would have to be made with an error-free master document, but no such thing can exist. Economic source material hardly ever goes through several corrected editions.[26] In view of the mountains of paper involved, this would be a clear impossibility. All these questions play a profound role in large scale computing and have been investigated there.

A singularly interesting and illuminating example has come to light recently, and gave rise to a "statistical detective story" due to Ansley J. Coale and Frederick F. Stephan.[27] The authors discovered in the 1950 Census of Population of the United States a surprising number of widowed fourteen year-old boys and, equally surprising, a decrease in the number of widowed teen-age males at older ages. There were also many female widows and divorcées at age 14! Excessive widowhood and divorce was also discovered among American Indians. Or, thousands of persons were recorded as being in first and second year of elementary school at ages of 13 to 15 years. The reasons for these oddities were not easily discovered, but it is convincingly shown that these were errors and that they have to be attributed

---

[25] So we conclude that in spite of our efforts to avoid them, there may very well be more than one misprint in this book though it is of much smaller size!

[26] It is not clear whether omissions in a table listing towns in Connecticut in the 1950 United States Census is a misprint, a mechanical error, or a statistical error. At any rate the table omitted two towns of 20,000 people, seven of 15–20,000, twelve of 10–15,000, seventeen of 5–10,000, while 30 others were listed inaccurately. This table has already been incorporated in other than Government publications. Cf. this omission together with that of about 5,000,000 persons from the same Census in Chapter XIV below, p. 258, and the reference to A. Coale there.

[27] "The Case of the Indians and Teen-Age Widows," *Journal of the American Statistical Association*, Vol. 57 (June 1962), pp. 338–347.

to mistakes in punching cards which had bypassed even the severe Census controls. The mistakes transformed, for example,

> Head of Household into White
> Wife   →   Negro
> Child   →   Indian
> Son- or Daughter-
>   in-Law   →   Japanese, etc.

Or, in determining sex, an entry in the race column of the punch card would transform White into Male, and Negro into Female. Another case is offered by the report in the same Census that many 13, 14, and 15-year-old children were entering the first year of grade or grammar school—again most unlikely occurrences which were clearly attributable to punching mistakes as were the others. Still another instance, reported elsewhere, is that according to the Census the number of husbands living with their wives differs from the number of wives living with their husbands. In a presumably monogamic society this must be an error, probably due to similar man-machine failure.

The complete unravelling of the origin, size, and effect of the errors discovered is necessarily complicated and can only be performed by highly experienced statisticians. In these cases the investigators were helped by the fact that the observations were oddities, most implausible events that could be judged as such on the basis of other data produced by the Census, as well as on that of direct, intuitive knowledge. Had the material dealt with financial data, incomes, production, etc., this would have been far more difficult, if possible at all.

The magnitude of the errors was naturally small in relation to the total population. But their "effect was anything but negligible. For example, the 1950 Census age distribution of American Indians contains more than 15 percent too many males 10–14 and 20–24; and the number of white males under 17 reported in marital status categories other than 'single' was determined more by cards punched in wrong columns than by actual marriages, divorces, or deaths of spouse" (p. 346).

This example describes effects of the interplay of men and machines under highly controlled conditions. It is clear that errors such as shown must occur wherever man and machine meet. This is the case even with pencil and paper, for example when questioners fill in answers obtained in interrogation. It is, as a rule, impossible for the user of statistics to evaluate their frequency and importance but there can be no doubt that they do occur.

The relative weight of human errors and machine errors will change over time. Now it is interesting that while machines can be made to be incredibly more reliable than humans, as far as their specific functions are concerned, they present their own problems insofar as they may *produce a (higher) type of mistake even when they work accurately,* as will be shown in Chapter VI below. Electronic data processing is only one manner in which machines are going to be used increasingly; computing machines—for true calculations—are another use of modern devices. Reliability of machines—which, if lacking, is one source of errors—is not a guarantee against other kinds of error they may be producing, though computing machines are technically the most reliable devices modern science and industry can make. Reliability of design is a task of new and overwhelming dimensions given to the engineer. It is nowhere as important as in the making of large scale electronic computers. The problem encountered there is a universal one: how to obtain a reliable machine (instrument, apparatus, organism, device) which is by necessity made up of unreliable components. Here *error* is *not,* as is otherwise the case, *"an extraneous and misdirected or misdirecting accident but rather an essential part of the process under consideration."*[28]

The economic system is certainly made up of unreliable components and it is not designed by anyone with a view toward making it reliable (for fulfilling some specific economic purpose). It is therefore certain that the description of the system cannot give an "accurate" picture, both for reasons of *what* is being described as well as by what *means* this is being done.

Finally we note that the idea that instruments have their own imperfections and contribute accordingly to the uncertainty of

---

[28] The logical problems are investigated in J. von Neumann, "Probabilistic Logics and the Synthesis of Reliable Organisms from Unreliable Components," in *Automata Studies,* C. E. Shannon and J. McCarthy, eds. (Princeton University Press, 1956), pp. 43–98.

the measurement took time to be developed. The great Tycho de Brahe was one of the first astronomers to make specific allowance for the imperfections of instruments. To overcome them, he repeated the same observation many times. The time is now certainly ripe for economists to emulate Tycho.

8. THE FACTOR OF TIME

Economic observations cannot be made continuously. They have to be made in successive, discrete intervals of time. When these are far apart, this creates another source of error aside from the fact that there may not even be the same agents and observers in both moments. This is usually the case when field work is required, as for a census of manufacturers. Frequently an added uncertainty of classification arises in two points of time, for example, because of the appearance of new commodities, new industries, etc. It is also commonly found that statistics reporting sums over a stated period often are not attributed to the proper time interval. In making production statistics at the lower administrative levels, it often happens that the material arrives in an irregular manner from the various sources (firms) and is then more or less arbitrarily attributed to one week or month rather than to another. Or, later corrections or supplementary information are simply put into the data of the current month instead of being used properly for correction of previous records. As is well-known to those who have ever had to do with production statistics, this happens frequently, in particular also in foreign trade statistics.[29] Sometimes, over longer periods, changes in the quality and appearance of products may occur, which lead to variations in classifications that may not become known for quite some time. The sources of error in this category are numerous and the errors highly significant. Though they are amenable to correction and though most statistical officers make efforts to remedy these deficiencies, they are never overcome and their magnitude remains great.

Furthermore, time plays a very important part when the phe-

[29] It is easy to see that this affects such sometimes delicate operations as correction for seasonal variations. It may make these both wasteful and meaningless.

nomenon to be recorded is sufficiently complex and therefore needs a considerable amount of time to be observed and the observations to be recorded. It is impossible to be 100% accurate in counting a large population for a certain day or week, or to determine the inventory and the sales of a large corporation, let alone the inventories of the Navy or Army. What is counted is *attributed* to the stated point in time and it must, of course, have an error that will increase, the larger the setup to be measured and the finer the time interval to which the measure is to apply. When objects to be accounted for are moving about considerably, it may be impossible to obtain a desired precision. For example, planes, railroad cars, tanks, and in particular people, move at much greater speed and more often than the papers recording their whereabouts move from one desk to another. For such organizations special communication arrangements are necessary in order to obtain a higher degree of precision. In organizations where the quantities to be recorded are moving at a slower pace, ordinary systems of communication are perhaps sufficient. This may be of very great practical significance in the design of the organization and its statistical description.

An illustration is offered by the Federal debt of the United States. For June 30, 1962 it is given as \$286,330,760,848, or a gross per capita debt of \$1,586.07. Accounting practices and the law require that such a figure be reported. Yet, it is clear that *as a statement of physical reality* it cannot be correct to the last digit or even million at that precise point of time. If it were, we would have the remarkable accuracy of one in twenty-thousand billion,[30] more than any natural process can deliver! For bookkeeping purposes, this "accuracy" has, of course, to be maintained in its own limited meaning. As statistical information, it

[30] This is 10^{-11}; one of the finest physical measurements is that of the wave length of light, 10^{-8}. There are not many physical measurements giving more than five significant digits. Compare with this the following statement from the official Bulletin of the Chinese Embassy in The Hague: "According to the figures of the Population Bureau of the Ministry of the Interior for the first half of the year 1948 the population of China is now 463,493,418, only 695,325 more than the figures for the second half of 1947 showed and 2,487,133 more than the figures for July 1947." Reporting in such detail is, of course, not restricted to the Chinese, nor to population counts.

is an impossibility and there is no conceivable use for which such accuracy would be needed. Three or four digits is probably the maximum accuracy of primary data that ever needs to be considered in the vast majority of economic arguments.

In the testimony of June 16, 1949, at the Hearings before the Joint Congressional Committee on Atomic Energy,[31] it was brought out, to the great consternation of the public and the Committee, that the weighing of all the gold in Fort Knox could be achieved only with an error of something like $\pm\$20,000,000$, yet the official record for June 30, 1960 was given as $\$12,483,415,000$. This means that the gold stocked there is known at best to only four significant dollar digits instead of the alleged eleven, which is a more reasonable assumption. The fact that better information was expected than can technically be provided demonstrates how much people underestimate the difficulties associated with fulfilling standards of measurement and how easily unreasonable standards are set up.

The matter of the accuracy of determining the physical supply of some materials can be of gravest importance. It does not matter much for monetary stability whether the gold in Fort Knox is accurately known. But it may be vital in a possible arms control scheme to know precisely—down to the last few ounces —how much Uranium U_{238} or how much Plutonium is being produced or is stocked in a given country! One should recall that a few years ago the Atomic Energy Commission had the greatest trouble accounting for fissionable material in substantially larger quantities than a few ounces—in spite of the most rigorous checks and the neglect of all cost considerations normally preventing the maintenance of such precise records.[32]

Primarily, the difficulty is one of classification; in the present case it is a question of identifying a category *and* a time moment together. In the illustration above, it is impossible that for a particular moment of time the complete status of the debt be known in view of purchases, reimbursements, surrenders, de-

[31] See Eighty-first Congress, First Session, on Investigation into the U.S. Atomic Energy Project, Part 9, June 16, 1949, p. 412 (Government Printing Office, Washington, D.C., 1949).

[32] Very naive ideas how easy it would be to control and verify production of fissionable material internationally are found in the literature on arms control.

struction of documents, etc., all going on during the time interval which must elapse while making the count.

To make this point quite clear: If the debt was $12,483,415,000 and could be written on a simple piece of paper serving as the credit instrument, then the debt would be known precisely even to two decimals, since it is possible to write down the above figure faultlessly. But if the same total has been issued gradually over the years in millions of separate certificates, having different denominations, held at various times by the many people and institutions, then the different situation exists, commented on in the preceding paragraph.

It is in the light of such considerations that national election returns have to be viewed. It will be recalled that in the Presidential election of 1960 the winning candidate had 49.7% of the votes, the second 49.6%, with 0.7% going to others (a total of 68,832,818 persons voting).[33]

Successive observations (whether made by the same or different observers) give rise to time series; these are therefore each beset with errors of this kind. If the phenomenon measured is rather stationary (e.g., the number of industrial plants within a reasonably short time), the error can probably be reduced by (expensive!) repetitions of the measurement. But, as a rule, processes substantially changing in time are measured only once and cannot be measured more often. Thus the errors remain uncorrected and in extent unknown with each observation. No way of their elimination then exists as in physics where by repetitive study and measurement of the same phenomenon a real evaluation of error is possible. We are then confronted with unique phenomena (in time), as discussed in the next section.

A particularly nice illustration of how the time element can play tricks with statistics, showing at the same time limitations of complete counts (as compared with sampling procedures), is provided by the following case discussed by the late Oskar Anderson: "According to the census of January 1, 1910, Bulgaria had a total of 527,311 pigs; 10 years later, according to the census of January 1, 1920, their number was already 1,089,699,

---

[33] Such precise counts should be compared with the experiences mentioned on p. 40 and p. 258.

more than double. But, he who would conclude that there had been a rapid development in the raising of pigs in Bulgaria (a conclusion that has indeed been drawn) would be greatly mistaken. The explanation is quite simply that in Bulgaria, almost half the number of pigs is slaughtered before Christmas. But after the war, the country adopted the 'new' Gregorian calendar, abandoning the 'old' Julian calendar, but it celebrates the religious holidays still according to the 'old' manner, i.e., with a delay of 13 days. Hence January 1, 1910 fell after Christmas when the pigs were already slaughtered, and January 1, 1920, before Christmas when the animals, already condemned to death, were still alive and therefore counted. A difference of 13 days was enough to invalidate completely the exhaustive figures."[34] A time series of such counts would show a sharp kink and remain high until the celebration of Christmas was also adjusted! Incidentally we should be impressed by the power of the Bulgarian (or any other) government to count every little piglet right down to the last of seven digits for one and the same day! And how important it must have been that the last digit was a 9, not an 8 or 7 or anything else!

The problem of time is more serious here than in the natural sciences. There, not only do processes have more "stability" (e.g., astronomy), but also the classification of phenomena over time is much less in doubt, due to the high precision of existing measurements and the firm theoretical structure into which they are fitted. The problem of stationarity of economic time series is very troublesome and highly technical, as becomes strikingly clear when modern, advanced methods of time series analysis are to be employed to economic and social data. These seem, as a rule, to exhibit "trends," i.e., show an apparent evidence of nonstationarity. While difficult to deal with, their challenge can be met, provided its nature is properly assessed.[35]

[34] Cf. O. N. Anderson, *Einführung in die Mathematische Statistik,* (Vienna, 1935), p. 14.

[35] Cf. O. Morgenstern, "A New Look at Economic Time Series," in *Money, Growth and Methodology,* ed. by H. Hegeland (Lund, 1961), pp. 261–272.

The forthcoming work by C. W. J. Granger (in association with M. Hatanaka) *Analysis of Economic Time Series* (Princeton, 1963) contains the development and application of the most modern techniques and in-

9. OBSERVATIONS OF UNIQUE PHENOMENA

Many economic observations concern events that are unique and *not* reproducible. One is usually confronted with historical processes. Sometimes the same event is observed more or less simultaneously by several independent but differently placed observers, all together producing discrepancies in their statements. It is then necessary to decide which one is to be trusted (with his own observational errors still remaining), or whether averages are to be taken, what kind of averages, etc. This is the typical situation in the reporting of foreign trade which is examined below in Chapter IX; there some enormous discrepancies are discussed in detail. The same problem occurs occasionally also in physics and astronomy, e.g., in the field of extraordinary sound propagation, the measurement of explosions, the accounts of eruption of volcanoes, spring tides, and the observation of novae. Statistical theory adequate for full consideration of all issues raised under these conditions apparently does not exist and will be difficult to develop.

This field, therefore, deserves particular attention. To begin with, it is seldom true that events are to be viewed as absolutely singular and can only be observed a single time. Of course, each economic event is *in ultima analysis* historically unique. So is every physical experiment. When we construct time series, consisting of such events, there is not necessarily complete uniqueness of observations, because—depending upon the length of the time interval and the speed with which the respective forces described operate—the successive observations may be interdependent. For example, the observer may have learned how to make better observations or he may show fatigue after a series of measurements.

In the economic domain it is not at all impossible to *design* statistics with a view to improving the quality of reporting and to discovering the quality of the agencies making basic observa-

---

cludes a thorough discussion of the role of nonstationarity. Cf. also Granger, "New Techniques for Analyzing Economic Time Series and their Place in Econometrics," (to be published) and C. W. J. Granger and O. Morgenstern, "Spectral Analysis of New York Stock Market Prices," *Kyklos,* January 1963, vol. XVI, pp. 1–27.

tions. Even the observation of events that are strictly non-repeatable and for which no long homogeneous time series can be assembled, may be designed. The situation in economics is possibly again more difficult than in the natural sciences, but the differences are not in kind but rather in execution.

True uniqueness must not be confused with the *pseudouniqueness* which consists in the mere fact that a given event is *measured* only once, although repeated measurements would be perfectly feasible. In the sciences the same phenomenon is usually reproduced and measured time and time again in order to increase the accuracy. This is done in astronomy, e.g., measuring the distance of planets and stars, determining their masses, etc. In physics the knowledge of the principal constants is forever being sharpened,[36] until at a later stage they can be derived from rigorous theory—a distant goal in economics indeed! Physicists, chemists, engineers carry a wide knowledge of these constants in their heads and can quickly look up others in handy tables. Neither those working in theory nor those engaged in applications could exist without this knowledge which is their daily bread.

In the social sciences the attempts to determine and sharpen constants are comparatively rare: in fact the possibility of their very existence is usually doubted or even denied outright. It is often maintained that it is one of the characteristics which divide the physical and social sciences that the former do possess constants while the latter do not. This issue is far from simple.

[36] As an excellent example we quote N. Ernest Dorsay, "The Velocity of Light," *Transactions of the American Philosophical Society*, New Series, xxxiv: Part i, 1–109, 1944. I owe my acquaintance with this study to Professor A. G. Shenstone of the Physics Department of Princeton University.

This work is a model of a physical investigation of measurement, and also contains a useful introduction into the theory and practice of measurement. The detailed description of the various experiments, their limitations, their results, as well as the historical account of the gradual evolvement of the measures is indeed exemplary. It would be excellent if economists, at an early time in their training and careers, could become acquainted with such work showing them the extreme trouble to which physicists must go in order to be able to accept data. Similar quantitative work ought, of course, to be done in economics. When comparable standards have become the rule in economic research, economics will be placed on surer ground, while at the same time its extraordinary difficulties will be better appreciated.

Economists have tried ever since Ricardo's time, to find laws expressed in the maintenance of certain fixed relationships such as the ratio of income obtained in an economy by labor and capital. The most celebrated and most closely investigated constant is the Pareto distribution expressing income inequality. Its essence is the assertion that a certain kind of inequality will establish itself in all countries at all times, this inequality varying only within very narrow limits.[37] Similar important work has been done by R. Gibrat[38] but has not yet found its deserved wide recognition. This kind of work points to the possibility that it may not be unreasonable to expect the discovery of economic constants, in spite of the fact that economic life is not stationary, it being subject to the continuing impact of technological progress and the concomitant change in organization.

Economic constants, whether Pareto's $a = 1.5$, the capital/output ratio, or the ratio of income between labor and capital etc., all are based on observations and measurements. Hence they have to be reconciled with the errors in the data and since these are likely to be considerable, these different ratios and constants lose much of their definiteness, which accounts for the fact that there is so much controversy in this area.

10. INTERDEPENDENCE AND STABILITY OF ERRORS

The factors we have discussed seem to be the main sources of error; some of them are particular to economic and social statistics. In estimating the value of some specific economic statistic, it would be necessary to account for the possible occurrence of these various sources of error and to estimate quantitatively the influence of each upon the final figure. It is not enough to enumerate the possible factors that influence the outcome although this is the first indispensable step in the right direction. Sometimes this alone will instill a healthy sense of realism.

---

[37] The equation for the distribution is $n = k \cdot y^{-a}$, where n is the number of recipients of an income of y or more, k and a are constants, $a \approx 1.5$. An excellent survey of the literature, which continues to grow, is in C. Bresciani-Turroni, "Pareto's Law and the Index of Inequality of Incomes," *Econometrica*, vol. 7 (1939) pp. 107–133. Pareto's assertion was that a would be about 1.5 which appears to be borne out by the statistics.

[38] *Les Inégalités Economiques* (Paris, 1931).

This estimation is a vast program for most occasions. It is extremely difficult to fulfill, because it is not customary in economic statistics to indicate the successive errors as statistics are processed and become (1) more *inclusive* through summation and aggregation, (2) more *complex* by the inclusion of different statistics into indexes, and (3) more *refined* by being subjected to sometimes involved and lengthy mathematical-numerical operations, such as time series analysis, solution of large systems of equations, etc.

However, it is one thing to *explain* that there is inaccuracy in economic and social statistics and to show where it arises. But it is another thing to arrive at *quantitative estimation of the error* or even at stating orders of magnitude which are needed for appraisal and rigorous scientific work. Every effort must, therefore, be made to obtain strictly quantitative estimates, especially in view of point (3) above, i.e., because of the fortunate possibility of highly complex mathematical operations with the data.

Such quantitative estimates require a *statistical theory* which now exists only for a part of the whole field for which error estimates are required. The difficulties are truly enormous when *several errors are simultaneously present* and when it is necessary to account for each one separately. The case is difficult enough if, for a given observation, there is the possibility of two sources of error that cannot be separated. When the number of error sources increases, one may easily arrive at a perhaps insoluble position. The problem is akin to one familiar to the economist: how to determine the value of each factor in a joint production, the famous question of "imputation" (or Zurechnung) which is treated extensively in the theory of n-person games.[39]

The enumeration of possible sources of errors carried on in this section suggests that these may be *interdependent* in various complicated forms. Frequently, one type of error will predominate in one field of statistics while another field will be primarily affected by a different source of error. For example,

---

[39] J. von Neumann and O. Morgenstern, *op. cit.*, especially pp. 34–37, 435.

investigators of personal incomes, tax returns, etc., will encounter the factor of lies frequently, while production statistics may be influenced chiefly by errors having their origin in faulty classification, though the desire to hide some information may also be present.

As long as error theory has not been sufficiently developed to cover the complicated cases of many simultaneous sources of error and their shifting nature of interdependence, one must proceed on an heuristic and common-sense basis.

An illustration of this, yielding a certain quantitative estimate[40] concerns "arbitrage," or derived exchange rates. There it is found out that the numerical data do not agree with other evidence, according to which dealers utilize even minute differences in prices of different currencies in order to profit. The data on exchange rates show, instead, that significant price differences persist over long periods, which is incompatible with the other, qualitative, directly accessible evidence. This leads to the alternative of either having to throw away a fairly strong, widely accepted theory or of discarding statistical material every economist would normally use without much hesitation—a most undesirable dilemma. It might also be resolved by placing doubt in the data and reconstructing the theory at the same time. This kind of interaction between theory and observation is a desirable development in any science.

Checks of this type, involving several sets of statistics related by some preliminary theoretical postulates, may open the way toward handling situations involving several simultaneous errors. For example, if two or more processes are known to be interrelated in a rigid manner, say technologically, and the data for one process are trustworthy, then the measurements of those other processes may be estimated on the basis of this interrelationship. Such cases are infrequent but not too rare. Their study opens a way for checking, e.g., the accuracy of production statistics. Other procedures are available, or could be developed, to estimate whether errors in one type of statistics may offset

[40] This is contained in O. Morgenstern, *International Financial Transactions and Business Cycles*, National Bureau of Economic Research (Princeton University Press, 1959). That study produced a number of further illustrations; cf., also Table v below, p. 148 and the attending discussion.

errors in another type so that the quality of an aggregate formed from both sets can be enhanced.

It is possible that the influence of one error which drives a number in one direction is exactly offset by the influence of another error doing the opposite. In that case, by coincidence, the errors could cancel out—if their "extent" or "strength" balance—and we obtain a "true" figure for our observation. But we have not *made* a true observation! The notion that errors do cancel out is widespread and when not explicitly stated, it appears as the almost inevitable argument of investigators when they are pressed to say why their statistics should be acceptable. Yet any statement that errors "cancel," neutralize each other's influence, has to be proved. Such proofs are difficult and whether a "proof" is acceptable or not is not easy to decide. The world would, indeed, be even more of a miracle than it is if the influence of one set of errors offsets that of another set of errors so conveniently that we need not bother much with the whole matter.

Qualitative description of errors is an indispensable preliminary step. It makes possible, for example, at least conclusions as to whether certain aggregations or computations would tend to cumulate or to offset the errors. This would be valuable information even if no further numerical estimate is possible at the moment. Apparently, economics will have to go through a stage of such qualitative description in order to arrive at more precisely expressed quantitative measurement of the errors.

These descriptions of errors may also give some information about one aspect of economic statistics not mentioned so far: the *stability of the error estimates*. It is widely believed that more recent statistics are more accurate and trustworthy than earlier ones.[41] This is probably sound, in a vague, general way, but only when sufficiently large intervals of time are taken. The tests or illustrations in Part II below reveal, however, many instances where this interpretation of the statistics is not correct. It is certainly not true when an economy is in a state of vigor-

---

[41] This view is held, for example, by W. C. Mitchell, "Business Cycles as Revealed by Business Annals," introductory chapter in W. L. Thorp, *Business Annals* (National Bureau of Economic Research, New York, 1926), p. 20. This opinion is shared by many others.

ous development, signified by the introduction of many new products, changes in quality of existing products, and a rapidly advancing technology.

In particular, statistics of the value of foreign trade—an enormously important field—are virtually worthless where countries practising discriminatory exchange rates are concerned; many nations do so right now and did not in earlier years. Domestic statistics do not necessarily improve either. The separation of visible items in the balance of payments from the invisible ones is just as arbitrary now as it was a hundred years ago, and this has nothing whatsoever to do with monetary standards, policies, trade practices, and the like. Neither the lapse of time as such nor the fact that a statistical office gains in routine is an assurance that the statistics automatically improve. Sometimes governments change radically and bring forth the deliberate falsifications associated with Nazi and Communist practices of government already mentioned above. Or "strategic" considerations play havoc with reliability.

Furthermore, new statistical methods have been introduced over time that have their own new sources of errors (e.g. sampling, use of questionnaires). Or statistics are collected on a larger scale than before and new fields are opened up to statistics where they may encounter objection, evasion, etc., entirely absent in other fields treated in earlier times.

If an estimate of the error is made in a given field and for a given moment of time, it should be well understood that the comparison over time still requires a separate justification. The error will usually change. In particular, one should guard against transferring the experiences from one field to another or against assuming that the errors of observation will tend to settle down at a desired level.

Qualitative explanations and enumerations of kinds of errors are found in the literature, for example, in the work of research institutions, such as the National Bureau of Economic Research, though this institution has not faced up to the issue in the fundamental manner in which it deserves to be treated. The mere repeated "checking" of the transcriptions of figures from some source and their correct transfer to other papers is no substitute[42] for the determination of errors of observation and their significance for deductions and inferences. Attempts of the latter kind ought to be encouraged and should *precede* any large enterprises of collection and interpretation. It is also necessary that worthless statistics be completely and mercilessly rejected on the ground that it is usually better to say nothing than to give wrong information which—quite apart from its practical, political abuse—in turn misleads hosts of later investigators who are not always able to check the quality of the data processed by earlier investigators. This is especially important if data are to be used in extensive aggregations. When elaborate calculations are needed that are difficult to set up (aside from monetary expense), this misleading information may make the use of high-speed computing machines meaningless.

Thus, new problems arise irrespective of whether the errors are quantitatively known or only more or less vaguely described qualitatively. These additional problems will be discussed in Chapters V and VI. It will be seen then that, in addition to determining errors of observation, the fineness of the measurement at which these errors occur has to be stated. This can only be done by bringing theory to bear on the matter.

Since different kinds of errors are interrelated at the moment of time when an observation is made, the question arises how they behave over a period of time. Most economic data are given in the form of time series which is why the analysis of time series assumes such great importance. When the errors in one period are related to the errors in previous periods then we say that the errors are "auto-correlated."[43] Even if there were no errors in the time series, successive observations tend frequently to be auto-correlated as, for example, the volume of production in May depends on that in April etc. In other words, economic time series normally are not strings of random num-

---

[42] This type of control over figures is of course trivially necessary in any case. It represents an effort to be precise and perhaps this kind of *"precision"* should be distinguished from *"accuracy"* of the kind under discussion in this book.

[43] If ϵ_t is the error in a statistic, auto-correlation occurs when $\epsilon_t = f(\epsilon_{t-1}, \ldots, \epsilon_{t-n})$; e.g., $\epsilon_t = a\epsilon_{t-1} + u_t$, where u_t is a random term.

bers, each independent from the other. Could it be that the same occurs with errors, and would that simplify our problem? In particular, even though our data may be poor, are not at least their month-to-month *variations* significant, so that the reported $\pm\frac{1}{2}$ or 1% changes in, say, Gross National Product, prices, production, employment are really telling us their implied or pretended story?

Auto-correlation of errors occurs for a variety of reasons. One frequent cause is *bias* in statistics persisting over time. Many facts will lead to statistics overstating or understating the "true" figures by a (more or less) constant amount or percentage.

Causes of *bias* are the elements described in this chapter: omission and double-counting; classes of items that should be included are consistently overlooked; others enter more than once, possibly under different disguises. Faulty definitions, in the sense that a figure is taken to measure something which in fact it does not try to measure or faulty application of a definition when the method for collecting data is constructed may each lead to bias. A steady tendency to hide information on the part of respondents or a consistent tendency to optimism or pessimism could lead to bias. So could the method used by the collectors of data in dealing with ambiguous and incomplete responses.

In order to lead to auto-correlation bias has to be persistent and in the same direction; but if the presence of bias is usually difficult to discover, its amount is still more so. Only careful examination of the procedure used in obtaining a figure would permit it, and even then sources of bias, such as failure to include certain items, may still escape detection. When two series purporting to measure the same thing differ in fairly constant fashion, it is evident that bias is present in at least one of them, but what the bias in each is still defies simple examination.

The seriousness of bias may or may not be great. It depends on the uses to which the data are to be put. If the absolute figure is important, bias can render conclusions completely meaningless.

Several other sources of auto-correlation of error terms may be present in economic data. When basically the same data or methods of assembling data in one period are related to those in previous ones, it is likely to arise. Such practices as using the same factor (such as weights derived from a census) in "blowing up" sample results to obtain population figures period after period, often may lead to auto-correlation. When parts of a figure are based on fairly rough estimation procedures, as occurs in foreign trade statistics and national income figures, the estimating errors in successive periods may not be independent of each other. Use of samples whose membership in one period is not independent of that in previous ones could also produce auto-correlation.

Even more difficult to detect than bias, and impossible to estimate if one does not know the "true" figures, auto-correlation in general, like all sources of errors, can vitiate the usefulness of data unless their uses are broad enough to overcome the poverty of data. Frequently it is maintained that certain statistics, particularly of the national income, are subject to bias and other auto-correlation of errors. These feelings are apt not to be demonstrably based on close study of the data and are seldom incontrovertible, but the comforting conclusion is still drawn that as a result of the auto-correlation *changes* in figures whose absolute sizes have little precision, possess amazingly high degrees of accuracy. While it is true that auto-correlation of errors will tend to make first differences of series less meaningless, economic statistics are usually subject to a host of other sorts of errors. The difficulties we had in this chapter in describing the numerous error components in strict separation from each other is a clear illustration of the degree of their interrelatedness.

It is unlikely that errors are so conveniently related and so stable in their relationship that they turn out not to matter in the end. The burden of proof that small variations of consecutive economic observations are significant must always rest with those making such statements. When one is ignorant of the exact nature of the errors afflicting statistics, one must not presume that these unknowns are so related that their effects cancel out.

Unfortunately, it is not sufficiently recognized that the burden of proof in the case of such assertions lies with the makers of statistics. We shall not hesitate to repeat that economists and the public will do well to insist that those who make claims that their statistics actually show what they purport to show give acceptable evidence that such is indeed the case. But it is at least as important that the users of statistics do not employ them in a manner which their quality does not warrant. There has to be adjustment on both sides.

Perhaps the most important use of the idea that *changes* in figures are significant as they come is in the determination of *turning points of business cycles*. First, it is questionable whether any procedure relying on visual inspection of time series is adequate for distinguishing "cycles." Indeed it is even claimed that often simultaneously several cycles of different lengths and amplitudes mixed together with each other can be discerned unequivocally by visual inspection alone. Second, even if this remarkable capability could be assumed, the observer would still deal with time series whose changes must be compared with those of other time series to such fineness that ultimately a precise *month* is identified as an upper or lower turning point of the aggregative business cycle.

When the time series are formed of large aggregates, such as Gross National Product or national income, it is impossible to determine any particular month as a turning point as the analysis in Chapter XIV will demonstrate. When many individual series are studied separately and their individual, so-called "specific cycles" are marked off visually, there appears to be a somewhat better situation since many series will tend to turn at about the same time and because some series are clearly of better quality than others. However, a sharp kink in a series does not guarantee that this series is of high accuracy. The only thing shown is a sharp kink. Even if several series have sharp kinks at about the same time, the conclusion that an aggregative statement about this situation is warranted is not thereby proven. More information is needed in order that one may have confidence in the assertion. Even very small errors in the series make the determination of turning points hazardous. Moreover, the accurate and sharp series do not necessarily have high significance for finding business cycle turning points. And, vice versa, the important series are often of poorer quality (employment, production, profits, foreign trade, etc.).

Yet sharp, monthly turning points are being determined on a subjective, qualitative basis with an alleged high degree of confidence, though over the years there are frequent revisions of the dates, some due to revisions of the data, others due to different opinions. In fact the dates chosen are usually the outcome of veritable "negotiations" among the "observers." Taken by itself this would not necessarily be objectionable, since there is ample room for expert judgment in the makeup and evaluating of economic statistics.[44] However, when recourse is had to these methods, numerical precision of the kind implied here is illusory. Instead of a precise *point* in time—for so complex a phenomenon as the turning about of business of a whole country—a much larger interval has to be chosen as an approximation. This poses a dilemma: current business cycle analysis demands that a time unit not larger than a month be used, yet the quality of the data will not support such fine-grained measurement.[45] It is, of course, questionable whether the notion of a strict business cycle is applicable; most likely it is an unwarranted oversimplification of an exceedingly intricate development.

Leads and *lags* between time series are also of a much less precise nature. The confidence with which statements about these important phenomena can be made is again dependent upon the error component of each series. Though it is recognized that leads and lags are not always constant, this is usually attributed to properties of the economic system rather than to the limitations inherent in its statistical description. Our observations regarding business cycle turning points will become clear when the reader has examined the examples of economic data in Part II. They show clearly that the alleged accuracy

[44] Cf. the references in Chapter XIV, footnote 13, p. 254.
[45] It is remarkable that the question of the accuracy of economic observations is treated only in a subsidiary manner in the standard work by A. F. Burns and W. C. Mitchell, *Measuring Business Cycles* (National Bureau of Economic Research, 1946). The ensuing controversy over "Measurement without theory" has also largely bypassed the issue of this aspect of the data.

cannot possibly be obtained and that, as a consequence, we are far less certain when business turns than we are made to believe and would like to know. Consequently measurements about the lengths of cycles, of their relations to each other, historical comparisons, etc. are beset with considerable uncertainties. Unfortunately they are not reflected in the current literature on business cycles.[46]

In my *International Financial Transactions and Business Cycles,* Princeton, (1959), I have made use of "reference" cycles and "specific" cycles determined by the National Bureau of Economic Research, accepting the Bureau's findings (though with many misgivings and questioning in general the quality of my data). Upon further consideration it appears that the limitations of the National Bureau method and its results should have been stressed even more strongly. The (objective) method of spectral analysis of time series referred to in footnote 35, p. 47 of course also deals with the same raw material. But no precise points are determined for the fluctuations. Instead, only frequency *bands* are found which in itself already expresses a more realistic viewpoint. In addition the search for leads and lags as well as for correlations is placed on a novel basis by that method.[47] There can hardly be any doubt that the powerful new techniques of spectral analysis will put the study of economic fluctuations on a new basis, in spite of the fact that there has been no magic improvement of the data.

We may properly conclude this chapter with the remark that it is not easy, and never has been easy, for the human race to accept the view that, whatever its state of knowledge at a given time, such knowledge is exposed to error. The extraordinary success of classical mechanics and its influence upon the whole

---

[46] A good example to the contrary is the interesting paper by L. C. Trueblood, "The Dating of Postwar Business Cycles," American Statistical Association, *Proceedings of the Business and Economic Statistics Section,* 1961, p. 16.

[47] It is now possible to consider the case where a series may lead another one in one frequency but at the same time lag it in another. Of particular interest is M. Hatanaka, "A Spectral Analysis of Business Cycle Indicators: Lead-Lag in Terms of all Time Points," *Econometric Research Program,* Princeton University, February 1963.

outlook on the world, has fortified this reluctance. Since economics also was shaped according to these ideas ever since Walras and Pareto, the notion of error played no role.

In physics errors were recognized for a very long time; but they were held to be a secondary nuisance, to be neglected and to be ignored by the theory. "The assumption was that errors could be made 'as small as might be desired,' by careful instrumentation, and played no essential rôle. Modern physics had to get rid of these unrealistic schemes, and it was indispensable to recognize the fundamental importance of errors, together with the unpleasant fact that they cannot be made 'as small as desired' and must be included in the theory."[48]

Physics has learned the hard way to achieve the new outlook on the world. Economics has still a long way to go before it will be ready and able to make a corresponding adjustment. The difficulties are perhaps greater since the use and application of economics is so strongly influenced by, or even dependent on, laymen, who so often demand certainty where there can be none.

In the field of theory, I refer, however, to the theory of games of strategy which has brought the element of uncertainty to the fore, a fact that is already showing its influence upon the new generation of economists. Quite apart from the stimulus it has given to the theory of utility based on uncertain prospects—which for the theory of games is, however, only a side issue—the theory of games demonstrates that the classical idea of sharply defined unique equilibria has to be abandoned. These have to be replaced by more complex notions such as that of multiple "standards of behavior," each consisting of alternative, equally possible, accepted schemes of distributing the results of economic processes.

[48] L. Brillouin, *Science and Information Theory*, 2nd Ed. (New York, 1962), p. 304.

CHAPTER III

SPECIOUS ACCURACY

SINCE "accuracy" is a constant aim of most agencies making or using statistics,[1] it is necessary to point out the frequent occurrence of what shall be called *"specious accuracy."* Of this we distinguish two fundamental kinds which, to make things worse, often go hand in hand.

1. IRRELEVANCE

The first kind consists in giving "accurate" information to an extent that is entirely irrelevant for whatever immediate purpose may be considered or for any other conceivable purpose. This assertion is possible even though by far the largest part of economic statistics is gathered without having been committed to any particular use. Normally these statistics are just raw material available for untold many possible purposes. But the present nature of economics and its probable future development for a long time to come (though progress has been rapid lately) make it most unlikely that a kind of frequently encountered alleged "accuracy" could be used with which most figures are usually presented by their gatherers. More precisely, irrelevance is connected with the nature of the economic model and the corresponding "fine structure" (or lack of it) of the theory of the user. The more rudimentary the latter, the less precision is required of the data. (This will be examined in more detail in Chapter V below.)

Roughly speaking, specious accuracy is often found in providing information down to several decimal points when no conceivable use can be made of such detail—even if the data, given to this degree, should be entirely free from error, which is usually impossible. By necessity, such data are combined

---

[1] Excepting the possibility of "fabricated" and "doctored" statistics and their misleading presentation used by pressure groups and other irresponsible manipulators. However, we need not be concerned with their products, although they often receive wide circulation. Cf. the reference to Russia in footnote 11, p. 21.

with purely verbal argument in qualitative reasoning or in computation with other only very crudely known quantitative data. Besides, the carrying of many places (being itself a constant source of errors) is expensive, wasteful, and time-consuming because of the increase in, or maintenance of, computational levels which are unjustified. This type of specious accuracy occurs in most economic publications, even in those of large, respected research organizations. It abounds in the publication of government primary statistics. The point may seem trivial, but one only needs to consider both factors in conjunction: expense and usefulness. The first is of tremendous importance; costs are enormously increased by printing six, nine and even more digits page after page, when perhaps, at most, two to three digits can ever be checked or used. These great masses of figures are then processed, with great costs in man hours consumed in computing, checking, proofreading, etc. Finally, statistics emerge of an alleged fineness which no present or future theory can handle. Though we must hope that future theory and analysis will be far more powerful than the present ones, centuries will elapse before, say, information about the total number of cows in the United States down to the last 100 is of any consequence.

This unjustifiable detail is, as has already been mentioned, the consequence of political pressure. It is perhaps not surprising that it is being applied to complete census of people and animals. But when it also makes itself felt in sampling, it discredits sound statistical procedures of potentially great scientific interest. The pressure usually leads to breakdowns of the sample to such small units that the sampling error exceeds what is being measured.

It is perhaps no exaggeration to say that from the savings in expense of producing, processing, printing, and computing unnecessary digits of basically doubtful statistics, large-scale research in economics and statistics could be financed. (One of its consequences would be to condemn this kind of specious accuracy!) Further examples are the interpretations of, say, indexes of prices, production, employment etc. to several decimals, which are irrelevant from every point of view. But this type of reporting or analysis gives the presumption of a particularly high, even "scientific," quality of the work and is apparently believed to lend greater credulence to the conclusions.

For example, a few years ago an aviation trade journal "estimated" air cargo for five years thence to 1/1000 of 1 percent! Or the U.S. Army published *enemy* (!) casualties for the Korean war also to 1/1000 of 1 percent—at a time when our own losses were not well known even by the thousands of men! (Cf. the reference in footnote 13, p. 23 to the researches of H. Delbrück.) An even better example is given by the official publication of the Austrian Finance Administration, which states that the population of Salzburg province in 1951 was 327,232 people = 4.719303 percent (!) of the entire population of Austria.[2]

An entirely different situation is encountered, of course, when, say, a system of equations based on numerical data has been solved and the computed coefficients are investigated. This will often involve the carrying of figures of six or more digits to take care of computational needs and errors of rounding. Such digits can have a limited, precisely definable meaning.

It is pointless to treat material in an "accurate" manner at a level exceeding that of the basic errors. The classical case is, of course, that of the story in which a man, asked about the age of a river, states that it is 3,000,021 years old. Asked how he could give such accurate information, the answer was that 21 years ago its age was given as 3 million years. There is a fair amount of this in economic (and other social) statistics.[3] This kind of statistic is exceedingly harmful; it persists although it will not stand up even under a simple common-sense criticism. Economic series, reported in billions, are often aggregated with others, reported in millions or thousands, by simple addition. The result is a new series which gives the impression that the aggregate has been measured, counted, or determined to far more digits than is actually the case.

[2] *Amtsblatt der Österreichischen Finanzverwaltung,* no. 45, 8 Feb. 1960, quoted by H. Christoph: "Missbrauch der Statistik, allerdings auf hohem Niveau," in *Berichte und Informationen,* vol. 16 (1961), p. 12.

[3] A nice, well-known example is that in order to determine the precise height of the Emperor of China whom none of his subjects has ever seen, it suffices to ask each of 300 million Chinese what he thinks the height is and average their opinions. This will necessarily give a very precise figure.

It is always easy to impress by specious accuracy of this kind or any other. The pretension of knowing how to handle it, is widespread in human affairs. It is often easy to do so, which probably accounts for its occurrence. What can be simpler than to state that a substance weighs 0.000001 kg. rather than give its weight as 0.001g.?[4]

A rigorous elimination of this seeming "accuracy" is necessary, even though it is likely to arouse great opposition from vested interests.

2. FUNCTIONALLY FALSE STATISTICS AND MEANINGLESS STATISTICS

The second kind of specious accuracy is perhaps even more dangerous. It is functional speciousness. Here data are given which even when they have only a very small margin of error are nevertheless useless. This is the case, for example, when the exchange rate of a country with exchange control is given at the official rate (quite accurately to any desired number of decimals!), while at the same time the vast majority of transactions take place at different rates that are not disclosed or cannot be determined. The same applies to price indexes, cost of living indexes, etc., which often include prices of commodities that are no longer traded in, have changed their function in the household, or are even no longer in use, and so forth. This is partly a question of the price reporting, partly one of the construction of an index, a problem of a higher type than we are concerned with here. Individual prices of commodities may be quoted accurately and in detail, though they may be monopoly prices with large quantities of the commodity being sold at secret rebates (cf. Chapter X). This applies even to some central bank discount rates.[5] Such data enter other statistics, often in a decisive manner, e.g., in determining sales volumes for entire industries, the value of foreign trade, etc., spoiling all the composites.

---

[4] The point is sometimes made that the unwarranted digits nevertheless have an important function, i.e., that they help in the discovery of errors. But there is no firm evidence to this effect.

[5] Secret central bank discount rates and other widespread practices invalidating statistics are discussed in my book *International Financial Transactions, op. Cit.*, Chapter VIII, pp. 363–367, 429–441.

In addition, there are the *meaningless statistics.* They are not meaningless in the sense that they are given with specious accuracy or are difficult or even impossible to interpret theoretically. Their nature is best characterized by an illustration. Consider, for example, "profits" as reported in balance sheets and operating statements of corporations. Here "accurate" data may exist[6] which taken by themselves are not directly useful and, therefore, have to be combined with others in order to produce desired information. Thus, profits are computed by comparing purchase prices and sales prices, both of which may be of doubtful statistical character.[7] While this procedure may sometimes produce meaningful statistics about profits, it is not always sound. When prices rise, repurchase prices of factors may have to be compared with sales prices and a significantly different "profit" will result. What could be more trivial than to understand that if in times of rising prices the purchase price rather than the higher repurchase price is taken as the basis for amortization, a fictitious profit results? This "profit" is nothing else but consumption of capital, of substance. Some widely used statistics, however, are produced by means of the inappropriate procedure, neglecting the change in the framework into which the concepts must be imbedded. Furthermore, the incorrect methods used differ widely from one corporation to another as well as for different industries. Aggregations of such figures produce statistics that may be full of errors of this particular brand, if not wholly devoid of meaning.[8] In still larger aggregations they enter combinations with valid figures which are free from such meaningless components, thus depriving the latter of their hard-won value.

An illustration how even good statistics may become meaningless and functionally false is offered by the credit market. There one observes brokers' loans to customers with which the

---

[6] Cf., however, Chapter IV below where the question of accuracy in accounting is raised.

[7] Neglecting, for the time being, other aspects such as amortization, overhead, etc.: cf. Chapter IV.

[8] The point is, however, that this type of information is used in business and government for spending, saving and taxation. It becomes crucial for decision-making and has a great bearing for determining values of securities and in the appraisal of corporations.

latter buy stock on margin. One may find that the increase in such loans has been modest as a consequence of government restrictions placed upon them. But the interrelation of all credit flows reduces the value of this observation, because when this type of credit gets short, people sometimes take out even second mortgages on their houses in order to use these funds in a rising stock market. Thus the frame within which a statistic has to be judged requires consideration. In this case an error of another kind than that of measurement is on hand.

A much deeper concept and thereby better understanding of "accuracy" or "correctness" of statistics is thus required. We are here confronted with an *"error"* which is of a somewhat *higher type* than those enumerated in Chapter II, which occur at a strictly basic level. This topic might, therefore, better be examined in connection with the economic models or economic theory, rather than on the same level with the other properties noted. Yet it is necessary to point out these difficulties here. Often, time series are constructed of which some parts are subject to these limitations while others are not. It is easy to figure out what this entails when non-homogeneous data of this kind are used in continuing statistical-numerical operations.

Among meaningless statistics would have to be counted all those that are presented by processing good basic data in an incompetent or willfully distorting manner. The first possibility is of no relevance here; the second occurrence was already commented upon on p. 9 (cf. especially the reference in footnote 5), and needs no further discussion. There is, however, a further category where more elusive properties have to be observed. As an example we refer to the computation of *rates of change* of various statistical entities. For example the rates of growth of employment, national income, foreign trade, or the rate of decline of unemployment, of a deficit of the balance of payment, etc. are computed for short runs, not to mention the changes in costs of living, prices, consumers' spendable income and so on. Now if the simple observation is made that by necessity *all* these are affected by errors, even if these be very small, say ± 2, ± 3, ± 5 percent in those quantities for which rates of change are being computed, the rates are spectacularly different—indeed often involving even a change in sign—from those computed without any error of observation. A specific example is discussed in some detail below in Chapter XV which deals with the rather primitive but very popular notion of "growth" of a nation's economy as expressed by changes in national income.

It is, of course, difficult to distinguish clearly, and to everyone's satisfaction, between primary statistics and those of a higher type which result from manipulations of the former. It could be argued that there is no ultimate, lowest level, since even in the simplest enumeration some theory enters (certainly arithmetic!) and that even the most ordinary tables and numerical forms have to be designed, etc. While this is true, it is a far cry from recording, on the one hand, some ordinary business transaction, a shipment of goods, the number of automobiles in stock, the number of travelers on a plane, etc., to constructing, on the other, a price index, the basis of which has to be a theory of consumers' expenditure, involving complex economic and mathematical reasoning. And the latter, as also the most ordinary sample, at some point have to fall back on the primary level of recording and counting. In other words, everything rests, in *ultima analysis,* on primitive observations (data), just as all mathematical computations are reducible to the four elementary arithmetic operations.

A well-known difficulty, relating both to *time* and to the *meaningfulness* of the observations, lies in the already-mentioned change in the property of the object measured. This is evident in comparing production volumes over time when new products appear or fundamental technical changes and improvements occur. This has often been pointed out regarding big quality changes, e.g., in automobiles, etc. Difficulties are also created in accounting for entirely new products, activities and occupations, especially when aggregations of several are to be made, as is eventually inevitable. It is very easy for entirely meaningless "basic" aggregative statistics—each component perhaps individually of high accuracy—to be constructed. Each may look innocuous and appear to rest on a sound common-sense basis. In order to avoid the lack of meaning it is usually necessary to go outside the field covered by the observation itself and to fit it into a wider context. Many generally-used statistics require this type of attention, but it would lead too far to deal with this question further. We would then be entering the field of application of statistics while our main interest is far more modestly concentrated on essentially unanalyzed data and "primitive" observations.

⌯ CHAPTER IV ⌯

BUSINESS ACCOUNTING AS A FORM
AND SOURCE OF STATISTICS

1. The Nature and Components of Business Accounts

BUSINESS accounts constitute the single most important source of information about the economic activity of a nation. The amounts of figures produced are immense and it is therefore no wonder that in the United States, for example, literally millions of people are involved in their production. These figures are further processed, analyzed, and studied, and almost all business decisions are ultimately based on the information obtained from accountants. These data are all numerical. They deal with money, that wonderfully universal means for effectuating almost all transactions in a modern society. Therefore there would seem to be little doubt about the universal usefulness of accounting data for all purposes of economic analysis, business, and government. One might further assume that the long and continuing practices of accounting would have made the basic figures as well as the statistics built upon them unreservedly useful for their intended purposes. But no rigorous and undisputed standards of accuracy and reliability have been established.

The main reason for the difficulties is that, apart from providing records to guide management, the basic purpose of all business accounts is to measure *capital* and its *yield*. Although "capital" would seem to have an easily accessible intuitive meaning, it is the most elusive concept of economics. The literature on this subject is immense, and there is little agreement among economists how "capital" can best be treated conceptually and what constitutes a satisfactory measurement of this Protean entity.

Unfortunately, the contacts between economic theory and accounting theory and practice are far thinner than one would like and have reason to expect.[1] As a result, both have suffered. Here we can only indicate the nature of the great task that faces economic science to bring about a better interaction of the two disciplines.

In this chapter we shall look at accounting information only as it currently presents itself to the investigator whose principal concern is to apply a very simple notion of accuracy to economic data as they are given.

Excluding deliberately fraudulent financial accounts presented (rarely) in balance sheets and operating statements, and neglecting periods when accountants produce (more frequently) meaningless statistics—for example, because of lack of consideration of price movements as described in Chapter X—most financial statistics will generally be regarded as highly, if not completely, accurate and satisfactory. Yet such a view cannot be shared without strong qualifications. The questions of functionally false and often meaningless statistics arise, which were touched on in section 2 of Chapter III. A similar situation is shown when we realize that there is no distinction between profits due to a price rise of the product and due to increased earning power without such price movement; yet the two phenomena differ in meaning. The first, whether caused by a special demand situation or a general inflation, is an event taking place on the market, i.e. outside the firm, the second is due to the firm's technological progress and improved management.

First, we point out, financial statements for very large enterprises cannot be 100 percent free of error; this would contradict the probabilistic nature of the world. The same is true of accounts for smaller business units, mostly because they are usually made by insufficient or technically inadequate computing forces. Accountants, however, work untiringly toward a continuous reduction of this kind of error. In this they are now greatly aided by modern electronic data processing. Although the basic problem of accuracy seems to be treated little in ac-

---

[1] We shall quote only the following: M. Moonitz and C. L. Nelson, "Recent Developments in Accounting Theory," *Accounting Review*, Vol. 35 (1960), and E. O. Edwards and P. W. Bell, *The Theory and Measurement of Business Income* (Berkeley, 1961).

counting literature,[2] the practices developed in this field are all directed, at least because of the pecuniary interest involved, toward minimizing errors of the more obvious type. At the same time, however, often rather meaningless statements may be produced, particularly when aggregates are formed, by the addition of financial data from different balance sheets.

Second, both balance sheets and operating statements, i.e., profit and loss accounts, represent a mixture of figures that belong in widely separate categories. Yet these figures are treated conceptually and arithmetically as if they were completely homogeneous.

We shall concern ourselves briefly with the first point, and somewhat more extensively with the second.

Ad 1. The size of the business for which accounts are to be rendered has a decisive influence upon the accuracy of its reports. When a corporation reports on physical events such as inventory status and accumulation, units produced, sold, delivered, etc., it encounters all the difficulties connected with statistics as outlined in Chapter II. These difficulties are inevitably reproduced since, by necessity, financial expressions are attached to physical units known only within statistical limits. There simply cannot be a financial statement which is not ultimately the report of some physical event: money passing from one hand to another, when payment is made for goods and services; or a record made of physical entities allegedly in the possession of a business. The record, however, may contain an additional element, namely that of *evaluation* of the physical entity. Large corporations run into special difficulties due to

---

[2] Cf., however, W. A. Paton and A. C. Littleton, *Introduction to Corporate Accounting Standards,* Monograph 3, American Accounting Association (1940), F. Sewell Bray, "The Nature of Income and Capital," *Accounting Research,* 1 (November 1948), pp. 27–49, and W. J. Vatter, "Limitation of Overhead and Allocation," *The Accounting Review,* xx (April 1945), pp. 163–176. There are more writings of this type, some of them trying to reconcile accounting theories with economic theories. Some connection with our topic is also found in the interesting work by G. J. Staubus, *A Theory of Accounting for Investors,* Publications of the Institute of Business and Economic Research, University of California (Berkeley, 1961). Whatever divergence or reconciliation may exist, the main point made subsequently in the text about the mixture of qualitatively different kinds of numbers will hold.

size, distance, and spread of operations, etc. In that respect they have problems smaller in scale than, but similar to, those of the Army, Navy, and Air Force. However, control may be better in business, since reporting is a more professional and pecuniarily important activity; in military establishments, especially in the lower ranks, it is often only an unpleasant added duty.[3] But even in the very largest corporations the problem is very much smaller than in the Armed Forces. A company producing, say, 30,000 different articles, many in great quantities, is a giant in industry. But it deals with only a small fraction of the number of different items involved in the inventory and cost accounting of any one of the three military services. That number easily runs up to 100 times as much. The Armed Forces thus have to cope with problems that are far more complicated than those encountered by *any* business organization. Besides, they lack the guidance of a market that sets prices and of the profit motive which make the conduct of business comparatively easy.

In small businesses and in agriculture the advantage of having to keep track of smaller numbers of items is frequently offset by the lack of records, time, and, usually, also of understanding of the task. It is no exaggeration to state that a vast majority of shopkeepers and farmers do not know the status of their business, either in its physical or financial form, except in a very crude manner.[4] Their statements are, however, the basic units from which some of the most important totals are as-

---

[3] Some years ago there arose doubt as to whether the United States Army did indeed possess a large number of a certain type of tanks and if so, where they were! Yet the Army is an establishment with a highly developed, bureaucratic recording system and most thorough accounting procedures. This incident, whatever the facts in the case, shows the type of difficulty also encountered, without doubt, by large businesses. It would be interesting to learn how often similar instances occur, as they undoubtedly do, in our largest industrial enterprises. These firms also have great difficulties in finding out where their inventories are and what they consist of. This is one neglected aspect of the inventory problem which really consists of finding the optimum size of inventory under varying conditions of expected demand.

[4] The term "financial status" used here only makes sense if a definite method of determining it is presupposed. Here we mean it in the conventional sense. However, there may be no objective method at all, but only an accepted standard.

sembled which give information about the nation's business. This condition is to a high degree a function of the state of education in terms of accepted theories and practices of accounting. Data from countries with a large farming population and many small business establishments are subject to extreme doubt merely for this reason. For the rest, it is a consequence of the type of business organization and the impossibility of keeping full records even if the educational level is adequate.

This is only one indication why business accounts of different countries are seldom comparable. Even with the most careful adjustments due to different social and economic structures, they can be made comparable only in a limited sense. In addition, accounting practices vary considerably, sometimes depending on the legal framework within which business operates and sometimes due to the prevalence of particular theories and practices regarding the treatment of profits, depreciation, etc.

Ad 2. The financial records of business present the basic difficulties; these arise from the innermost nature of accounting theory and practice. Because of these complexities, it is impossible to deal with them in great detail in this book.

Figures produced by financial accounts of business enterprises fall into two classes: Class A figures record possession or handling of *monies* (either cash or equivalent forms such as bank [sight or demand] deposits), and Class B figures involve *valuations* (such as costs, profits, obsolescence) which are necessarily the outcome of theories, opinions, conventions, tradition, examples set by others, etc. Figures belonging to these two classes unfortunately occur mixed together both in balance sheets, which give a summary of a *condition* of business at a stated *moment* in time, and in operating statements, which give the *result* of having run the business for a stated *period* of time.

Figures of Class A will generally be available to an exceptionally high degree of accuracy. They are invariably given to second decimals[5] and many checks are provided in the form of

---

[5] Cost calculations within large firms are often carried to many more decimals, whether it be production or financial operations (e.g., arbitrage). The value of such calculations depends, however, not on the number of decimals but on the soundness of the underlying theory about "costs." They are, therefore, figures of Class B.

counting and recounting of cash and bank balances, money due from customers, money owed to creditors. These figures can be viewed as direct statements about fairly easily ascertained *physical* things such as cash, currency, and bank deposits. There is no problem here that would be peculiar to accounting or finance; the enumeration and counting of these items involves an ordinary statistical process, though for very large firms we may have a problem similar to that of determining the national debt actually outstanding as of a particular date. (This was discussed above, p. 44.)

Next in line, belonging to Class B and already much less definite, are *assets* that require a sale and transaction before they assume the monetary form given them in the accounts. Here, by necessity, estimation, or more properly speculation, enters: assumptions are made about prevailing prices, marketability, what prices may be obtained at the sale, etc. And so it goes on along a more or less continuous scale in which always less and less definite figures occur (but which are usually still given down to two decimal points!), until finally the pure estimates are entered into the balance sheet: for example, "goodwill," value of "real estate," etc., are sometimes demonstratively shown to be wild estimates when set at $1.00, etc.; sometimes stated with great detail, presumably arising from carefully considered valuation procedures; or as records of past expenditures, sometimes an "asset" is created in order to achieve a desired balance.

An illustration, showing the difference in practices even among corporations nominally in the same kind of business, is given in the following: For 1959 the Coca-Cola Company evaluated in its balance sheet goodwill, formulae, and trademarks at $40,198,392, but the Pepsi-Cola Company evaluated the same items at only $4,012,107. The E. I. Dupont Company valued its patents and goodwill at $41,882,149; but the Union Carbide Company, its main competitor, entered only $1.00 in its balance sheet for exactly the same items! Similarly, R. H. Macy showed $1,300,000 for goodwill, but Allied Stores showed only $1.00. This list could be lengthened to include most of the country's important industries. Aggregates are formed for the respective industries by simple addition of the respective items in the balance sheets of the individual companies. The aggregates are clearly deficient in their logic so long as they are not clearly identified as expected values. This is not done.

There is thus a peculiar mixture of trying to attribute firmly a certain amount of money to some asset or liability and the outright statement (as in the case of the $1.00 for land or goodwill) that the attribution is not to be taken seriously.

To illuminate the true character of the various posts in a balance sheet, we proceed as follows:

It has already been stated that a balance sheet is the attempt to state the conditions of a firm at a given moment of time. The different component parts, shown in so many dollars have, however, different probabilities of being realized and in that sense "true." If we take "cash on hand," the probability of this cash being convertible into cash of the stated amount at the date of the balance sheet (or at least immediately thereafter) may be considered to be one. (In the terminology of probability theory a certain event has that probability, an impossible event that of probability zero, all others falling between these two limits.) If we take as the next position "Government securities," shown for a certain number of certificates, to represent a certain amount of dollars, the probability of realizing this amount or more will be high, but less than one, since the market may not produce that much money when sold. Say, it will be .98. Going on to "accounts receivable," the probability may drop still further to, say, .85, or, depending on the state of business and the nature of the firm, even lower. When we come to "inventory," the probability of being capable of realizing at least the stated amount (always within a given time period, which is a further complication, to be neglected here) will fall even more, say to .75. Finally we come to "goodwill." If it is stated at a high, precise figure, its associated probability will perhaps be low. When it is given at one dollar, then that amount may have probability one.

So we see that for each item a "true" dollar value should be shown besides the given value. Such a dollar figure will have a probability distribution attached to it, the amount being obtained by adding (integrating) the various possible dollar values multiplied by their respective probabilities. This gives, in other words, the so-called "mathematical expectation." The probabilities can be determined in the customary way on the basis of experience as frequencies, though for some items they may have to be arrived at by more direct estimation. This point need not be discussed here further, since either procedure would yield numbers between zero and one.

Looking more closely at the above expected values, further refinements are necessary. An example will be helpful: if inventory is given as $1,000,000 and the probability of realizing it or more is .75, then the same physical inventory, set at a value of, say, $900,000, would have a probability of .85 to be realized. Surely all could be sold for, say, $500,000, hence it is worth this amount with a probability of one. Thus, the first stated probability is *marginal;* and for the particular item, in this case inventory, a probability distribution has to be determined and the mathematical expectation computed on that basis. For those cases, as cash, where the marginal probability is one up to the figure stated and zero above, the probability also is one for the total amount given. Dealing with the goodwill case, $1.00 has probability one of at least being realized, but since this is a deliberate understatement, probabilities for higher amounts and the corresponding mathematical expectations could also be computed.

A portion of the assets side of a balance sheet would thus have several columns for each item: The figures in column 3 would be comparable among each other and be subject to the ordinary arithmetic operations. As far as the liabilities are con-

TABLE 2

PROBABILISTIC STRUCTURE OF ASSETS

	Stated $ (1)	Marginal Probability (2)	Mathematically Expected Value (3)	Standard Errors $ (4)
Items				
Cash	1,000,000	1.00	1,000,000	0
Securities	2,000,000	.95	2,075,000	50,000
Inventory	5,000,000	.80	5,400,000	600,000

cerned, similar considerations apply. There the mathematical expectation will equal the stated amount in several categories, but it will differ sometimes significantly from the stated amount when capital, surplus and other reserves are considered. We shall not investigate whether a balance sheet of this probabilistic design necessarily must "balance" and what the nature of possibly needed balancing items would be.

The principle having been made clear, we dispense with further discussion at this juncture[6] although considerable expansion of this approach is possible and necessary.[6a] This shall be done at another occasion.

The comparability of balance sheets of different firms is assured, as long as each indicates the probabilities it uses in order to arrive at the mathematical expectation. This holds under the restriction that the probabilities (i.e., the transactions) are not interrelated.

It is, of course, unlikely that balance sheets will be drawn up in the indicated manner; this is a matter for the future. But it is clear that present balance sheets already contain an element of expectation and speculation. Indeed, some accounting theorists emphasize this point, though without introducing also the probabilistic approach which is indispensable, since there cannot be an expectation without a probability attached to it. This would be meaningless.

At any rate, we note that a seemingly simple statement of the condition of a firm at a given date is in fact a very complicated matter and subject to the occurrence of many errors whose nature and amount are usually shrouded in mystery.

It follows that *profit and loss* statements cannot be easier to interpret. Indeed, they are beset with even more difficulties. In profit and loss statements some receipts and transfers of money such as interest received and monies transferred to surplus are again of highest accuracy, but what a "profit" or "loss" is, as al-

[6] The reader familiar with the linear expected-utility hypothesis of von Neumann-Morgenstern will discern some interesting connections with those ideas. In particular, the familiar problem of what it is that the firm wishes to maximize appears in a different, sharper light.

[6a] Insurance companies determine expected claim payments and hold reserves calculated on the basis of variance or "ruin probability." But this concept is not carried through completely.

ready mentioned, depends on some theory which can never claim to be as convincing as a statement of the hard facts that certain sums of money were received and others were paid out.[7]

Specifically, the notion of "cost" does not fall into the first category of immediate physical observations. It would lead too far to go into the wide variants of cost theory as understood either by economists or by accountants. But it is clear that in the absence of a convincing and complete theory there is no unique and objective way of accounting for costs when overhead, amortization, and joint costs have to be taken into consideration; of course, this is the case everywhere. These difficulties prevail even when prices are stable. "Cost" is merely one aspect of a valuation process of great complexity. Even if accountants should uniformly follow the same practices (i.e., hold the same "theories") or be compelled by law to apply certain procedures, these rules would never be sharp enough for a unique financial interpretation of the conditions and events of a business. Hence, wherever costs enter into financial accounts, non-objectively measured data are produced, having their own sources and forms of error. And where would "costs" not enter?

2. THE NOTION OF ERROR IN ACCOUNTING

From such data of widely different properties there results a final *figure*, given down to two decimals, to which the ordinary concept of an "error of observation" can hardly be applied. Yet the total of assets or liabilities is not an entirely meaningless figure. In particular, such figures cause people to act one way or the other. Sometimes their acts are based on careful, lengthy computations, carried on with great attention to detail and precision. Yet the underlying information is such that the meaning of these calculations is in grave doubt.

Costs thus arrived at do not necessarily determine how much profit or loss will be shown or how many dividends will be paid! These decisions often *antedate* the making of the corre-

---

[7] A good, short survey of many of the underlying difficulties, and comparisons of the wide differences of opinion both among economists and accountants and among accountants themselves, is given by H. Norris, "Profit: Accounting Theory and Economics," *Economica*, XII (New Ser.) (1945), pp. 125–33.

sponding balances, the determination of "cost," "net," etc. Considerations such as the behavior of other firms, tradition, expectations of the future, prestige, etc., all play an important role. This will determine how much to pay out as dividends or what to put into surplus and to retain. The idea that "profits" are an automatic consequence of costs of production and sales on the one hand and receipts from sales on the other is naive and has nothing to do with business reality. Economic theory does not deal with the real world if it does not take into account these practices.

Balances of most companies (probably incomparable in a rigorous sense) at a given time often have the same direction of bias, i.e., they are constructed by application of the same ideas and "theories" about depreciation, inventory evaluation, costs, etc. When prices move up or down, the same kind of optimism and pessimism prevails, although not everywhere to the same degree. In such times views and practices differ among firms which are then apt to produce incomparable results on that account alone.

Apart from the incomparability is the fact that when price movements are not correctly understood and accounted for in balances and in determining profits, the business fluctuations are likely to be aggravated. This is an old idea, going back at least to 1878, and is apparently due to Lujo Brentano. It has been developed by others, chiefly under the impression of the German hyperinflation after World War I, notably by F. Schmidt.[8] The essence of these views is that the adherence to inflexible accounting procedures produces apparent gains and losses and that subsequent decisions based on these are to the detriment of the firm and, indirectly, to that of the economy as a whole. We shall not dwell on this matter further. The inability to take proper account of price movements is a fact that cannot be denied in the light of countless examples from business and accounting literature. Thus there is a source of error in business accounts of an especially elusive nature. They belong to the

---

[8] "Die Industriekonjunktur—ein Rechenfehler!" (1927), republished as *Betriebswirtschaftliche Konjunkturlehre* (1933). An exposition, with further references, is in W. A. Jöhr, *Die Konjunkturschwankungen* (Zürich, 1952), pp. 438–458.

category of functionally false statistics, of which they are probably the most significant illustration.

In times of highly stable prices, and if accounting is consistently carried out according to the same accounting theory, balance sheets and operating statements give, for the same individual firm, some information which may even be itself consistent, although it does not show what it purports to show. This is quite apart from outright falsified balances, which we do not consider although they undoubtedly still exist. It should, however, be noted that a "lie" is, in this context, not a simple and obvious concept. It is unmistakable when a false cash position is fraudulently given or when physical inventories are reported that do not exist. But when a more optimistic attitude is deliberately taken in interpreting the success of a year's operation—for example, by small amortization or using purchase price when the price level is rising—it is hard to classify this statement as a "lie." Instead, it may be viewed as an error in judgment, and as such, to be proved or disproved by later events.

There is an intermediate category between the (subjectively) completely truthful reporting and outright falsification. It may be called "adjusted reporting," one form of which is well-known also as "window dressing." It consists, for example, of short-term borrowing (for a few days) in order to show a substantially better cash position than otherwise would be the case. This has always been a common practice, at least in Europe, especially with commercial banks, and occurs when year-end balances have to be exhibited. In the United States, on call dates the commercial banks often arrange their affairs so as to have little or no borrowing from the Federal Reserve, so that they be found in a satisfactory cash position. This procedure is counteracted by the call dates (except for December) now falling on days which are not fully determined in advance. The banks are therefore subject to a moderate amount of surprise.[9] Nevertheless, this kind of reporting problem persists.

---

[9] This, incidentally, is a good example of the use of a random or mixed strategy—in the game theoretical sense—in order to arrive at the truth when evasion or manipulation by the questioned is to be feared. Cf. p. 22 above.

An individual balance sheet is therefore a configuration made up of parts, each of which can be represented graphically as in Fig. 1. Here each column is ordered according to the decreasing probability of realizing the stated amount shown on the vertical axis. Each column to the *right* contains the smaller columns to the left which have a higher probability. Fig. 1-(a) has only a single column which is, with probability one, the cash on hand. Fig. 1-(b) shows that of the total government securities, y_2, the smaller amount, y_1, can be counted on with probability one, but the difference between y_2 and y_1 only with probability .95, and there is none lower, the market being what it is. The other items are similarly treated. The average value of a balance sheet item is then based on a properly chosen, probably weighted, average of these segments, and would be the value of the mathematical expectation of the total amount shown in the last, righthand column. We call the amounts with probability one the "kernel" or "core" of the balance sheet. All others are farther and farther away from the core.

A representation of figures in the balance sheet of a single firm can be made as in Fig. 2. A single hard core such as cash on hand (with probability of one) to which the ordinary ideas of errors apply, is surrounded by successive layers of other figures, with lesser and lesser probabilities attached to them. In each area the values from each item in the balance sheet will be shown which have the same probability. Thus the core does not only consist of cash, but of all those amounts whose probability of being realized also is one; from there on we proceed in decreasing order as described above.

Aggregation of several balance sheets, for example, of firms in the same industry, can now be made on the basis of expected values with better assurance that homogeneous figures are used than otherwise. But in outward (monetary) appearance balance sheet items as currently drawn up are indistinguishable in their presentation even down to the last decimals. In their magnitudes the total of the less and less definitely known figures, obtained by applying various theories and having attached to them various probabilities for conversion into cash, far exceed those for cash on hand; in other words the more truly reliable figures are only a small percentage of the balance sum.

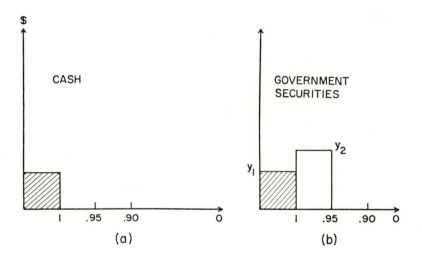

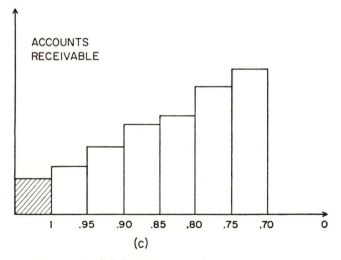

Figure 1. Probabilistic Structure of Assets

Figure 2. Composition of Balance Sheet

An aggregation from several balance sheets is, therefore, the summation of such information; but only the *arithmetic sums of the "kernels"* can have a claim to an "accuracy" to which the customary notions of error can be applied.

The lack of definiteness of each configuration is quite different in character from that "fuzziness" of natural and social data which is due to our inability to determine them more sharply. But, as already mentioned elsewhere, even in physical theory (more specifically in quantum mechanics) it was necessary to show that certain types of measurements, or rather combinations of measurements, are *in principle* impossible. Perhaps analogous notions will have to be evolved for parts of economics, with correspondingly grave consequences.

It will be a serious task to develop a statistical theory capable of dealing with such a situation: an ordered mixture or sequence of firm figures with guesses and estimates of increasing uncertainty. This sequence is not random but has its own rules, conventions, and some amount of stability. The aggregation of such figures produces a certain measure of information, though not of the commonly imagined kind. The usual notions of error do not apply to these situations in any obvious and intuitive manner.

84

Summarizing, we see that adopting a correct statistical view of the true, limited nature of information produced by financial statements has profound *operational significance*. It must be realized that at present combinations of financial statements yield far less information than is implied by the nature and extent of the numerical operations carried out with these figures. For example, if the stated value of an asset depends on non-disturbance of the market by a sale of this asset, then the figures for all or many firms, showing such assets, are clearly non-additive (if the assets are at all estimated in close agreement with their market prices!). Yet additions are made for different firms and finally larger and larger aggregates are constructed when, for example, the capital invested in an industry is described, or when its total assets, inventories, etc., are discussed. Such figures give a very inadequate picture of physical or economic reality, even when a business balance is (correctly) interpreted as being equivalent to a still photograph taken in a stream of events that often moves swiftly.

The reader should contemplate the extent to which financial information guides action: earnings per share are a standard measure, share prices are expressed as multiples of earnings and thereby are judged as to whether they are "out of line" or not. Profit ratios, i.e., profits in their relation to invested capital, are compared for firms in the same industry or for different industries. The advisability of new ventures is judged by forming ideas about expected profits—which, however, are determined by the same questionable procedures discussed above. The circularity in method is striking but it will be a permanent part of our pattern of thinking until the time when economic theory develops observable measures for profits which are free from these objections and until accountants produce substantially new ideas of constructing balance sheets composed of conceptually homogeneous figures. That time appears to be distant. But accountants could begin to use the existing tools which probability theory provides and which allow the determination of expected values, as outlined above. The users of balance sheets, especially the investor, should be the first to insist on the introduction of a modern spirit into this sadly stagnant field.

Though what was said here is applicable to accounting problems in any country, they are larger in one nation than in another. This raises the question of the international comparability of balance sheets and profit and loss statements. The fact is that they are seldom comparable. Disclosure of business operations differs widely from one country to another. It is probably highest in the United States, less in Great Britain and Germany, and shrouded in mystery in Italy and elsewhere; and it must not be forgotten that in Switzerland, as has been remarked, secrecy is a national virtue. Government requirements and tax laws differ and their enforcement differs even more. In some countries consolidated balance sheets are published, in others not. Depreciation is carried out in a widely differing manner. Profits shown in published balance sheets have only a remote resemblance to the profits shown internally and sometimes even to the national governments. This list could be lengthened.

Consequently, international comparability of business accounts is an exceedingly difficult matter which we shall not discuss further at this juncture. It suffices to point out that international comparisons of profitability of invested capital, return to investment, ratio of price per share to earnings, etc., cannot be made with confidence on the basis of the published records. They all require deep probing in which the above considerations about the statistical properties of business accounts is mandatory. The greatest difficulty is faced by economists in divers countries, confronted with material of such varying characteristics, trying to derive economic laws which should be universally applicable.

Business is transacted in the illusion of dealing with "accuracy" where there is none in an ordinary or scientific sense; nor does there exist a substitute notion. We know far less about the economy as a whole even in the financial field than one imagines when the nature of the financial figures (other than those of Class A above) is considered. This has deep significance in judging the possibilities and effects of policy, of prediction, and is, of course, of paramount importance for economic theory.

The financial figures are only representative descriptions of the physical events behind them which in their entirety make up business—the production of goods and commodities, their transportation, the rendering of services, communications, the storage of supplies, merchandising, etc. We have seen that the observation of all these highly diverse physical facts and their changes cannot possibly be free from error and, as a consequence, the same applies to their representation by financial figures. The economist must be aware of these conditions when he tries to formulate the laws that govern the economic behavior of individual firms or whole nations.

❧ CHAPTER V ❧

ECONOMIC DATA AND

ECONOMIC THEORY

WE DO NOT intend to enter upon a deep philosophical or even thorough methodological discussion of the basis of empirical science in the field of economics.[1] We simply propose to make a number of comments about the relation of economics to data showing the properties previously outlined.

1. DATA AND INFORMATION

The chief thing is to understand that there is a fundamental difference (in the field of economics) between mere *data* and *observations*. The latter are naturally also data, but they are more than that. They are selected. They are supposed to arise from planned observation, guided by theory, which however need not necessarily be tied to controlled experiments. *Observations* are deliberately *designed;* other *data* are merely *obtained.* Together they constitute economic information which is related to the entire body of information, partly deriving from it, partly illuminating that section of problems that is not yet understood. Theory itself is never based solely on ordinary data in the above sense, i.e., merely obtained information with largely unknown but probably exceedingly wide error margins. Theory, moreover, is constructed and invented; data are merely

[1] A most authoritative modern treatment of the problem of theory construction and the relation of theory to measurement to be found anywhere in contemporary literature is by H. Weyl, *Philosophy of Mathematics and Natural Science* (Princeton, 1949), especially p. 139 ff. and p. 151 ff. Though not a very recent book (its main part was written in 1926), it is still a standard work; the appendices to the English version deal with profoundly important recent developments, especially the role of combinatorics and the nature of Gödel's discovery in logic. This book had, incidentally, a profound influence on J. von Neumann at the time it first appeared, as well as on many other kindred spirits.

There exists, of course, an immense amount of literature on the nature of statistics, its relation to science, etc. A very good treatment in a truly modern spirit is J. W. Tukey, "Statistical and Quantitative Methodology," in *Trends in Social Science,* edited by D. P. Ray (New York, 1961).

gathered and collected even though this involves always *administrative* planning. But economic theory is nevertheless to a very high extent in addition related to non-constructively obtained material, such as personal experience. This is quite different from astronomical observations and the making of a theory in the sciences. The small body of economic theory that is placed deliberately upon an empirical basis is thus not necessarily resting upon a very substantial basis.

It is desirable to set forth systematically the relationship of such terms as "observation," "data," "statistics," "evidence," etc. Our use may not find general acceptance, but, in order to achieve precision, clarity of the terminology is essential. The ordering of the concepts is illustrated in Fig. 3. A is the body of data consisting of gathered (numerical) statistics; B represents other data, such as historical events or (now) non-measurable data, e.g., "expectations"; C is the theory based partly on A and B, as well as on deductively obtained facts (perhaps not accessible to direct observations; this class may, as yet, be empty in economics). The intersection of A and C, and B and C, and, if it exists, of A and B and C, is called *scientific information* which is thus made up of quantitative observation (i.e., the intersection of A and C) and *description* (i.e., the intersection of B and C).[2] *Data* are thus something much wider than scientific information; the latter alone is related to theory. Data become scientific information only through this connection. Otherwise they are nothing more than possible building stones for theory. Should they ever be used, they assume a state characterized by the relation into which they enter with other data and their explanation by the theory. Most economic quantitative (statistical) data are of the class A minus C type; i.e., they are represented by the non-shaded area of A in Fig. 3. While they may illuminate something they do not do this automatically. These data as such tell no story, or they tell many different and conflicting stories simultaneously; either condition is equivalent to the lack of a theory.

Observation and description are *planned* processes, in which the initial stimulus comes from some existing theory, however

[2] The intersection of A and B and C also constitutes observation.

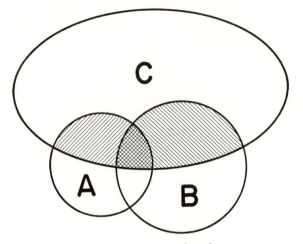

Figure 3. Data and Scientific Information

rudimentary it may be. This is true even when it is intended to produce observations (quantitative or not) aimed at overthrowing the initial theory in order to replace it with a better structure. This is the normal process of scientific progress.

In economic life, continuous processes automatically produce currently great masses of statistical data which often become useful for the above purpose. These are the statistics of foreign trade, of stock prices, etc. Sometimes even unique phenomena produce their own quantitative record as a byproduct. Therefore, there exist great masses of economic statistics which as such do not constitute scientific information; they may be raised to that level by being connected with this field. These statistics as well as their counterpart in the field of non-quantitative (historical) description are *potential* scientific information.

In the *natural sciences* there are only few, but perhaps important, automatically *accruing* data. Almost all are the product of planned conduct, strictly guided by theory. Many measurements, it is true, are initiated without much help from a formal theory, especially when a field is very new. It is, in general, difficult to decide in advance what new measurements the desired future theory will demand. But a theory is always the ultimate aim; and even when the data are not yet strictly connected with theory, they are systematically produced by experimental scientists.[3]

In a new field, or when a fundamentally new research tool is invented, almost anything "goes." Thus, when the telescope and the microscope became available, looking at any planet or star, or at any drop of water made sense because it would immediately disclose new worlds. Now, several hundred years later, the precise spot at which to look has to be carefully computed to justify the observation. Electronic high-speed computers are for the social scientist comparable to those two instruments of physics and we are still in that early phase where almost any computation that has been entirely out of reach thus far might make sense and bring a startling discovery. But this will not be true for long.

The immensity of the present revolution is only gradually becoming apparent. The development of computers has progressed at a speed which was only possible because the early computers themselves contributed to the solution of the design problems the newer ones posed. This is not the place to discuss the probable influence of computers upon economics,[4] but one illustration will take the place of many: In 1934, Ragnar Frisch described for his work on confluence analysis[5] how by careful programming and the use of the best desk computers of that time it was possible to make about 100 multiplications of six decimal digits *per hour*, checks, corrections, and occasional rests included. This was an accomplishment indeed and a fair num-

---

[3] To give an illustration: Many years ago a great number of spectroscopic measurements were made by numerous physicists, the results of which did not fit into any then existing theory. This condition lasted until W. Pauli took the great step in announcing the "exclusion principle" which with one stroke brought meaning to seemingly disconnected results of measurements: a theory was established and a new order prevailed. Further experimental work was called for and was given a firm basis.

[4] Cf. my paper, "Experiment and Large Scale Computation in Economics," *op. cit.* Since published in 1954, many of the developments anticipated then have taken place, but fewer in economics than in computer advance. However I am convinced that economics will eventually be as profoundly affected as I have there suggested.

[5] R. Frisch: *Statistical Confluence Analysis by Means of Complete Regression Systems* (Oslo, 1934), p. 96 ff.

ber of computations could eventually be handled. Compare this now with the large, fastest computers, in existence since about 1960. An IBM 7090 can easily handle 10^4 or 10,000 multiplications *per second,* or 36,000,000 per hour, if well programmed. A computer will run faultlessly for such periods. An even faster computer, the "Stretch" can extend this again by a factor of 10 and deal with more than 9 digits in the decimal system. All computer work requires careful programming and, in terms of the actual computing time, the time spent on programming *new* computations is very long. But whatever it be, that time is immaterial compared with the previous inability to compute at all or to reduce the needed time by a factor of a million or more. Clearly a revolution of such dimensions cannot fail but to transform the social sciences fundamentally.

2. ECONOMETRIC THEORY

Although it is impossible on methodological grounds to distinguish sharply between economic and econometric theory, such a distinction persists at the present. Like any other economic theory, econometric theory attempts to construct models of economic reality which it casts in mathematical form, thereby necessarily involving a high degree of idealization. We do not propose to discuss specific attempts or results at this occasion. However, it must be pointed out that efforts along those lines did *not* begin with a critical examination of the quality of the data; neither has this aspect occupied econometricians decisively in more recent times. Yet, this need will have to be faced.

Econometric theory has, instead, considered another possibility: discrepancies noted between the model and the data entering into equations may appear to be due to influences of specific factors not considered in the equations, to "hidden variables" rather than to errors and inaccuracies of the data. This, then, poses a theoretical problem of accounting for the other factors[6] rather than one of "mere" correction of the basic

---

[6] As set forth in the programmatic writing of T. Haavelmo, "The Probability Approach to Econometrics," *Econometrica,* Vol. 12, Supplement (1944). Cf. especially Chapters III and IV. Since then a considerable number of publications has followed, especially by writers belonging to the

information. The two approaches are necessarily inseparable from each other; but they need to be further characterized in their mutual relation to each other.

The differences between "true" and "observed" variables is not necessarily that of overlooked economic forces showing up as alleged random disturbances. The differences may be far more elementary and lie in the data themselves on the basis of which the econometric theory was presumably established. The word "elementary" must in this connection be used in both its meanings: as *simple* from a technical point of view and as *fundamental* from the point of view of theory construction.

So long as no specific assumptions are made about the degree of error in the basic observation of economic phenomena, it is not feasible to make useful statements about the "randomness" of the information given as due to the alleged presence of other factors hitherto neglected in the formulation of the model. To the extent that stochastic theory is at all possible, it must be designed so as to allow us to distinguish and to decide between the two sources: firstly, errors of observation and secondly, failure to account for disturbing factors that ought to form part of the theory and enter into a more adequate set of equations. In a strict sense, these neglected factors (variables)[7] too become known only through information *also* beset with errors of ob-

---

Cowles Commission. However, little if any attention was paid to the property of the underlying primitive observations and basic data. We shall not enter upon this discussion, much of which is concerned with the problem of identification, the validity of the simultaneous equations approach, estimation, least squares, etc. I refer only to the Symposium on Simultaneous Equation Estimation, *Econometrica*, Vol. 28, October, 1960, pp. 835–871, where most of the relevant literature is discussed. The discussion there clearly reveals the great uncertainties that still prevail in this area, even when the data are assumed to be better than they are.

It is noteworthy that none of the currently available textbooks on econometrics brings any thorough discussion of the accuracy of data and the implication for econometrics. The topic is hardly ever mentioned. To view the present discussion in proper perspective, the reader may want to reconsider the last paragraphs of Chapter II above.

[7] Modern scientists take a dim view of "hidden variables" though many feel reluctant to abandon this view. "Hidden variables are an invention; they can neither be observed nor measured. If we cannot observe them, let us admit that they have no reality and may exist only in the imagination of their authors." L. Brillouin, *op. cit.*, p. 315.

servation. Hence, there is never a possibility of completely transforming the *observed* parameters into *true* parameters by accounting fully for excluded factors. "True" parameters can, on principle, only be theoretically determined.

Consider, for example, the important problem of whether linear or non-linear production functions should be considered in economic models. Non-linearity is a great complication and is, therefore, best avoided as much as possible. True non-linearity in the strict mathematical sense is avoided in physics as far as possible; even quantum mechanics is treated as linear on a higher level. Many apparently non-linear phenomena, upon closer investigation, can well be treated as linear. For example, the pendulum can be treated by linear methods when swings are small; when they are large a non-linear method becomes necessary. The distinction is largely a matter of the precision of measurement, which is exactly where the weakness is greatest in economics.

It is astonishing that economists seem to hesitate far less to introduce non-linearity than physical scientists, where the tradition of mathematical exploration is so much older and the experience with observation and measurement so much firmer.

Often linearity or proportionality will simply have to be assumed, because otherwise such formidable mathematical difficulties arise that the handling of economic models becomes virtually impossible. Clearly, it is ultimately a question of *fact* whether any significant violation of reality has occurred, if linearity is chosen. Can it be settled on the basis of our present knowledge of "costs," production, input-output relations, etc? This is greatly to be doubted. Present information is so vague and so much beset with doubt, that a final decision of such major problems one way or the other is, as a rule, quite impossible without further, profoundly better, new measurements.

Economic theory of all types is ultimately designed to make *predictions.* It must be understood that any such process, whatever its ultimate possibility, involves four steps: (1) the initial data, (2) the model, (3) the computations, and (4) the comparison of the numerical results with reality. Each one of them has its own sources of errors: the initial data are available only with a certain degree of accuracy (which it may be impossible to determine), the model is an idealization of reality, the computations can produce errors that are added to those existing at the start. The numerical result with all its cumulative errors will be compared with, and "checked" against, a "reality" that is again only revealed up to an (unknown) error factor. This is then hopefully called "verification."

Clearly, it is difficult to state whether discrepancies in the final comparison are due to a concentration of successive errors, to a faulty underlying theory which either does not account properly for the factors recognized or perhaps omits significant forces, or finally to imperfect information about the later reality. (For further discussion, see Chapter VI.)

A theoretical model as such can never tell us whether other factors have been overlooked and should have been included. Such indications can only come when a theoretical model is put into relation with experience. As we saw, the question then is to decide whether discrepancies are due to a faulty model or to lack of definition of the information. Most likely, one will encounter a combination of the two, namely some admixture.

To put this issue in different words: Is the application of an economic program, i.e., of a particular economic theory, more sensitive to changes in the model or to changes in the data (the quality of our information)? This is a far from trivial question to which at present the answer is not obtainable in general. At best we can hope to give satisfactory answers only from case to case.[8]

3. THE DEGREE OF FINE STRUCTURE OF ECONOMIC THEORY

Economic theory has in its various parts, as all other theory in any field, either more of a *fine* or more of a *coarse structure*. This implies that, in order to be corroborated or falsified, a type of observation is required that corresponds as closely as possible to the given degree of fineness of the structure.

The usefulness of economic data, therefore, cannot be gauged without relating them to the uses (theorems) to which they are to be fitted.

---

[8] It is easily seen how the justification of the widespread use of large linear programs would be dependent on a resolution of this dilemma.

The error of observation, in order to be meaningful, has to refer not, as thus far discussed, to a mere figure, whatever it might be, but to one that is specifically related to the *level of accuracy* required by the use. The use is not immediately open to intuition but can only be inferred from the basis of the known structure of the theory. As Einstein stated, one single new fact could suffice to invalidate the whole theory of relativity.[9] Thus, relativity theory is in this sense shown to be of exceptionally fine structure (the remark in footnote 3, page 9, notwithstanding). What economic theory or "law" would now be, or ever has been, overthrown by one single new fact?

To put it differently: the statement that the dollar-sterling exchange rate was at a certain date $4.86 for one pound sterling may, on the one hand, be more than adequate for an investigation into some phases of the movement of exchange rates (where one decimal may be satisfactory or even more than enough, as in the study of a large scale inflation). On the other hand, it may be wholly inadequate for the study of mutual relations of exchange rates, gold points and short term interest rate differentials between the two countries (where two, three or even four additional decimals ought to be known accurately). At each level there is an admissible error of observation. It must be referred to specifically.

This has been the development in physics and astronomy, too. For a long time, it was quite sufficient to know the distance of the earth from the moon, the sun and from other planets only roughly. Now there is an interest in making the measurements far more accurate. The new improvements of measurement would perhaps have meant little 200 or even 100 years ago. Now the need to know the location of any point on earth precisely down to $\pm\frac{1}{2}$ mile is important to those who may sometime fire an intercontinental ballistic missile from a distance of 5,000 miles with a CPE (circular probable error) of less than ½ mile. Previously, such accuracy of earthly measure-

[9] Obviously it would have to be a fact exceedingly difficult to find! New physical facts (of scientific interest!) are not easy to find; the discovery of important ones is often rewarded by the Nobel prize.

An interesting discussion of what a "fact" is can be found in M. Polanyi, *Personal Knowledge; Towards a Post-Critical Philosophy* (Chicago, 1958), especially pp. 134 ff.

ments not only did not matter but would have been absurd and too expensive to establish.

A simultaneous development has to occur in the theory, in its application, and in observation. The first is affected by the latter; it proves its value if it remains unaffected when either more points of observation are brought to bear upon it or when the existing measurements are refined and sharpened. It can also happen that a theory is in no perceptible way influenced by any additional and/or finer measurements. This will be the case when it is not related to the facts at all or only in such a hazy way that it deserves no consideration whatsoever as an empirical theory. It is likely that parts of accepted economics fall into this category. For example, no amount of improved observations of a modern economy will have any bearing upon the Walrasian system which, using the inadequate conceptual-mathematical notion of maximization, describes only a hypothetical case of economic organization, far removed from reality however coarsely or finely described.

The fine or coarse structure of economic theory has little if anything to do with *micro-* or *macro-*observation. The distinction holds for all fields, whether one deals with the individual consumer and firm, or with the national income. It is very likely, however, that the essentially phenomenological statements about large economic aggregates are now far more coarse than those about, say, costs in an individual firm—unless the latter are merely tautological definitions!

Thus, since there exists no integrated system of theory in any one area, be it physics or economics, there are simultaneously several degrees of acceptable levels of precision of measurement. In physics it is possible, for example, on the one hand to have a measurement of the "Ritchie constant" with an accuracy of 10^{-14}, but on the other to know the age of the earth and of the universe only approximately with a deviation of several billion years, and to make acceptable cross-section measurements in nuclear physics with only a 50 percent (!) accuracy. *In the overall, a measurement in physics with 10 percent accuracy is a very good measurement.* The reader should compare this with the alleged ability of the economist to measure changes in national income, consumers' spendable income, price levels, imports, etc., to an overall accuracy of ten to one hundred times better—even in the average!

Newton established the law of gravity and verified it with an accuracy of about 4 percent (it was later proved to be accurate to about 1/10,000 of one percent).[10] We conclude from such shining examples in the history of physics that the economist need not despair that good, workable theory is impossible unless the data are of the presently alleged high accuracy which even the physicists now do not enjoy in general. But the theory will look different from what is now being advanced.

Theories can be classified according to the requirements they make upon the data with which they are concerned; some are demanding, some are not. But in each case a clear evaluation of the situation must be made since otherwise meaningless associations are established.

For example, while it might be desirable to have simple models of the economic world, there is an anachronism of proposing naive Keynesian models of only a few variables, yet to insist that the data to which they are to be applied—aggregations of vast scope—be known to hundreds of one percent accuracy when, in fact, the second digit is already in doubt. This will change, of course. In less time than a generation one will wonder how such proposals could ever have been taken at face value.

[10] E. P. Wigner, "The Unreasonable Effectiveness of Mathematics in the Natural Sciences," *Communications on Pure and Applied Mathematics,* Vol. xiii (1960), p. 8. This brilliant paper might well be studied by anyone concerned with clarifying in his mind the role of theory formation and to see in particular how "false theories . . . give, in view of their falseness, alarmingly accurate descriptions of groups of phenomena" (p. 13).

❧ CHAPTER VI ☙

NUMERICAL-MATHEMATICAL
OPERATIONS IN ECONOMICS
AND THE PROBLEMS
OF ERROR

*"Der Mangel an mathematischer Bildung gibt sich durch
nichts so auffallend zu erkennen, wie durch masslose
Schärfe im Zahlenrechnen"*[1]—C. F. W. GAUSS

I. GENERAL CONSIDERATIONS

IN THIS CHAPTER we examine briefly a field of perhaps uncommon problems; but they are of far-reaching significance. Some of these problems have been of interest to mathematicians and statisticians for a long time, as the development of the calculus of errors and observations shows. Now, however, they assume entirely new aspects and proportions because of the magnitude of operations that have become possible since the construction of high-speed electronic computers. These problems are of great relevance to time series analysis, input-output studies, linear programming, etc. Many of these activities lead to the attempted solution of high-order systems of linear equations. They are even more important for still more complicated mathematical and numerical setups.[2]

Both statisticians and economists are interested in application, the statistician to see his data fitted into a theory that will explain their meaning, and the economist to apply his theories

---

[1] "The lack of mathematical insight shows up in nothing as surprisingly as in unbounded precision in numerical computations."

[2] Cf., O. Morgenstern, *Remarks,* "Session on Input-Output Analysis and Its Use in Peace and War Economics," *Proceedings of American Economic Association,* May 1949, pp. 238 ff.; and O. Morgenstern and T. M. Whitin, "Aggregation and Errors in Input-Output Models," National Bureau of Economic Research, *Conference on Input-Output Relations* (Princeton University Press, 1955). In the latter volume, C. F. Christ discusses the subject matter closely following the present Chapter VI (from the 1950 edition). The entire complex is taken up at much greater length in my paper "Experiment and Large Scale Computation in Economics," in *Economic Activity Analysis,* O. Morgenstern, ed. (New York, 1954), pp. 483–549.

in such a manner that they become numerically useful. Their cooperation produces the activity known as "econometrics."

The fitting of *new* data into economic theory has been a very loose and uncertain process. There does not seem to be one single instance where this process required vast numerical operations of the type considered here. Where they would have been necessary on a really great scale in the past, as, say, in the analysis of time series by means of Fourier series, they have not been carried out to the extent required by a sufficiently large number of long time series. The difficulties were in the lack of use or design of proper machines, combined with a widespread skepticism among economists concerning the usefulness or appropriateness of the complex mathematical techniques. Even ordinary serial correlations with distributed lags were not made in really large numbers, mostly because the necessary experimental work seemed forbiddingly extensive. All this is now changing.

The other type of work lies in the direction of application of economic theory and its numerical evaluation. This has been done mostly by computing coefficients of elasticity of demand for certain commodities (the work mainly of H. Schultz) and similar kinds of work. More recently, efforts have been made to determine the consumption function for various cases. But there do not seem to be many applications involving a very large body of economic theory, sequences of theorems, etc., each requiring large-scale, continuous mathematical operations. Numerical evaluation was, however, at least mentioned by Pareto in a famous passage of his *Manuel*, where he pointed out that, according to his general equilibrium theory, for 700 commodities and 100 persons not less than 70,699 equations would have to be solved—a patent impossibility then or now.[3] Incidentally, it is noteworthy that the impossibility of numerical application of his theory did not disturb this leader of mathematical economics or his followers. It would, of course, be an enormous achievement to be able to describe mathematically economic phenomena and their interdependence even without immediate numerical evaluation—an accomplishment generally

[3] Vilfredo Pareto, *Manuel d'Economie Politique* (Paris, 1927, second edition), pp. 227 ff.

believed to have been made by Walras, Pareto, and others. But eventually the numerical evaluation must always be attempted and constitutes the final aim, however far removed it may be at any given time. The application must be possible *in principle*. The latter raises a neat issue: there must be given a *proof* that the equations have a solution—a solution of a specified kind such as, for example, excluding negative prices and negative production. If that cannot be done, nothing further needs to be said. If it can be given, the additional question poses itself whether the solution can be *computed* in a concrete case of application. This is the aspect with which we are concerned in this chapter. In Pareto's case, the question is to be answered in the negative, even if he could have shown that a solution exists. This neither he nor his immediate followers have done.[4]

To make this point quite clear: though it may have been proved mathematically that a system has solutions of a desired kind, it does not necessarily follow that a numerical-practical application is always possible. As an extreme example, the application may require so many computational steps that they cannot be performed in a time interval that makes the application still useful. This is of importance in meteorology, where the weather may change before the (otherwise correct) prediction has been computed.

Pareto's 70,699 equations are still beyond our reach—whatever their worth—though the model itself deals with but a tiny "economy." Hence a whole economy is entirely inaccessible for computation, unless drastic simplifications are introduced. This leads to the process of aggregation, mentioned elsewhere, which presents one of the most important but also most troublesome problems in economics. Aggregation is the formation of larger entities from myriads of components. This reduces the number of equations that have to be set up. A balance has to be struck:

[4] The turning point is the work by A. Wald inspired by Karl Menger in 1933–34, "On Some Systems of Equations of Mathematical Economics," *Econometrica,* vol. 19, 1951, pp. 368–403, translated from *Zeitschrift für Nationalökonomie* (1936). The idea frequently encountered, that a proof is not needed, since the economy can be regarded as a huge analogue computer which actually solves Pareto's system is, of course, worthless. It would have to be shown first that Walras' or Pareto's equations (or anybody else's for that matter) are the *only* ones that can describe the economic system. This is evidently not the case.

too little aggregation leaves us with more detail than we can handle, though it would be highly desirable to possess the information; too much aggregation mixes the unmixable and gives us models that are easy to handle but with low, if any, power of resolution. Modern computing devices allow us to think now of much more detail than could ever be considered seriously a generation ago, or even a decade ago. By aggregating, errors of a new kind are introduced; gradually, more attention is being paid to these. The situation is fluid and will remain so until much more experience has been gathered in this whole area.[5]

The first endeavors to solve a really complex economic problem numerically are apparently due to W. W. Leontief and Herbert F. Mitchell, Jr., as well as to George Dantzig and his group, then in the U.S. Air Force.[6] These authors naturally, and tacitly, assumed that their equations, which were based on a simplified Walrasian model, did have significant solutions—a point we shall not pursue in the present context.

These efforts (especially the first one of solving 38 simultaneous linear equations) enormously exceeded anything numerically attempted in economics up to that time (or elsewhere in the social sciences, as it appears to be the case).[7] Even

---

[5] Reference is made again to the important work of M. Hatanaka, *The Workability of Input-Output Analysis* (Ludwigshafen am Rhein, 1960) which deals with several of these problems.

[6] Cf., W. W. Leontief, "Computational Problems Arising in Connection with Economic Analysis of Inter-industrial Relationships," *Proceedings of a Symposium on Large-Scale Digital Calculating Machinery,* (Cambridge, Mass.: Harvard University Press, 1948) pp. 169–75; H. F. Mitchell, Jr., "Inversion of a Matrix of Order 38," *Mathematical Tables and Other Aids to Computation,* III: 161–66, July 1948; and George Dantzig, *Programming in a Linear Structure* (U.S. Air Force, February 1948); and unpublished application. Mention should also be made of computations by the Bureau of Labor Statistics in connection with applications of input-output data collected by the Bureau. By the present time this literature has swelled beyond all bounds.

[7] Large computations made by hand or with the aid of special analogue computers were, of course, routine matters in astronomy, physics, and meteorology long before this time. There were also systems of up to three hundred equations that had been solved (meaningfully) by manual operations. But these were usually systems of equations of a very highly special (sequential) character where the problem discussed in this chapter did not pose itself. We shall not pursue this aspect any further here.

time series manipulation thus far carried out, however involved, had not been of this order, although some procedures already applied for small samples would rank high in comparison had they been applied to a greater number of long series (e.g., harmonic analysis, Fourier analysis, etc.).

Large-scale numerical operations depend on the type of computing machines available (both technically and financially). The advent of electronic high-speed computers has brought about possibilities of entirely new dimensions. It still cannot be foreseen how far-reaching their influence upon economic research will be, though we begin to discern developments. They also produce qualitatively and quantitatively new problems that have a direct bearing upon the questions discussed thus far in this book. These new problems will have to be faced by economists who may have occasion to use these new instruments.

Apart from deeper connections (discussed in the next section) between the accuracy of data and the extent and intricacy of numerical operations, the considerable expense will make it imperative that only very high-quality data be used. Although this is obvious, it is not impossible that the fascination of being able to explore hitherto inaccessible regions of economic activities may lead to premature computations which the quality of the material does not warrant. This danger is great because of the general lack of consideration of errors in econometrics and in economic statistics even under far simpler computational and common-sense conditions. The best indication is that, even now, routine computations are performed on ordinary desk computers which the data do not justify.

A good illustration is offered by the frequent routine and mechanical elimination of seasonal variations from time series that are highly suspect; that is, the seasonals are not very clear or distinct and that data are poor at the same time. In these cases, the mathematical-statistical operations are often of a much finer nature and structure than can be tolerated by the data. If, for example, observed seasonal variations are uncertain or weak and the data have the probably not-uncommon error of, say, ±5–10 percent, methods for their computation and elimination, presupposing data with a smaller error, are inapplicable. Time and money used for such purposes are wasted. Instead of mechanically "correcting" time series by a *relatively* too powerful analytical procedure, it would be better to concentrate efforts toward an improvement of the "raw" basic information itself. (For an example, compare Chapter XIII, p. 234.)

Another important illustration for computations that are not warranted by the quality of data is the computation of rates of change, such as growth rates of a country measured by Gross National Product or national income (cf. Chapter XV).

The caveat against computing sharply with poor data (cf. the words of the great Gauss taken as motto to this chapter!) is not in conflict with the remark, made in the last paragraph of Section 1 of Chapter V, to the effect that the possibility of large-scale computation gives a new freedom to economics and the other social sciences, the kind of which could not have been envisaged even a generation ago. But this freedom has to be used with the inevitable constraint imposed by the rules of numerical analysis. Some of these constraints are novel in view of the new dimension which computing has assumed. This ability to compute is, incidentally, one of the most revolutionary features of our age.

2. THE FOUR SOURCES OF ERROR

We shall now discuss briefly the main forms in which problems of numerical computation are related to errors. In this account, we have mainly large-scale operations in mind such as would necessarily arise in any application of economic theory, be it by inverting matrices of high order, for linear programming, by computing multiple correlations, by solving of problems arising from the theory of games such as finding the best strategy, etc.

The general problem was set forth and thoroughly discussed, for the first time, in a pioneering paper by J. von Neumann and H. H. Goldstine, "Numerical Inverting of Matrices of High Order,"[8] which we shall follow rather closely. There the following four classes of error are distinguished:

[8] *Bulletin of the American Mathematical Society* 53:1021–99 (1947), Part II *Proceedings Am. Math. Society*, vol. 2 (1951), pp. 188–202. Cf.

(1) The underlying (economic) problem can be expressed only with idealizations, simplifications, and omissions. The mathematical formulation will, by necessity, represent only a more or less explicit theory of some part or aspect of reality and not the full reality itself. This point shall, however, not be discussed further but go unquestioned, since we are not concerned with any particular economic or social problem or theory but merely with the methodological situation; it is convenient not to enter upon this aspect any further. The matter is indisputable at any rate, since this is the essence of theory formation or model building. However, the choice of the model is a problem of serious nature since the same basic description of interrelations among economic quantities is amenable to a variety of interpretations or theoretical models.

(2) If the representation according to (1) is accepted as providing a satisfactory model, this means that the simplifications and idealizations are found agreeable and cannot be viewed as sources of error. In other words, the possibility that the model overlooks "significant" variables is excluded. But the chosen description will "involve parameters the value of which have to be derived directly or indirectly (that is, through other theories or calculations) from observations. These parameters will be affected with errors, and these underlying errors will cause errors in the result of our calculation" (p. 1024). This group comprises the *errors due to observation*. *"Their influence on the result is the thing that really matters."* (p. 1027) We shall return to them later.

(3) The third point is of a more technical nature because its significance depends on the mathematical formulation of the model: the formulation (cf. (page 94)) will in general involve transcendental operations such as functions like sin or log, or operations like integration and differentiation, and implicit definitions like proper value problems, etc. Many of these would inevitably occur in the various models used in economic theory. In order to be approached numerically these transcendental operations have to be replaced by elementary processes

---

also: V. Bargmann, D. Montgomery, and J. von Neumann, *Solution of Linear Systems of High Order* (Princeton, 1946) (Report of U.S. Navy Bureau of Ordnance, Contract NORD 9596).

(depending upon the computer's facilities, whether man or machine) and the implicit definitions by explicit definitions (corresponding to a finite constructive procedure that resolves itself into a linear sequence of steps) (p. 1024). Also convergent, limiting processes have to be broken off or truncated at some point where the level of the approximation is held to be satisfactory.

These procedures replace the *strict* mathematical statement of (1) by an approximate one. This produces the third source of error. It is intuitively clear that when these operations are very numerous this source assumes great significance. A good economic model cannot be very simple, so that the application of large systems of simultaneous equations or of equivalent constructs to economic data produces a highly complex situation.

(4) Even if we now, quite unrealistically, assume that none of the three preceding sources of error need concern us, there still remains a fourth source deriving from the physical limitation of the computations: "No computing procedure or device can perform the operations which are its 'elementary' operations (or, at least, all of them) rigorously and faultlessly" (p. 1025).[9] All computing devices are either analogue or digital machines. The first are afflicted with "noise" variables (errors and imperfections in any physical embodiment of a mathematical principle), the second with round-off errors. These occur in all performances of elementary operations which, in large-scale applications, will run into many millions. They are, therefore, the fourth and last source of error. Analogue computers have their place, especially in simulation of complicated economic relationships, such as the interaction of changes in sales prices, advertising expenditure, share of the market, costs of production, etc. But they are far superseded in importance by digital machines. The noise variables of the former are forever present and for complicated devices exceedingly hard to determine.

---

[9] We forego giving an account of the argument which needs to be stated separately for so-called analogue and for digital machines. Although of profound importance, it would lead too far at this occasion to enter upon the highly technical detail. The reader is referred to the first paper quoted in footnote 8 on page 104.

This need not be further described. The round-off errors of digital machines are by necessity the result of the fact that a given computer may be limited to, say, eight decimal digits (even if it uses the number system of base 10). Multiplication of two eight-digit numbers gives a sixteen-digit number which, in order to be carried by the machine, has to be rounded off to eight digits. In large computations this process is repeated hundreds of thousands or millions of times. The question therefore is whether the "result," i.e., the final numbers, is still meaningful or represents only "noise," this being the result of rounding off. Whatever the carrying capacity of the computer, it must be limited to 8, 10, 16, . . . digits. In view of the magnitude of the computation, the round-off problem exists as described. This is an illustration of the remark on p. 42 that *errors are being produced even when machines work faultlessly:* the computer works as designed, but has to round off numbers in order to be able to work. This is, of course, independent of the kind of computer; even with pencil and paper alone one would have to do the same thing. Consider 100 equations of only 1–2 digits for each parameter. Without ever rounding off, one would easily arrive at numbers with 10^{99} digits, which is more digits than there are particles in the Universe.

3.   INTERPRETATION

Still following von Neumann and Goldstine, we turn now toward the interpretation of these four sources of error.

We need not concern ourselves with errors due to theory since no specific theory is being discussed at present. Yet it is clear that they would be fundamental, although they are not really part of the mathematical or computational problems.

Quite different is our interest in the errors of type (2), that is, the errors due to observation. "They are, strictly construed, again no concern of the mathematician. However, their influence on the result is the thing that really matters. In this way, their analysis requires an analysis of this question: what are the limits of the change of the result, caused by changes of the parameters (data) of the problem within given limits? This is the question of the *continuity of the result as a function of the parameters* of the problem, or, somewhat more loosely worded, of the mathematical stability of the problem" (p. 1027). It is mainly from this point of view that the present book has been written. In other words the stability of the problem has to be explicitly investigated whenever one is confronted with a well-defined economic model. This is not being done in the usual econometric studies. The problem is by-passed. Even if the model should be satisfactory, it does not follow necessarily that its numerical evaluation and application secures useful results. It is here where much additional work is required. An attempt in that direction is made below.

It is worth emphasizing that as great a mathematician as J. von Neumann never tired of repeating the fact that the errors of observation are what really matter. This is entirely in the spirit of Gauss. It is also noteworthy that von Neumann was firmly convinced that the intimate contact between mathematics and reality would produce, from time to time, decisive progress in mathematics.

The errors of approximation or truncation (3), as well as those of "noise" and rounding off (4), need not be discussed here in detail, although (4) forms the main subject-matter of the investigation to which we refer. However, this much ought to be said: the strict mathematical problem of (1) is replaced by an approximation (3). Therefore, the actual computation deals with (3) and not at all with (1). Now the point is that the continuity or stability of (1) does *not* guarantee that of (3) as well. This is particularly interesting in cases where partial differential equations are arbitrarily well-approximated by partial difference equations.[10] Such approximations may occur in economics, for example, in various models purporting to show economic growth and other dynamic behavior, and the stability will therefore have to be investigated in each individual instance in order to obtain meaningful results. Errors of type (4) become highly significant when very large numbers of computational steps are involved. This too would necessarily be

[10] Finite difference equations begin to play an increasing role in the work of many economists. The example given by von Neumann and Goldstine, *op. cit.*, p. 1028, shows, however, that even arbitrarily good approximations of stable differential equations by difference equations need not at all guarantee the stability of the latter too, no matter how good the approximation!

the case, when an economic problem leads to the inversion of high order matrices, i.e., when more than ten rows and columns are involved and no or few zeros occur. Input-output studies will easily involve very much larger numbers; in fact, $n = 100$ or $n = 200$ would be highly desirable. Large sets of linear economic equations have already been solved, but the issue under what precise circumstances such computations have produced meaningful answers is still with us, in particular since, as noted above, the "results" are compared with "data" whose error components can at present only be guessed at so that there is no satisfactory control.

This brief exposition has served to indicate the interrelationship between accuracy of observations and the possibilities of their extensive application through theory and numerical evaluation. We hope that we have shown that numerical operations with economic data—which are obviously intended and necessary—impose their own requirements. *Without knowledge of errors, the feeding of economic data into high-speed computers is a meaningless operation.* The economist should not believe that "correct" solutions of many linear equations and of other computations, such as multiple correlations are necessarily *meaningful.* This is true even when only two linear equations in two unknowns are involved. The following example,[11] which could of course be generalized, shows what enormous differences very slight errors of observations (i.e., of type (2) above) will produce in the solution.

The equations

$$x - y = 1$$
$$x - 1.00001y = 0$$

have the solution $x = 100001$, $y = 100000$, while the almost identical equations

$$x - y = 1$$
$$x - 0.999999y = 0$$

have the solution $x = -99999$, $y = -100000$. The coefficients in the two sets of equations differ by at most two units in the *fifth* decimal place, yet the solutions differ by 200,000.

If one recalls how easily equations are sometimes written

[11] Taken from W. E. Milne, *Numerical Calculus* (Princeton, 1949), p. 30 ff.

down purporting to show economic relationships and how shaky is our determination of the parameters, it will be realized what difficulties have to be overcome in constructing and applying an empirically significant theory. If the number of equations is even moderately large, it becomes far from trivial to find out whether or not the determinant actually vanishes.

We proceed to investigate the stability of a model somewhat further in order to show the influence of errors. But instead of generalizing the above case of two equations to a larger number, but devoid of economic meaning, a simple three-equation economic model is taken in which the variable coefficients are allowed to undergo changes. The changes can be interpreted as errors of observations. The model is from L. R. Klein's *Economic Fluctuations in the U.S. 1921–41* (New York, 1950). Its meaning and adequacy are not being questioned; the point is merely to provide a widely-known illustration from economics. It would be possible to select other models, perhaps of greater realism, with many more variables and using more recent data. But Klein's model suits the present purpose because it is limited and it is therefore easier to appreciate the magnitude of the changes in the solution of the equations which occur as a consequence of different perturbations in the variable coefficients of the three-equation system.

The system is Klein's Model I in the full information maximum likelihood version (L. R. Klein, *op. cit.*, p. 69):

(1) $C = 16.78 + 0.02\pi + 0.23\pi_{-1} + 0.8\,(W_1 + W_2) + u_1'$

(2) $I = 17.79 - 0.23\pi + 0.55\pi_{-1} - 0.15K_{-1} + u_2'$

(3) $W_1 = 1.60 + 0.42(Y + T - W_2) +$
$0.16(Y + T - W_2)_{-1} + 0.13(t - 1931) + u_3'$

(4) $\qquad Y + T = C + I + G$

(5) $\qquad Y = \pi + W_1 + W_2$

(6) $\qquad \Delta K = I$

where C is consumption
     I is net investment
     π is profits
     W_1 is labor income originating in private employment

W_2 is labor income originating in government
K is end of year stock of capital
$Y + T$ is net national product
Y is net national income
T is indirect business taxes
G is exogenous investment
t is time in years.

Eliminating the identities (4)–(6), we get three equations:

(7) $C - 0.02\pi - 0.8W_1 = $ Constant

(8) $-C + .77\pi + 1.0W_1 = $ Constant

(9) $-.44\pi + .58W_1 = $ Constant

The coefficients were subjected to the following changes:

(1) The coefficients of π in the three equations (7)–(9) and those of W_1 in equations (7) and (9) had "errors" added to them varying from $\pm 5\%$ to $\pm 40\%$.[12] The system thus adopted was used to solve numerically for values of C, π, and W_1 using data on exogenous variables for 1935. Table 3 shows the changes in the respective solutions, expressed as a percentage of deviation from the "correct" solution—that is, the one obtained when no errors were added—when errors are added only to the coefficient of W_1 in the first equation.[13]

TABLE 3

RELATIVE CHANGES IN SOLUTION VALUES OBTAINED WITH "ERRORS"
IN THE COEFFICIENT OF W_1 IN THE FIRST EQUATION.
PERCENT DIFFERENCES FROM CORRECT FIGURES

% Error	C	π	W_1	% Error	C	π	W_1
+5	4.4	10.9	3.1	−5	−4.0	−10.9	−3.1
+10	8.6	23.4	6.9	−10	−8.0	−21.1	−6.0
+15	14.1	36.7	11.1	−15	−12.0	−31.3	−8.8
+20	19.5	50.8	15.1	−20	−15.0	−39.8	−11.3
+25	25.3	66.4	19.5	−25	−17.6	−48.4	−13.8
+40	45.8	119.5	34.9	−40	−26.9	−71.1	−20.4

[12] Since this was done purely for illustrative purposes, we did not maintain in this experiment all restrictions on, and connections between, coefficients and the "constants" in the system.

[13] For C and π these were the largest of the changes in solution arising when errors were added to only one of the coefficients to be varied.

(2) The same computations are carried out when errors were introduced in *all* five of the coefficients varied. Table 4 shows the largest deviations obtained in this way. Finally, Figure 4 gives a graphical presentation of the changes.

Only a few comments are needed, since the tables and the chart offer no particular difficulties for interpretation. To begin with, this numerical experiment involving 30 matrix inversions is important in view of the great role that econometric models are beginning to play in practical applications for the purposes of government and business. It is furthermore significant since a theory is lacking which would allow us to determine easily and with reliability how sensitive an economic model is in regard to error-induced changes in the variable coefficients. The suspicion is, of course, that the sensitivity is great; if confirmed this would very much reduce the confidence one can put into these and similar models.

The two tables show that this is, indeed, the case. Even when

TABLE 4

LARGEST POSITIVE AND NEGATIVE RELATIVE CHANGES IN SOLUTION
VALUES OBTAINED WITH "ERRORS" IN ALL COEFFICIENTS.
PERCENT DIFFERENCES FROM CORRECT SOLUTION

% Error	C		π		W_1	
	Posi- tive	Nega- tive	Posi- tive	Nega- tive	Posi- tive	Nega- tive
5	8.6	−7.0	19.5	−18.8	11.3	−9.1
10	19.3	−12.8	42.2	−35.2	25.2	−16.4
15	33.3	−17.5	66.4	−50.8	43.4	−22.6
20	52.4	−21.9	94.5	−64.9	68.2	−28.0
25	79.5	−25.3	125.0	−78.9	104.0	−32.7

The positive changes in C and W_1 were obtained with positive errors on the varied coefficients of the first equation, negative error in the varied coefficient of the second, positive error in the first and negative error in the second coefficient of the third equation. (A positive error is understood as increasing the absolute size of a coefficient.) The negative changes are obtained with the signs of all these errors reversed.

The positive changes of π are obtained with: positive errors in the coefficients of the first equation; negative errors in the coefficient of π in the second and third equation, positive error in the last coefficient of the last equation. The negative changes are obtained through reversal of the signs of the coefficients.

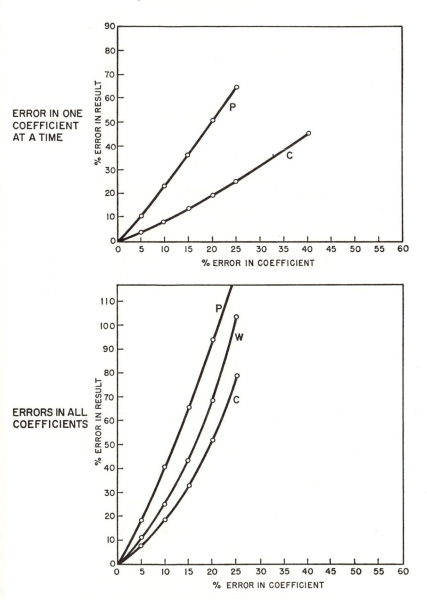

Figure 4. Positive Changes in Solution Values Obtained
with Errors in Coefficients

an error is only introduced in the coefficient of W_1 (wages) the consequences are considerable. A 10% error—which is not excessive!—produces a deviation from the error-free result of $+23.4\%$ (in profits) if positive, and a -21.1% deviation if negative. This is a great range which is also reflected in the changes of the other variables, though the effects are less. When all coefficients are allowed to experience error—the obviously most natural and realistic case—the situation is much worse, as Table 4 and Fig. 4 show. For profits the range is between $+42.2\%$ and -35.2% (still assuming only a $\pm10\%$ error) and for consumption and wages the results are not much better. If the error goes up to more realistic levels, the divergency from the "correct," i.e., error-free solution increases rapidly. This situation would become still worse if another model were taken, where instead of only three equations we might deal with twenty, thirty, or more. Extensions to larger numbers of equations are, of course, highly desirable and the tendency in making models is precisely in that direction. Research along the lines carried out in this section is urgently needed. It will be difficult work, especially when the problem is attacked at the level of scientific sophistication that it demands, combining statistical argument with purely mathematical studies of calculating with very large sets of numbers.

At this place, a word of caution is in order: the weakness of econometric, mathematical models, when subjected to numerical application, is *not* due to the fact that they are mathematical or that a numerical application is made. Rather we are confronted with a property of our reasoning and of our ability to observe and to measure the phenomena which we want to explain. The properly handled mathematical formulation has the virtue of showing us clearly where the limitations of our knowledge are. We are induced to push on to achieve a balance between seeming though unwarranted precision on the one hand and the vagueness of purely verbal argumentation about phenomena which are essentially numerical on the other. Should we give up the mathematical formulation of our thought, we would fall back on an inferior type of reasoning and, surely, the results cannot improve. Should we ignore the statistical inputs (but how could we?), we would be completely in the dark.

Thus the issue is precisely as stated earlier: the crucial problem lies with the accuracy of the data. If they are reliable, it will not be very difficult to evolve suitable models, preferably mathematical and capable of describing many interdependencies. Without reliable data our confidence must remain low. "Intuition" and "experience" and the like, unless they can be brought into sharp focus, are not substitutes. Either we have knowledge (of a certain type and quality) or we do not.

It is hoped that considerations which have led to the above illustrative computations will induce economists to pay proper attention to the relation between the accuracy of input data and the meaning and reliability of the values obtained by solving for the unknowns. In that connection the reader should recall that a 10 percent accuracy is a rather average, i.e., common, accuracy obtained in physics!

Summarizing: Each particular numerical operation, if it is at all of sizeable proportions, has to be studied separately with respect to its validity. This is true whether one deals with the solving of equations, with time series analysis or any other field. Whatever it may be, there is nothing to be gained from the almost mechanical use of modern computing devices. Instead the most recent developments in the field of applied mathematics will have to be brought into the picture. Norbert Wiener, the eminent mathematician, has expressed corresponding ideas: "It is already becoming clear in the use of these new machines that they demand purely mathematical techniques of their own, quite different from those in use in manual computation or in the use of machines of smaller capacity. For example, even the use of machines for computing determinants of moderately high order, or for the simultaneous solution of twenty or thirty simultaneous linear equations, shows difficulties which do not arise when we study analogous problems of small order. Unless care is exercised in setting a problem up, these may completely deprive the solution of any significant figures whatever. It is a commonplace to say that fine, effective tools like the ultra-rapid computing machine are out of place in the hands of those not possessing a sufficient degree of technical skill to take full advantage of them. The ultra-rapid computing machine will certainly not decrease the need for mathematicians with a high level of understanding and technical training."[14]

It is of paramount importance, however, to understand the nature of the data and to obtain quantitative error estimates. The research worker in this field will realize that there does not exist enough experience, especially not in the social sciences, which could guide him. The more comprehensive the scope of theory and of application, the more uncertain is the procedure and the meaning of the result, both of which must be continuously subject to searching scrutiny.

It would be tempting to conclude this chapter with a survey of the economic problems which may be suited to large-scale computations. Such problems exist both in the field of theory (especially when considering the theory of games of strategy) and in that of economic statistics. This would not be adequate without an account of the possibilities of modern computing devices and their logic. Therefore, we would be led too far away from our modest field.[15]

[14] Cf., N. Wiener, *Cybernetics,* (1948), p. 154. In that important work more information is found on the topic discussed (and it is written in the spirit of Gauss, cf. the motto above to the present chapter); the fact that it is reprinted unchanged in the revised and second edition of 1961 (p. 131) is a clear indication that in spite of the tremendous progress of computers and computation techniques during the last decade, nothing has changed in respect to the observations made above. And how could that be otherwise?

I might add that Professor Wiener, after reading the first edition of the present book (1950), remarked that "economics is a one or two digit science," a comment worth pondering over, especially by those who report changes in national income, prices, etc., up to six, seven, or eight "significant" digits or to hundredths of one percent.

[15] Compare however my "Experiment and Large Scale Computation in Economics," *op. cit.*

CHAPTER VII

DATA AND DECISION MAKING

1. Quantitative and Qualitative Elements in Decisions

THE PRECEDING CHAPTERS have dealt with the nature and difficulties of economic observations. This has led us to expect that the picture we can make of the economic world around us is much less precise, far less definite, than we would like it to be. In the second part of this book some examples will be given which will bear out this expectation.

In the main, we have restricted ourselves to a common sense level of examination of economic statistics and other data. Modern statistical theory, which has shown such tremendous development over the last few decades, can only be applied profitably with all its subtleties and refinements after the common sense clarification of the data has progressed. There is a great deal of work to be done constantly that is of a preliminary but nevertheless not of a trivial character.[1] In the discussions of the previous chapters, it became clear that the making of economic statistics, to a far higher degree than heretofore, must be subject to scientific design. This would rapidly show that a proper design is impossible without taking up in a fundamental way the matter of multiple errors and their propagation throughout the system. We have noted the great variety in the degree of accuracy that can be associated with the various kinds of observations, these always related to some prospective use of the data. We have seen that this variety applies also to physics and other sciences, where exceedingly fine measurements occur together with gross estimates. Now it is a difficult thing to have to make *decisions* on the basis of information of greatly mixed quality. This is one of the most interesting and, I believe, as yet least explored problems, and it presents itself in the fields of theory and of practice. In the former it is a little more clearly defined. There the maximum precision of measure-

---

[1] I refer again to the interesting paper by J. W. Tukey, "The Future of Data Analysis," *loc. cit.*

ment needed is dependent upon the power and fine structure of the theory using the measurement and determines the methods and standards by which to develop them.

The most frequent use of economic observations is, however, for practical purposes, i.e., for government and business decisions most of which are of great consequence for the community as well as for the individual. This kind of decision making is exposed to several types of uncertainty: *first,* there is the formulation of the goal and the decision of the opponent, which sometimes is Nature, sometimes a human or a group of humans; *second,* there is the uncertainty whether all necessary information has been gathered and whether its quality has been correctly evaluated; and *third,* there is the uncertainty whether the proper conclusions have been drawn from the scattered parts and pieces, integrating the information into a satisfactory picture.

This is not the place to discuss the problem of decision making *de profundis.* That task belongs to the theory of games of strategy. The difficult problems that this theory examines are posed even under the severely simplifying assumption that each participant in a game is completely informed and is capable of carrying out all necessary computations. Here, on the other hand, we are interested in the question of what the information is like which is actually being used. In general, it is worse than normally (naively) assumed and, whatever its state, it is always put together from pieces of very uneven quality. It is this latter property which creates so many interesting and novel problems. We know rather precisely the prices on the stock exchange, even their hourly variations and the turnover; we know much less and much later how much is being exported to what country, and still less certainly (and even much later) what the gross national product of the country is like. All this information is dated; some comes to us rapidly and correctly, other less rapidly and incorrectly, often subject to many revisions, these only made with great delays. There can never be a complete synchronization of all kinds of information to which we have access.

In making a decision, e.g., to buy or sell a particular stock, we know its past prices very precisely; we know the balance sheet of the company and may have some information as to what happened since the last one was published; we study the statistics (if any) of the market in which the company operates; we compare it with other companies in the same industry, the industry with others. We study the condition of the stock market, e.g., by finding out what the money flows are and what other buyers and sellers in the market are doing or are planning to do. We try to assess the total situation of the economy—hence our interest in gross national product, the political events and their probable influence upon our stock in question, and finally the international situation. Not everyone always goes through all these steps, and seldom deliberately, but this is nevertheless an illustration of the information components on which many a decision rests. Some components are well known, others have varying, sometimes unknown, elements of error; others are based on pure estimation of a kind where not even the standard methods of assigning objective probabilities will work. All this is to be combined into one coherent basis for a decision. Depending on the concrete circumstances the various components will have different weight. When buying a pound of sugar, few of the components will matter. But when a large company is to decide whether to build a new plant, or to issue new stock, many more components of the information picture become relevant, especially those where it is crucial to realize that the value of the information (if it even is a number!) may be quite different from its apparent exactness. Rates of change in the various components, often so desirable to know, can be fairly exact; they can also lose most of their meaning, as for example in the case of gross national product.

In order to make the use of economic statistics more rational, it is necessary that *quantitative error estimates* be made and be currently published with all statistics of major importance. For all others, the way should be left open to determine them at any time. The government should be persuaded to state publicly each time a new gross national product figure is made available that it is known only with an error[2] of, say, ±10 per-

---

[2] In his paper, "Statistics and Objective Economics," (1955), reprinted in *Fact and Theory in Economics, The Testament of an Institutionalist* (Ithaca, 1958), M. A. Copeland reports (p. 72) that thirty odd years ago

cent, employment figures with no lesser uncertainty, that foreign trade and balance-of-payments figures are subject to corresponding doubts, etc. This would have beneficial influences. Such error estimates should be made as soon as the data are produced, even though later revisions may be anticipated. Revisions often take years to come to rest. In the meantime, information about the initial conditions under which the statistic was made is lost. A late error estimate is at any rate far less useful than an earlier one, since most statistics are wanted when first produced (if not earlier!), and it is then that they have their greatest significance for, and impact on, decision making. Even when it is very difficult to make direct error estimates, i.e., when one has to fall back on personal judgment, the effort is still indicated. Indeed, this applies to some of the most important economic statistics. There will then still remain observations where even this is not possible. Clearly, these should be set aside in a separate category, to be dealt with differently.

Publication and wide discussion of (trustworthy!) quantitative error estimates would prove a powerful force working towards their reduction and at the same time cautioning people in their use for scientific and, perhaps, also political purposes. This will, of course, not improve statistics of the past, those mountains of figures that require to be explored, but it will make clear that such explorations are far more dangerous than commonly assumed.

The fundamental reform that will have to take place is to force the government to stop publishing figures with the pretense that they are free from error. There are no such figures, no matter what the layman may think and no matter what the producers of economic statistics may assert.

A further consequence of a growing consciousness of the intrinsic quality, or lack of it, of economic statistics would be the reduction in money costs. It would then appear less desirable

---

national income statistics were reported with a $\pm x$ percent error, but that this practice had been abandoned. Although aware of many limitations of economic statistics, Copeland does not advocate the publication of error estimates. For time series he maintains that their changes are more important than their absolute values. This restates the common and convenient views refuted above, and is in conflict with our findings in Chapter XV below and elsewhere throughout this book.

to carry, absurdly, many more digits than is warranted—a great reduction in printing costs.[3] Thus, specious accuracy would be encountered less frequently. Also, many currently applied operations on these statistics would be simplified, if not dropped altogether as being meaningless. This would be most desirable until useful data with known observational errors are available, errors small enough to warrant the application of refined, complicated, and expensive manipulations. The knowledge that powerful methods of analysis and extraordinary computational facilities exist but cannot be properly applied to many economic statistics in their present form will itself act as a strong stimulus to improve the underlying material.

The awareness and publication of error estimates, however crude and tentative, will also introduce greater caution into *operating* with such data. As we have seen in Chapter VI, the multiplication or division of two error-free, determinate numbers is a very different thing from multiplying or dividing two numbers each one of which has a considerable margin of error. If this process has to be repeated many times, and different elementary operations must alternate with each other, in order to arrive at the desired final figure, e.g., at gross national product "corrected" or "deflated" for price changes, the assurance with which the final, desired result can be stated deviates very much from a similar computation with sharply given numbers. These observations apply even when very few elementary steps of computation have to be taken. The difficulties described in the preceding chapter (especially those arising from rounding off) come about in *any* case if the calculations are lengthy. If the computations also deal with figures known only within fairly wide limits, or with mixtures of such figures, the difficulties are compounded. All this, of course, is not particular to economics; it is part of all scientific work. The difference is only that in economics little, if any, awareness prevails of how this situation should be dealt with. The textbooks are silent on this point.

Operations of this kind, restricted as they are, have to be

---

[3] It is left to the reader to estimate how large the economies would be and whether this was really a crucial point made in this book, as some reviewers of the first edition believed!

combined with others where no numbers are available, where only qualitative statements, subjective probabilities, or estimates of orders of magnitude may be possible. We are lacking well-founded techniques by means of which to put together into a meaningful picture, and in an objective way, the information contained in the various components. This need arises also, though to a lesser degree, in the natural sciences; but for decision making of a practical-political kind one is inevitably confronted with such demands. And usually very little time is available during which to come to a decision.

Finally, considering that theories of decision making are very difficult, even when it is assumed that the results of all possible interlocking decisions—the so-called "payoff-matrix" of game theory—are clearly known, one can form an idea of the obstacles that have to be surmounted in real life. The answer is, of course, that "intuition," "experience," and "know-how" have to take the place of calculated rationality. This is both true and meaningless. It is simply another way of saying that no satisfactory method is known with which to accomplish consciously what has to be done, since in most concrete circumstances decisions simply have to be made. They cannot be postponed until the complete intellectual clarification has been achieved. Even where it is possible to become more precise, to improve information, to reduce error by letter and further measurements, and to make measurements where only guesses have been available, a point is reached where the additional effort has to be compared with the added gain for the final act of decision. This remains a very difficult point to determine so long as the above mentioned methods for combining quantitative and qualitative elements in the act of decision are lacking.[4]

However, the following is of importance: Even though a residuum always remains that cannot be quantified, it can frequently be made smaller. It is through constant expansion of measurement where there was none, better measurement where

[4] This is particularly significant for, and characteristic of, sequential military decision making: weapons characteristics are carefully computed, the number of weapons needed is harder to determine, how many should be used even more so, where and whether they be used is often vague and so on, to the top political decision itself. For a discussion, see my *Question of National Defense* (New York, 1959; 2nd Ed., 1961).

it was poor, that we extend our knowledge. Where we have measurement we do not need intuition to determine the characteristics of what was measured. Our intuitive efforts can then be better concentrated on the areas that still remain inaccessible for measurement. It must also be recalled that measurement is the result of a theory, but is based on something intuitively given. In the natural sciences it was always very difficult to arrive at numbers. To measure temperature was a great achievement, although everyone has immediate personal knowledge, when one body feels warmer than another. In economics the situation is in many ways much simpler. Here we can *start* with many numbers which the various economic processes produce. We already have interest rates, prices, quantities produced, sold, bought, etc., etc. It is not necessary first to make these into numbers. They are not perfect, they have errors and other faults, they have to be modified and sharpened, but they make a much easier start for a developing science than the qualitative phenomena of nature, which step by step had to be made numerical, a process that is never completely finished. In economics too, we have areas that are not immediately numerically described, so that numbers have to be introduced. Utility, a fundamental notion for describing economic behavior, is a classical case, and, as in the natural sciences, it has taken a long time and many vain efforts to accomplish this.[5] Further such transformations will undoubtedly follow, each one a necessary step towards making economics a better science.

It is perhaps not a digression, though it may appear to be one, that similar problems arise in neural behavior. If it is recalled that modern computer design has greatly profited from the study of the human brain it is proper to look to the brain for guidance in the above matter. The human neural system also is not quantitatively sharp in the conventional physical sense of measurement. Yet the mind comes, sometimes very quickly, to sharp decisions, when, for example, I quickly withdraw my hand from a hot plate, though the nerves measure the heat only within wide limits and apparently by different methods than counting the number of degrees. Often, several such experi-

---

[5] Cf. footnote 6, Chapter IV.

ences are combined into one precise act. It will, of course, take much time until a real understanding of these phenomena is achieved and an application to other fields can be made.

2. GOALS AND SOLUTIONS

(1) *The goals* of business enterprises and of economic policy have to be described by numbers. We shall discuss briefly how well this is accomplished and what *kind* of numbers are involved.

As far as *firms* are concerned it seems obvious that profits are to be maximized and that these are easily and clearly identifiable numbers of undisputed accuracy, i.e., a certain amount of money, a certain rate of earnings. But the considerations of Chapter IV have shown that "profit" is an elusive concept. Firms may instead also want to maximize something else. If that be sales, then there is a lesser problem of ascertaining that number. If they aim at optimizing combinations of profit with "social standing" and service to the community or nation, etc., problems of measurement arise as mentioned at the end of the preceding section. In general, however, money profits are a frequent aim and the mistake in too narrowly considering these as the purpose of a business enterprise is small. This applies as most likely when the firm is of nondescript, medium size. Curiously, when it is either very small or very large it usually exists in an environment where its survival will depend on many factors which may make an unrestricted pursuit of dollar profits difficult if not impossible.

Not wishing to discuss this matter further, we observe that the business community is, in general, satisfied with published earnings as a satisfactory measure of performance. Though inaccurate and fundamentally inadequate for the purpose, firms and investors are to a large extent governed by this information. This is what matters for describing the behavior of the private sector of the economy.

When the *goals of the entire economy* are concerned, the situation is quite different. Now there are no simple figures given. They have to be identified and evaluated. This is one of the fundamental problems of economic policy.

For example, if stability of the exchange rates is a goal, then a fluctuation of the rates between the gold points, when the gold standard is in force, is compatible with that aim. If the rates go beyond the gold points, the policy aim has not been reached. Now it is not too difficult to determine the gold points with considerable accuracy. Success or failure of that part of monetary policy easily becomes clear.

When there is no gold standard, the aims of monetary policy are more difficult to formulate. They could still be stable exchange rates in a free market. But that may involve (as in the other case) great variations in price levels, employment, etc., and policy restrictions may also be placed upon the latter. Or, it may be the express policy of the government to secure full employment. This requires a statement about the percentage of unemployment compatible with the notion of "full employment." Then one has to see whether that percentage is exceeded or not. It is not material here whether the percentage chosen is realistic. The problem is how accurately it can be determined. It will be shown (Chapter XIII) that such figures are of extremely doubtful validity. It is similar with price stability and even worse with "growth," especially in the short run and when considering large aggregates such as gross national product. There all will depend on the accuracy with which the goal has been formulated and on that of the measurement of the result in order to find out whether the policy was successful.

The statement of an economic goal without quantification is seldom of value. It is, of course, often politically convenient to avoid quantitative statements, since it is then easier to assert that the policy was successful. Few will demand that goals be stated very precisely; limits will be acceptable. These express the fact that the state of an economy cannot be expected to be very sharply determined, for example because of its complexity. The narrow gold point criteria are certainly an exceptional case. On the other hand, the use of limits is oddly contradicted by the precise use of growth rates, prices, foreign trade figures, and production indices, etc., where every change of one-tenth of a percentage point is hailed as significant. Of course, no such narrow fluctuations have any meaning whatsoever when the data have errors of the type discussed so far. Part II of this book will reveal that the errors usually are in excess of expectations.

To sum up: Economic policy has to state its multiple goals in fairly definite quantitative terms in order to formulate them properly at all. The results have to be measured against these goals; otherwise statements about success or failure are impossible. But while goals can be formulated sharply—though it may be unwise to do so and very often they are not—the events can never be described without substantial error. Our present practices in discussing success or failure of policies do not bear out these conditions.[6]

(2) *Solutions*, i.e., reaching properly formulated goals, require policy measures. These must be feasible, their effect should be predictable, especially when they intermingle with those of others. There are always many goals of national policy to pursue simultaneously which should be in harmony with each other. Some measures were instituted some time ago, others more recently; still others are planned to be taken in the near future. Thus their effects become apparent at different moments in time and from the aggregative data proper imputation should then be made to the shares each of these measures have in this continuing stream of actions. To all these policy measures must be added the basic, underlying behavior of all individuals and firms, plus random factors that cannot be neglected; in other words, some parts of the economy are being carried on unaffected by policy, or only touched by it in such an indirect manner that most people are unaware that they are acting within another framework. That framework is set by policy, such as new import duties, margin requirements on stock purchases, rules about drug inspection, limitations on planting in agriculture, etc. While those directly involved in the respective activities have knowledge of the measures and may even understand their effects, others, only little removed, cannot easily make the proper connection between their own activities and these more remote measures.

---

[6] Whether a policy measure has brought about a certain change is an entirely different matter. All we are considering at the moment is whether correlations can be made, not what meaning they have!

The problem of feasibility is the first problem the makers of policy have to settle. Will a particular measure lead to the desired result in the desired time? What are its costs? What are its side effects? How much of the measure is the proper dose? When this is settled, there still remains the question of alternatives. What other measures are there? Which is to be preferred over the other? Which is "optimal"?

Since all these questions can only be considered as having been properly answered when their quantitative aspects are spelled out, a picture is had of the true complications of the tasks of economic policy. It is in the light of these observations that the ordinary political procedures should be judged, the claims, assertions, exaggerations, the alleged references, attributions, etc. If we recall how inevitable error is in merely describing a *state* of the economic world, not to mention projected *changes* of states, and if we compare this with the limited, superficial, trivial, and sometimes deliberately doctored, picture of the economy the world is presented with, it becomes clear that there exists more than the one immediately apparent "reality."[7]

In the second part of this volume, some examples of economic statistics will be discussed which will illuminate our findings thus far. The reader will see the difficulties with which the economist is confronted if he is true to the standards of scientific enquiry.

---

[7] Though the discussion of a theory of economic policy is not our aim in this book, one neglected problem should at least be referred to. This is the problem of the restrictions that may be placed upon the tools of policy. Without a clear understanding as to what is and what is not admitted in order to secure a solution of a problem (in general), that problem has not been properly formulated. The question whether it is possible to "square the circle" cannot be answered unless it is specified whether this is to be done by using only ruler and compass, in which case it is impossible, or whether other instruments are also admitted, in which case it is possible. Similarly, it may be impossible, at a given state of our economic knowledge, to secure full employment when exchange rates must not become flexible, but possible if this condition is lifted. This entire question is discussed in O. Morgenstern, "When is a Problem of Economic Policy Solvable?" in *Wirtschaftstheorie und Wirtschaftspolitik*, V. F. Wagner and F. Marbach, eds., (Bern, 1953), pp. 241–250.

PART TWO

ERRORS IN ECONOMIC STATISTICS

❧ CHAPTER VIII ❦

INTRODUCTION

IN THE following chapters we shall make some specific attempts to measure or at least indicate levels of accuracy in several fields of economic statistics. This is only a preliminary attempt for two reasons. First, methods for estimation of errors other than sampling errors for an indifferent (i.e., not hostile) universe have rarely been applied to economic data, and therefore some rather indirect measures have to be constructed for each particular field. Even methods for estimating sampling errors specifically designed for the not so indifferent economic universe are lacking altogether. Second, since each field that we shall examine is a large one, it would take years of study and negotiation by a variety of experts to arrive at generally accepted indicators. Because of the lack of powerful theoretical aids, we have only selected smaller areas for illustration and in order to persuade others to initiate further studies.

We have undertaken this investigation so as to evaluate statistics used in studies such as those pertaining to time series analysis, to the construction of econometric models involving many simultaneous equations, and to input-output models. In all these areas mathematical techniques are applied to large bodies of data touching most of the economy. We would have liked to establish in the following few areas at least indications of acceptable and attainable levels of accuracy for future studies. Our piecemeal and perhaps somewhat devious attempts to study accuracy should at least indicate a step toward discovering errors of the several types discussed in Part I. We would have preferred to study directly the accuracy of, say, an input-output table by assigning a numerical error to each entry of the matrix. This would undoubtedly have been of immediate value for this interesting but rather specialized field. However, this is a tremendous task and it is first necessary to approach the problem in the simplest and most general manner which will give results; therefore, the specific selections in the following pages. The particular types of statistics chosen were mostly governed by the accessibility of the material and its significance in reporting. We regret the omission, so far, of manufacturing industries. It will be vital to the further progress of the theory of production and related fields to obtain estimates of error of the data needed in that domain.

Another approach to statistical data and other qualitative information is the study of their *internal consistency*. For example, when two production processes are technologically closely related—e.g., one product being a by-product, in fixed proportion, of another one, such as number of cattle slaughtered and hides obtained—we can obviously insist on agreement of a high order. If the series disagree, something is at fault; if they agree, they may, of course, still both be wrong. In modern industry such strict dependencies are not easily found or not easily isolated. Production is normally highly mixed and makes such simple internal checks quite hopeless. As soon as aggregates are formed, the situation becomes even more obscure; yet some amount of aggregation is unavoidable, in view of the tremendous detail of economic operations. "Consistency" tests can then only be established on the basis of some model. There has to be technological knowledge as in the above example, or economic relationships have to be established in terms of which alone a consistency test can be developed. For example, it is consistent with our economic knowledge that a sharp increase in the quantity of money normally goes together with a rise in prices, etc. Depending on the given degree of our knowledge, certain indications of economic activity are compatible, and at another level of activity they may not be compatible. For example, if the increase in the quantity of money is moderate, there may be no noticeable rise in prices; money may be absorbed by an increase in population, by an increase in the stages of production, or by hoarding. Thus if the two series diverge, this need not be an indication of inaccuracy in either one. But if the quantity of money is supposed to be increasing sharply and price indices show no rise, then at least one of these two indicators is faulty. The safest consistencies are always technological; for example, if it is asserted that the value of exports rises while prices are reported stable, and the shipping volume from our ports does not go up, then we can be fairly certain that at least one of these indicators is wrong. In this manner we can apply valuable checks and controls, but we are dependent on the state of economics and the constancy of technology. *The data by themselves tell us no story whatsoever, neither a true one nor a false one. They are silent.*

A specific case for testing internal consistency is offered by input-output tables to which previous references were made. These simply arrange in a rectangular scheme the sales and purchases among different industries. When the table is coarse, i.e., when few industries are distinguished, virtually every cell in this scheme will show some positive inter-industry transaction. But when, say, two hundred or more industries are considered, as one naturally strives to do, there will be many cells indicating either no mutual transactions or very small ones. The determination of the consistency of such data is theoretically possible but exceedingly difficult and expensive. However, such a procedure may serve as an illustration of how to proceed in other areas where economic data come under scrutiny.

The occurrence of zeros in input-output tables is of considerable, though more technical, interest. But it illustrates an important point. A zero means that (for a certain level of general activity) no measurable transactions occurred between two specified industries. This will often be plausible, but in many cases it will require deeper examination. We know from other economic information that a modern economy is intricately connected, i.e., that a great many processes enter into each simple process, often in entirely unexpected ways.[1] Engineering knowledge is also an indispensable aid in this search. Inspection of the larger tables now in existence shows that they contain many more zeros than can probably be justified. If this is the case, it has far-reaching implications: first, in throwing doubt on the other figures, and second, in complicating the mathematical operations. (Inversion of high order matrices

---

[1] During World War II, the production of optical instruments was temporarily greatly hampered by a shortage of babies' diapers. The reason was that diapers were an excellent polishing material for lenses. Surely in an input-output table a zero transaction between these two industries would have seemed more plausible than a purchase of diapers by optical companies!

with few zeros offers far more difficulties than those showing many zeros or, indeed, of those approaching the unit matrix.)

The errors with which we are concerned are errors of observation. It may be debated that the error is a deviation from a true standard, and, since we cannot know the true standard, it is fruitless to study the error. Statistically, if we were able to study many repeated measurements of the same event, the mean of these many observations would give the true observation (aside from bias, lies, etc.).

Our approach is for the most part an approximation of this method. We concern ourselves wherever possible with *discrepancies* between reports of the same event when it is measured repeatedly by the same observers or (almost) simultaneously viewed by different observers. We recognize that sometimes the discrepancies are not "errors" in the statistical sense, but are merely differences in definition—differences in emphasis in which components of a statistic are important. They are therefore measurements of different things. Nevertheless, we include these in our study of errors since the various measurements originate from and are used for the same purpose. At other times the discrepancies are true "errors"—there are actually omissions in the description of the same event due to difficulties in sampling or due to mistakes in taking a complete count. In what follows we do omit errors caused by rounding off or transcription. Such errors would certainly arise in the comparison of several sets of estimates and would be counted as part of the true "error" as termed above. They will be numerous because of the masses of statistics involved. But relative to the other factors involved, they are of minor significance. It is, however, a very different and most serious matter to consider the rounding off error when large scale computations are contemplated, as was shown above.

The distinction made here is the one between margin of *error*, which is the difference between one set of statistics and the (perhaps unknown) true standard on the one hand, and discrepancy due to *incomparability* on the other. These two factors could be isolated if (1) the true standard were known—perhaps only statistically by its mean; or (2) if a complete reconcilation could be made so that the difference in definition could be eliminated by adding and subtracting the proper factors. But in the practical case, if more than a single observation is available at all, one is faced with *alternative sets of data* which aim to describe the same phenomenon but which appear quite different. And it is difficult, if not impossible, to discover just where their difference lies. The social scientist in this respect is confronted with much greater difficulties than the physical scientist, for the latter deals only with non-definitional kinds of error, since terms are carefully defined, and there cannot be alternative and non-equivalent descriptions of the same phenomenon. Thus, before getting into the main part of this discussion, the importance of adequate and precise definition should again be emphasized. Alas, that is almost never achieved.

The following chapters contain illustrations. These were chosen because they seemed interesting and important. Each illuminates a whole area of economic activity. There is no claim to "cover" all areas of interest; this would be impossible. But it is believed that the following chapters each have a point of their own, and that together they give an adequate idea of the extent to which various kinds of errors occur in economic data. They will show that whatever field might be analyzed, whether by econometric methods or simply by viewing it in the general, intuitive manner in which most economic statistics are used, as either proving or disproving a theory, a development, or a policy claim, there is always so much uncertainty in the data that it is not easy to show that a point has, indeed, been made at all!

In the subsequent discussion, we do not specifically mention every argument that occurred in Part I when we analyzed the contributing error factors. Not all factors may be at work in each case described below; but together they all appear sooner or later. The reader will have no difficulty in making the identification where it is desirable to do so.

Specifically, we analyze:

a. *Foreign Trade:* certainly an area of immense importance and interest both from the practical and theoretical point of view. This field has been of central importance in the development of economic thinking.

b. *Prices:* There is no need to justify this selection. As will be seen, conceptual difficulties rank with those of ascertaining the truth.

c. *Mining and Agriculture:* Two ancient fields are examined, seemingly clear and simple. They are extensively researched and great amounts of money are spent on the collection of these data, yet great problems remain.

d. *Employment and Unemployment:* Here conceptual difficulties vie with those of counting and proper recording, all embedded in an atmosphere highly charged with purely political interests.

e. *National Income:* This notion has again come to place itself in the center of interest. "GNP" figures are almost a symbol of a country's economic condition.

f. *Growth Rates:* These have become perhaps the principal measure of progress in an international struggle of development in which the leading nations are rivals among each other. It will be seen that the reliability of these figures is, for all practical purposes, zero.

CHAPTER IX

FOREIGN TRADE STATISTICS

1. INTRODUCTORY REMARKS

THE STATISTICS of foreign trade are important in any study of a country's economy since every nation is related to the rest of the world through its commodity imports and exports. To these must be added capital flows, credit operations, gold movements for monetary purposes, migrations, etc. From the statistics pertaining to these areas, important consequences are drawn which are familiar not only to the professional economist but also to businessmen and politicians. Indeed a "passive balance of trade" is often deemed dangerous and frequently leads to an increase of tariffs, introduction of import quotas, export subsidies, and the like. The balance of payments is watched not only in its manifestations—strength or weakness of the currency—but in regard to the individual payment components which enter into the whole picture.

First it should be clearly understood that despite its wide and time-honored use, the "balance of trade" is an arbitrary and fearfully vague notion. The correct way of speaking, though much more cumbersome, would be to say that there is an *excess of statistically reported "visible" trade* in one or the other direction. What is "visible"—and in that sense a "commodity"—is what is being recorded as such at any given time. There is an obvious interest in observing the movements of particular commodities across borders, since this gives information for the industries concerned in their production, merchandising, and transportation. However, the addition of all these commodities need not necessarily result in a meaningful economic entity. That would be the case only if there were no services rendered across borders and if no capital movements took place. The division made along the whole array of items that make up the entire set of foreign transactions of a country is therefore accidental, arbitrary, and of only subsidiary economic interest. As long as, in more primitive times, say in the age up to and including the mercantilists, *primarily* the same kind of physical goods moved across borders and money was essentially metallic, there was no great difference between the two basic kinds of trade. But, as time passes, any restriction of measurement to visible trade becomes more and more artificial. The tendency for services to assume an ever increasing share in the total national product is at any rate very pronounced and a consequence especially of the most recent technological revolution. In the United States there are currently more people engaged in service industries than in production of physical commodities. This must eventually reflect on international trade, where over the years the volume of travel, transportation, communications, etc., unquestionably has assumed steadily greater proportions. Therefore, even if the "balance" of "trade" could be accurately measured, the economic meaning of this measurement would continue to shrink.

It is not difficult to make these observations and they are clearly incontestable. Yet there is a peculiarly continuing unconcern in speaking about the balance of trade as though it were a *necessary* and *sufficient* measure of the economic relations among the various countries. There can hardly be any doubt that this will continue, which shows that the valid demonstration of a severe limitation of a statistic need not have much scientific or practical impact where the social sciences are concerned. This then becomes itself an important characteristic of these sciences from a methodological point of view.

The following discussion bears mainly on the difficulties of ascertaining the quality of foreign trade statistics, whether they be used for relatively detailed business information or for the study of the overall trade among nations. The quality of these statistics also presents an interesting problem in the relation between data and theory. It will be seen that statistics on foreign trade and gold movements are exceedingly poor, and as a result large parts of the theory of international trade are open to doubt. This presents a real dilemma: economic theory has unquestionably postulated a fine structure in the international field; yet we cannot describe this structure adequately by relying on the data with which we are confronted.[1] This dilemma will be made amply clear by the examples to be discussed. The problem is, of course, not restricted to foreign transactions, but the general accessibility of foreign trade statistics makes this field particularly attractive. Extensive accounts of nearly identical events are given by observers in slightly different positions in time and space: those recording the physical quantity and the value of an *exported* commodity and those recording both again as an *import*. Such double reporting is not normally available for purely domestic economic activities, although most transactions could, of course, be recorded both as a sale and as a purchase.

Foreign trade is therefore a well-defined area in which to study discrepancies in reports. The problem is to differentiate between true discrepancies of reporting[2] and the influence of such items as import duties, transportation charges, time lags, classification of commodities, deliberate falsification for political reasons, etc. The separation of these factors is exceedingly difficult and will succeed only occasionally. When that is not the case, possibly big gaps remain in the respective reports.

The need for studies of this type has been noted by many writers over a long period of time. One of the earliest writers on this subject was the Italian economist, C. F. Ferraris, who developed (for gold movements) a test which did cast grave doubts on the validity of official returns.[3] Ferraris measured

---

[1] For example, in our study, *International Financial Transactions and Business Cycles* (Princeton, 1959), we found that the assertions, made mostly in the 1930's, that the gold standard mechanism imposed a rigid behavior upon the countries adhering to it, were not borne out by the facts as described by the data. So either the theory is at fault, or the data are inadequate (assuming that their confrontation was done correctly). See especially Chapter V and the discussion on pp. 565–573.

[2] See F. D. Graham, *Protective Tariffs* (Princeton, 1942), p. 28, footnote: "Much confusion arises from the fact that only a varying part of the total exports or imports of any given country is recorded in the statistics ordinarily published. . . . Official statistics, in fact, merely show the results of that portion of foreign commerce which happens to be easy of surveillance, or they reflect the statistical whims of legislatures." Yet Graham did not draw further consequences from this correct evaluation.

[3] See his almost totally neglected work, *La Statistica del Movimento dei Metalli Preziosi fra l'Italia e l'Estero* (Rome, 1885). See also his contribu-

the movement of gold from France to Great Britain for the periods 1876–1880 and 1881–1884, using the statistical sources of both countries. This showed the following large discrepancies (even after making allowance for transport costs, tariff duties, etc.):

GOLD IMPORTS IN BRITAIN

(in millions of francs)

	According to French export statistics	According to British import statistics
1876–1880	41.5	94.4
1881–1884	52.9	112.2

These differences are appalling and show that one is dealing with far from trivial troubles. Even if they were much smaller, they would call for study and remedial action. As we shall see, little has been accomplished, though the matter has been observed from time to time.

The long history of efforts on the part of various international organizations to standardize the classifications of commodities moving in international trade might lead eventually to increased validity at least as far as matching statistics is concerned. The reliability of data will depend on intensive analysis

---

tions to the *Bulletin de l'Institut International de Statistique,* vols. 11 and 12 (1899–1900), especially vol. 12, pp. 338–340. Another writer of note is L. Bodio, "Sulle discordanze che si osservano fra le statistiche commerciali dei vari Stati," *Biblioteca dell'Economista,* Ser. IV, vol. I, Part I, 1896, pp. 77 ff. Bodio had treated this problem already in 1865. Another important piece is U. Ricci, *Sulle Divergence fra Statistiche del Movimento Commerciale* (Turin, 1914). A more recent piece is the paper by C. Gini, "Le statistiche delle esportazioni," *Rivista di Politica Economica,* 1928, vol. V, where criticisms directed against Italian foreign trade statistics by Mortara and others are discussed. There have undoubtedly been similar studies made in other countries and on other occasions. In particular, reference is made to the paper by Sir Arthur Bowley, "Some Tests of the Trustworthiness of Public Statistics," *Economica,* vol. 8 (1928), pp. 253–278. He has shown wide discrepancies in the transit trade of Scandinavian countries. (I owe my acquaintance with this paper to C. Clark.)

—perhaps by commodities—into the data.[4] We will have more to say on this subject in section 3 below.

The most important causes for disparities between statistics of exporting and importing countries are the differences in:

a. Coverage of the statistics and definitions of commodities.

b. The methods adopted for showing "provenance" of imports and destination of exports.

c. Detailed definitions used in connection with a given method.

d. Methods of valuation and exchange conversion.

e. Inability (or unwillingness) of importers and especially exporters to furnish accurate information; it is usually more difficult to furnish correct data as to destination of exports than as to provenance of imports.[5]

In the following pages we shall first take up gold movements, partly for their intrinsic interest and the great role they have always played as a critical component in the items that make up the balance of payments, and partly because gold offers the simplest and most standardized of all cases where commodity movements are to be recorded. Then we shall examine some cases of commodity statistics other than gold.

2. STATISTICS OF GOLD MOVEMENTS

a. *Introduction*

In this section we will examine statistics of international gold movements for their reliability and usefulness.[6] An investiga-

[4] Recently, the Inter-American Statistical Institute has made some preliminary investigations along these lines: "Discrepancies in Foreign Trade Statistical Data as Reported by Trading Partners," prepared for the Third Inter-American Statistical Conference, Brazil, June 1955, reference document 3225a (mimeographed).

[5] *International Trade Statistics,* edited by R. G. D. Allen and J. Edward Ely (New York, John Wiley), 1953, pp. 117–118.

[6] This section is based, for the most part, on my monograph, *The Validity of International Gold Movement Statistics,* Special Papers in International Economics, No. 2, International Finance Section, Princeton University, November 1955, to which the reader is referred for more detail. That paper grew out of the work involved in a larger investigation undertaken for the National Bureau of Economic Research, *International Financial Transactions and Business Cycles* (Princeton, 1959). In the course of this

tion of this kind is justified for the light it may shed on the problem of the analysis of economic data in general, and, specifically, because gold movements are important in the study of international trade, especially in the behavior of exchange rates and capital movements. Gold movements are of particular significance for our understanding of the period of the gold standard, but they are also important for any other monetary system. The accuracy of the statistics on gold movements should probably be the least questionable of all the components of balance of payments statistics, certainly not to be compared with such items as security movements, the pure (and usually wild) estimates of tourists' expenditures, and immigrants' remittances.[7] It is therefore of singular importance to determine their worth. In the absence of fortuitously offsetting errors, the aggregate, formed of parts of widely diverse quality, cannot be better than the best part; in fact, it will in almost all cases be considerably below that standard.

In the case of gold, one is dealing with a clearly defined commodity of great significance. There are no technological changes in the product considered, and there is no serious problem of classification; it is easy to ascertain what constitutes gold, though not necessarily monetary gold. The statistics of gold

---

investigation, gold movements, gold points, their relations to exchange rates, etc., had to be examined. It was hoped that significant correlations could be computed on the basis of monthly data for exchange rates and gold movements for the important countries of the world during a period from approximately 1870 to 1939. However, studies by other writers of these relationships had already shown that it was very difficult, if at all possible, to obtain intelligible and significant relationships. The question therefore arose whether there might be troubles with the basic statistics themselves. Few difficulties are to be expected or found in the statistics of exchange rates. Statistics of gold points were non-existent; a collection of all accessible information about gold points for New York, London, Paris, and Berlin from 1870–1938 is given in Chapter V of my book mentioned above. The plentiful statistics of gold movements lent themselves to an investigation of their accuracy.

[7] The very great difficulties in obtaining reasonably reliable migration statistics are described by F. E. Linder, "World Demographic Data," in *The Study of Population*, edited by P. M. Hauser and O. D. Duncan (Chicago, 1959), pp. 321–360. Migration is a world-wide phenomenon, affects international transactions, the labor market, etc. Yet the coverage is only for about 32 percent of the world population and differs widely even among countries having such statistics at all.

movements have been and are being used by hosts of writers in their analyses of the conditions in various countries, in the studies of balance of payments, and for the verification and development of the theory of money and international trade. Most observations regarding gold in the field of the theory of international balances ultimately rely on information that can be culled only from gold movement statistics. Consequently, a test of the value and the significance of these statistics is of considerable interest and serves as an example for the statistics of foreign trade.

The "test" described in the next pages is entirely on a commonsense basis. The fact that no high-powered statistical procedures are used is explained by the peculiar circumstance that, as already commented on (p. 7), no techniques specifically appropriate for the subsequently shown situation exist, the tremendous development of statistics during the last decades notwithstanding.

In order to determine the value of statistics of gold movements, it is necessary to establish a standard of accuracy. This standard, by common scientific practice, can be derived only from the uses to which the data are to be put. The uses are, of course, governed by the "theories" for which the data are needed. If no theories existed, it would be impossible to say what "accuracy" of measurement of these quantities means. It will be seen in the following, however, that even for ordinary description, which is in itself not intended to be an application of high-powered economic theory, the statistics are so grossly bad that for most purposes they must be rejected.

Data on international gold movements are used not only for purposes of description and analysis, but also for policy guidance. The rates of interest of central banks, for example, frequently have been changed because of reported gold flows between countries. Such changes were justified by data which are of highly questionable character.

b. *Uses of Gold Movement Statistics*

The statistics of international gold movements are used primarily for two general purposes: (1) broad observations of long-run behavior of, say, gold and prices, using years as the minimum unit, and (2) the study of the fine structure of international economic interaction, as described, for example, by the variants of the theory of the gold standard and various theories of adjustment of balances of payments for which monthly data are indispensable. Obviously, the criteria of the usefulness of the data must be taken from the maximal requirements to be made for them.

We are concerned here only with gold movements across national borders. The separation of monetary gold and non-monetary gold used for industrial purposes, is neither simple nor conclusive,[8] although it would be desirable since the indirect effects of gold as an industrial commodity upon the price system and upon the international accounts are less important and direct than its monetary effects.

Gold statistics are derived from the statistics of monetary gold movements plus those of some gold stocks (in banks and treasuries). Important judgments hinge on them, including the nature and extent of the "gaps" in the balance of payments. Information about gold in possession of central and commercial banks and of treasuries is generally made available not only in the usual trade statistics but also in special reports. Nonetheless, such information is seldom trustworthy. At any rate, none of the available statistics shows the variations in the possessions of banks and treasuries as originating from contact with specific single countries (cf. footnote 20, p. 161); they are thus only useful for more limited investigations than those now under discussion.

A simple test of the data on official records of gold movements (as well as for other items in foreign trade) is the one developed (for gold) by C. F. Ferraris, mentioned above (p. 139). The following test uses Ferraris' principle and consists in taking A's exports to B according to A's export statistics and B's import statistics and B's exports to A according to B's export statistics and A's import statistics. Each of these two sets should agree within certain bounds that are set by such items as

---

[8] Some of the problems arising in this area are discussed by W. R. Gardner, "Merchandise Trade in the Balance of Payments," in *International Trade Statistics, op. cit.* For some comments on this work, see my review in *Econometrica*, Vol. 23 (1955), pp. 105 ff.

freight, insurance, and duties. To these some other factors may have to be added, mostly in the nature of lags; a reasonable allowance for clerical and printing errors must also be made.

c. *The Test of Validity*

The problem may be broken down into four parts: (1) the formulation of the underlying hypothesis, (2) the description of the sample and the results, (3) the explanation of the failure of the statistics to confirm the hypothesis and a discussion of certain difficulties even if it had been confirmed, and (4) the consequences of (2) and (3).

(1) *Formulation of the hypothesis.* The observations of gold movements from country A to country B are made in A's export and in B's import statistics. The two should coincide. In neighboring countries such factors as transportation costs and time lags virtually disappear; in countries more distant from each other, a time lag may have to be considered. Costs of transportation, insurance, handling charges, and so on, which all enter significantly into the determination of gold points, play no appreciable role here. Gold is so valuable that these costs all but disappear from the statistics, as is evident from the value of these items relative to the value of gold shipments.[9] Nevertheless, we shall not expect 100 percent agreement between the two statistics describing the same foreign trade operation, but will accept "reasonable" deviations. However, differences also due to other causes should be random. If they are not, there exists probably a special factor or bias that should be accounted for separately.

Thus, the expectation of practical identity of the two sets of data for neighboring countries, after allowing for a possible, but not necessary, time lag for others, constitutes the hypothesis of the following test.

(2) *Description of the sample test and its results: a*) The data used are the official statistics of imports and exports of gold, gold coin, bullion, leaf, etc. Sterling was chosen as the unit of measurement because most references to gold movements are in sterling, although the test, determining the ratio

[9] This does not contradict the fact that the profitability of shipments depends on very small changes of transportation cost, interest rates, etc.

between the two observations, is independent of units and could have been made in any currency.[10]

β) Figure 7 (discussed below, p. 153) shows two monthly time series over longer consecutive periods than were used for the sample in order to demonstrate that the choice of one source rather than of another, presumably equivalent, leads to widely different results concerning cycle turning points and the duration of cycles, the cycles merely determined in the conventional, intuitive manner of the National Bureau of Economic Research.

For each year, monthly data were assembled from both sources in a total of eight directions for the United Kingdom, the United States, Germany, and France. Canada was introduced only in her relations with the United Kingdom and the United States. This gives six pairs of countries plus two pairs involving Canada. Since each country's export and import statistics were examined and compared with the import and export statistics of each other country for the four years, there are 1536 possible monthly observations.[11] However, since only the differences between the reports enter into our subsequent computations, the number is cut to one-half, or 768 months. Quarterly and yearly values were obtained by summation from the monthly data. The monthly statistics are summarized in Table 5 in annual form.[12]

Table 5 gives exports and imports of gold in 1,000 pounds sterling from both sources, where available. There is also shown the ratio between the statistics from the two sources. If both sets of data were accurate, the ratios should be unity or very near to unity. But, the ratios do not cluster closely around 1; indeed, quite absurd and fantastic values occur. The spread, as is to be expected, was even greater for the quarterly than

[10] The period covered by the sample includes the years 1900, 1907, 1928, and 1935.

[11] There were, in fact, somewhat fewer entries, inasmuch as data were not available for each country for every month.

[12] Monthly data are not shown because of their bulk and in order to avoid any impression of erratic behavior of the sample. See, however, the monthly data of net movements in Figure 8. The quarterly data are reproduced in full in Table 2 in my monograph, *The Validity of International Gold Movement Statistics, op. cit.*, pp. 14–17.

for the yearly data, and would be still larger for monthly data were they shown.

An even more comprehensive picture is obtained from Fig. 5, which is, essentially, a frequency distribution. On the horizontal axis the ratios are shown and on the vertical axis the values of the transactions (using log-scale) are shown in 1,000 pounds sterling, the value taken from the first named country in each case.[13]

An additional hypothesis is suggested by Fig. 5: When gold movements are large the ratio will improve,[14] perhaps because greater care in reporting might usually be taken by both sides in such cases. Whatever the reason, the noted relation seems to be borne out by the yearly data. But it is noteworthy that the four largest values occur for 1935, and the really interesting gold standard period (pre-World War I) again fares badly. Even more noteworthy is the fact that the second largest movement, involving not less than 85 million pounds sterling of shipment between the United States and the United Kingdom, was, according to the statistics of the latter, only 75 percent of that which the United States reported for the same time—hardly a reliable piece of information!

(3) *Failure of the statistics.* The charts of quarterly data,[15] are even more revealing, showing departures from unity larger than would be admissible for reliable data. Even for 1900 and

---

[13] Figure 5 shows the frequency distribution of the ratios of Table 5 in the following manner: To take an example, in Figure 5, UK 35 US at ● means that the statistics of the United Kingdom indicate a gold movement to the United States in 1935 (summed over the whole year). The dot shows (from the legend in Figure 5) that the United Kingdom statistics were used to determine the ordinate, i.e., in this case the placement of the dot tells us that the cumulative amount transacted was given as £ 85,883,-000. The ratio at the bottom of the chart is taken from Table 5; that is, in the numerator are the data of the country whose statistics were not used for the determination of the ordinate (in this case the United States), and in the denominator are the data of the other country (in this case the United Kingdom). In the case of UK 35 US the ratio was .75, as Table 5 shows, and to this corresponds the abscissa of the dot ● on Figure 5. The other points on the chart should be interpreted in the same way.

[14] The chart omits the extreme ratios altogether for reasons of difficulty in plotting, but they can be seen in Table 5.

[15] See *The Validity of International Gold Movement Statistics, op. cit.,* pp. 20 and 22.

TABLE 5

Comparison of Annual Gold Movements and Ratio of Pairs of Statistics for Selected Countries for 1900, 1907, 1928 and 1935[1]

Unit: Thousands of Pounds Sterling

		U.K.-Germany	Germany-U.K.	Ratio Germany to U.K.[3]	U.K.-France	France-U.K.	Ratio France to U.K.	U.K.-U.S.	U.S.-U.K.	Ratio U.S. to U.K.	Germany-U.S.	U.S.-Germany	Ratio U.S. to Germany
1900	Exports[2]	4,903	2,065	1.12	2,360	671	1.76	1,082	3,896	.68	—	1,052	—
	Imports	2,544	5,490	.81	2,154	4,165	.31	5,872	738	.66	804	776	1.31
1907	Exports	3,162	7,176	1.25	7,208	3,224	.92	18,354	898	.99	210	558	2.25
	Imports	7,760	3,947	.93	5,204	6,590	.62	652	18,104	1.38	19	473	—
1928	Exports	21,047	116	—	19,969	—	.01	6,602	6,684	1.17	19	5,913	—
	Imports	52	—	2.22[4]	187	285	—	6,684	7,708	1.00	—	—	—
1935	Exports	1,373	149	—	49,845	77,164	1.00	85,883	117	.75	10	36	.80
	Imports	454	—	.33	81,000	49,631	.95	168	64,485	.70	—	8	—

(Cont.)

TABLE 5 (Cont.)

COMPARISON OF ANNUAL GOLD MOVEMENTS AND RATIO OF PAIRS OF STATISTICS FOR SELECTED COUNTRIES FOR 1900, 1907, 1928 AND 1935[1]

UNIT: THOUSANDS OF POUNDS STERLING

		Germany-France	France-Germany	Ratio France to Germany	U.S.-France	France-U.S.	Ratio France to U.S.	U.K.-Canada[5]	Canada-U.K.	Ratio Canada to U.K.	U.S.-Canada	Canada-U.S.	Ratio Canada to U.S.
1900	Exports	16	—	28.1	3,527	185	.47	—	—	—	645	204	.87
	Imports	130	450	—	368	1,667	.50	—	21	—	1,387	558	.15
1907	Exports	481	—	1.22	5,197	422	.94	—	1	—	2,795	3,955	.47
	Imports	641	589	—	1,035	4,879	.41	—	135	—	5,197	1,309	.76
1928	Exports	—	—	—	63,296	—	—	—	1,958	—	4,653	21,323	1.04
	Imports	—	—	—	31	—	—	1,958	1,014	1.00	21,038	4,854	1.01
1935	Exports	18	1,832	15.4	12	186,791	84.91	—	2,164	—	15	17,466	11.20
	Imports	—	277	—	192,005	1,019	.97	2,174	1	.99	19,573	168	.89

[1] The figures are those of the first named country for each pair. In some instances the sum of the monthly figures does not add up to the annual total given in the trade statistics. When this occurs the final figure reported, that is, the annual total, is used here. A dash means negligible amounts. For sources and further notes see Appendix to O. Morgenstern, *The Validity of International Gold Movement Statistics* (International Finance Section, Princeton University, 1955).

[2] The figures should be compared on the diagonal for each pair.

[3] The ratio is the proportion of imports from A to B to exports from A to B; e.g.: $\dfrac{B\text{'s imports from }A\text{ in }B\text{'s figures.}}{A\text{'s exports to }B\text{ in }A\text{'s figures.}}$

[4] Pairs of data with italicized ratios are excluded from the charts due to the smallness of the original figures or to the large size of the ratio.

[5] The pairs including Canada cover only July to December for 1900.

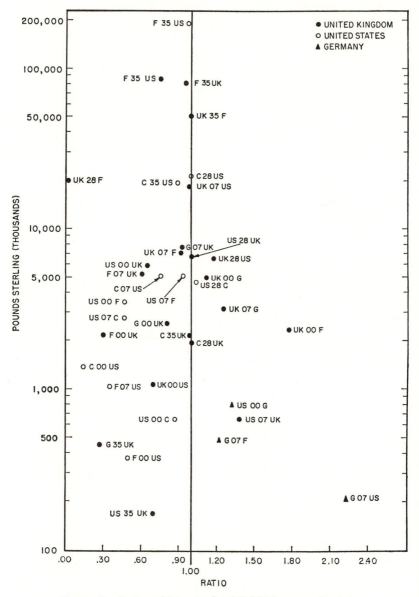

Figure 5. Ratio and Magnitude of Gold Movement Statistics
of Pairs of Countries, Yearly Sums

1907, the years of the classical gold standard, the results were catastrophic. There was no recognizable tendency or systematic bias of any sort. The statistics were simply contradictory. Although the quarterly sums for the period after World War I fared somewhat better (there were fewer entries), they are useless for purposes of more intricate economic reasoning. Nonetheless, they were used in thousands of publications, scientific and political, with all kinds of delicate "inferences" drawn.

If the monthly data of gold movements were correlated month for month with movements in exchange rates, short-term interest rates, and short-term interest rate differentials on the basis of the data included in our sample, or with any other available gold movement data, especially for the classical time of the gold standard before the first World War, the results would be very poor almost without exception. Correlations are not observed where they are expected. And in this case there are no potent reasons for permitting the lack of correlations to override the expectations. Furthermore, the results differ depending on which set of statistics is used, and there is no reason to prefer one set of these statistics over the others.

These observations apply even if the cycle turning points are determined only for gold movements and exchange rates or the other series referred to, or if the correlations are time series correlations involving all consecutive values. Since this is a question of application of series and is not directly connected with the test of the validity of the statistics, the material on which these remarks are based is not published in this book.

Further information about the inner nature of the discrepancies is highlighted in Fig. 6 which shows, for some randomly chosen cases, cumulative sums of monthly data from two sources. It is surprising that the statistics involving Canada and the United States are among the most unreliable; this is especially the case because of the shift of the discrepancy first from one, then to the other. We have no way of telling whether the Canadian or the United States statistics, or both, have to be rejected. The differences are particularly notable for the United States exports to Canada for 1907. But the other pairs of countries do not fare much better. They do have one thing in

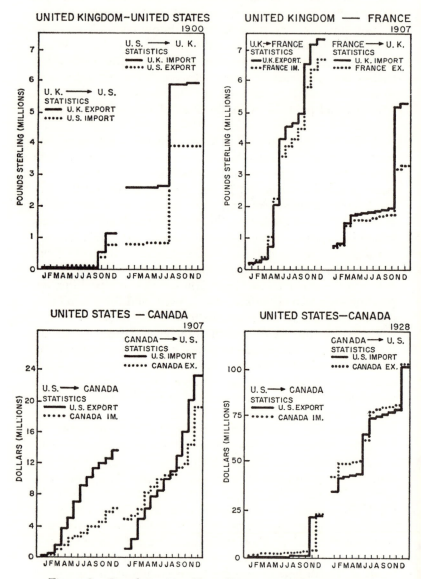

Figure 6.   Cumulative Monthly Gold Movement Statistics for Pairs
of Countries from Respective Sources 1900, 1907, 1928

common: when differences exist, very frequently they persist for many months in succession and often are not removed. This means that there are, apparently, at best no self-correcting forces at work making themselves swiftly felt.[16] In general, even if the direction of movement should be the same, the great *absolute* differences make it impossible to use these statistics for purposes of determining, for reasonably short intervals, the amounts of gold shipped and, possibly, of capital transfers. They can only be used for the crudest kinds of estimates and can play no major role in the fine-structured theory of international trade.

(4) *Further explorations.* Since most writers on international trade are particularly concerned with net movements, we insert a chart showing the net movement of gold from the United Kingdom to Germany for the periods from 1900–1913 and 1931–1936 on a monthly basis. The statistics are made up from the two possible sources: United Kingdom figures and German figures. In Figure 7, the two lines would coincide if the data were accurate, but this is the case only in rare instances. Anyone interested in the cyclical aspects of gold movements would be in a considerable quandary in trying to determine where the cycles are, what the amplitudes are, and into which particular month the peaks and troughs of the cycles fall.

The confusion of the statistics between the two European countries is much greater for the time before the first World War than it is in the early 1930's, but it is worth recalling that this latter period coincides with a time in which exchange control was applied quite strictly by Germany and so it would be expected that more accurate records would be kept.[17]

---

[16] There is a *lag* in several cases and there may be transit movements, as already mentioned. Elaborate statistical operations on these data may be indicated in order to discover lags, especially when more than two countries are simultaneously considered.

[17] A somewhat laborious extension of our procedures suggests itself: instead of forming cumulative sums (gross or net) merely for significant pairs of countries, all countries, or at least the most important, could be taken together and an overall total of imports and of exports could be formed. It might be hoped that in this way all major discrepancies would disappear. But even if a favorable result should be obtained, it is difficult to see how the all-important country-to-country data could be corrected.

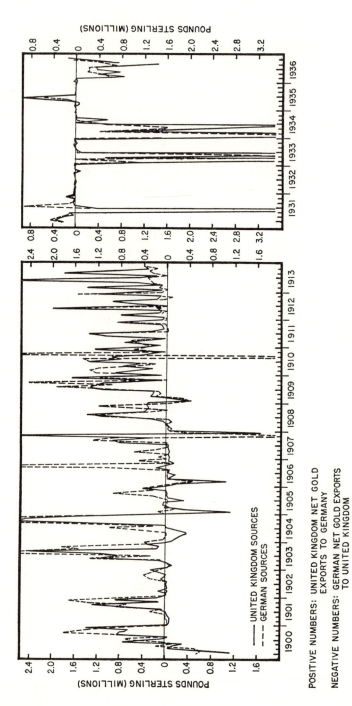

POSITIVE NUMBERS: UNITED KINGDOM NET GOLD
EXPORTS TO GERMANY

NEGATIVE NUMBERS: GERMAN NET GOLD EXPORTS
TO UNITED KINGDOM

—— UNITED KINGDOM SOURCES
- - - GERMAN SOURCES

Figure 7.   Comparison of Statistics of Monthly Net Gold Movements Between
United Kingdom and Germany, 1900–1913, 1931–1936

In order to facilitate the evaluation of the information contained in Figure 7, we have cumulated quarterly the discrepancies in the reported net gold movements for both cases. Figure 8 shows the quarterly cumulative values as well as the percentage of the cumulative discrepancies. Any one point of the series indicates how much gold is cumulatively unaccounted for from the beginning of this series up to that particular point of time. From January 1900 to July 1900 the cumulative net movement was from Germany to the United Kingdom. Germany then reported a net movement £310,000 *less* than the United Kingdom reported. From July 1900 on, the cumulative net gold movement was in the other direction (from the United Kingdom to Germany). From January 1900 to October 1907, for example, Germany reported a cumulative net gold movement to Germany of £29,000,000 in excess of that reported by the United Kingdom. This £29,000,000 discrepancy is 156 percent of the cumulative amount reported by the United Kingdom. Any other parts of the chart may be interpreted similarly.

The reader may judge for himself whether differences of these orders of magnitude mean anything. At any rate, what has happened in these arbitrarily chosen, short time intervals may easily have happened for other countries and for other intervals. For some purposes, the discrepancies may not matter, but if they do not, then it is because economic reasoning in these fields cannot be as sharp as it is often assumed to be.

The arguments used so far in evaluating the statistics were mostly qualitative because the lack of statistical theory makes the desired quantitative expression at present impossible. But in order at least to describe the data along statistically conventional lines, the significance of algebraic differences of the quarterly statistics of gold shipments between pairs of countries is shown in Table 6. The data used here include quarterly statistics of gold movements between all possible pairs, covering trade of the United States, Germany, France, the United Kingdom, and Canada for the years 1900, 1907, 1928, and 1935. Silver transactions between the United States and the United Kingdom are also included in order to provide at least one comparison of the two precious metals.

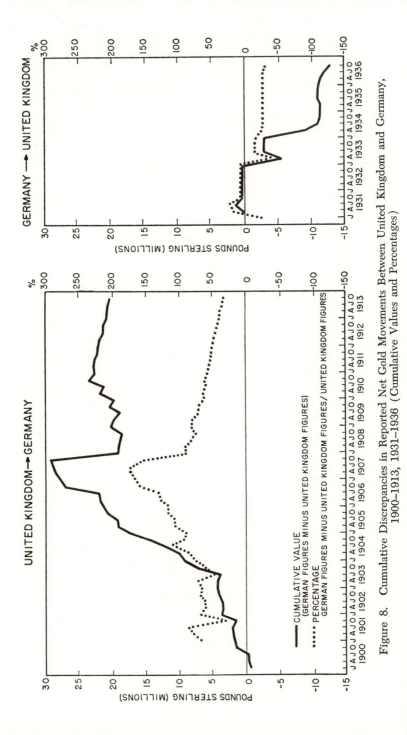

Figure 8. Cumulative Discrepancies in Reported Net Gold Movements Between United Kingdom and Germany, 1900–1913, 1931–1936 (Cumulative Values and Percentages)

TABLE 6

Test of Quarterly Gold Statistics
(1900, 1907, 1928, 1935)

| Pairs of Countries[2] | | Algebraic Differences[1] between Pairs of Countries and a Test of Their Significance | | | Standard Deviation of Sample Mean $\dfrac{\sigma}{\sqrt{n}}$ (4) |
		Average Differences[3] (1)	Standard Deviation[4] (2)	n (3)	
United Kingdom–	I	1,741.7	3,466	12	1,000.55
United States	II	168.5	600	10	189.74
United Kingdom–	I	1,696.6	5,230	12	1,509.77
France	II	727.0	2,302	8	813.88
United Kingdom–	I	−171.5	652	8	230.52
Germany	II	81.6	94	16	23.50
Germany-France	I	−45.1	109	8	38.54
Germany-United States	I	−67.5	83	4	41.50
United States–	I	38.4	2,458	5	1,099.37
France	II	832.4	2,326	7	876.85
United States–	I	97.7	272	13	75.43
Canada	II	303.4	912	14	243.75
Silver					
United Kingdom–	I	−13,810.3	27,959	14	7,556.48
United States	II	−6,426.8	4,854.1	12	1,402.92

[1] For each pair of countries there are four possible differences for each year of every series. There are four countries and six possible pairs of differences between them. In addition, the difference between Canada and the United States is introduced; and for silver the difference between the United Kingdom and the United States is examined.

[2] The series of differences in observations between each pair of countries is divided into two parts:

I. The difference between the observations of A and B with regard to the gold flow from A to B; i.e., the exports of A minus the imports of B.

II. The difference between the observations of A and B with regard to the gold flow from B to A; i.e., the imports of A minus the exports of B.

[3] Statistics of first country minus those of second. These algebraic differences are then summed and divided by their total number. In some pairs of countries, data are not reported for all years. This diminishes the number of differences to less than 16 (quarterly figures taken for four years) since years for which no data are reported are excluded.

[4] The computation of the standard deviation of the sample mean is sometimes conventionally restricted to $n \geqq 10$. We nevertheless include the values for smaller n since the tendency of the different computations appears to agree in all relevant aspects.

In this table, the first column shows the average differences with regard to the two directions of the gold flow between two countries. The second column shows the standard deviations of the population, the third the size of the sample, and the last gives $\frac{\sigma}{\sqrt{n}}$ the standard deviation of the sample mean.[18] Inspection of the first column of the table shows that the average differences between reports are much larger than can be explained by the known factors of freight, insurance charges, and the like. This indicates faulty statistics. One might take a general point of view that all measurements are subject to error and that the discrepancies indicated are natural consequences of this phenomenon; but, in terms of a simple theory of errors, the possibility of a bias is still present.

The result of the computations is clearly this: the statistics are so bad that a finer test is not warranted. The standard deviations of the sample mean show this directly. A reasonable interpretation of the situation is that it is impossible to determine what bias exists, which is to say that the reliable and the faulty statistics cannot be identified. This agrees entirely with what common sense has indicated. It may be possible to develop another approach to the problem of error and bias for the present case, but the explanation of the discrepancies, given in the following section, seems valid in any case.

(5) *Explanation of the differences and further difficulties.* What are the factors explaining these differences? We see here the consequences of the fact that economic statistics are in the rarest instances the result of scientific observations. They are usually only a by-product of other activities. There is also the difference in the position of the "observers"; this consists, for gold, mostly in the time interval which occurs when recording an export and when recording the corresponding import. When "lags" appear, they are not stable, sometimes going in one direction, sometimes in the other. Besides the genuine time lag due to transportation between distant countries, there are

---

[18] For the rationale of the calculations, see, for example, H. Cramér, *Mathematical Methods of Statistics* (Princeton, 1946), p. 345; or A. M. Mood, *Introduction to the Theory of Statistics* (New York, 1950), p. 133; or S. S. Wilks, *Mathematical Statistics* (New York, 1962), pp. 198–9.

others that are (a) spurious and due to inaccuracy, and (b) due to transit. Most likely, (a) holds more frequently.

All differences due to prices, freights, insurance, duty (zero!), exchange rates (except for Germany which, in 1935, had a variety of exchange rates) can be neglected. They are more or less known and trifling.

So there remain the "true" causes. We leave open whether the statistics were often, occasionally, or never deliberately falsified. Since we are dealing with gold transactions, in which a great deal of secrecy often prevailed, it is not impossible that such manipulation occurred. Inaccuracy as a consequence of privilege is a frequent occurrence; central banks, and sometimes even private banks, often could remove gold from ships in a great hurry, and the statistical records may then have suffered even unintentionally. Furthermore, the high value of the metal is not a sufficient cause for accurate entries, especially when the customs officials had no interest whatsoever in the valuation of gold. They may indeed have been under orders *not* to report.

There are even explanations arising from differences in classification, which, of course, become really troublesome with ordinary commodities (cf. below, p. 167). Gold and silver were often thrown together in the same cases and shipments, and frequently in such instances there were false declarations on the part of the shippers. Freight and insurance were cheaper on a "mixture" of gold and silver, and it was often easy to add a piece of silver to a gold bar in order to get a "mixture." In one country the mixture might leave as "silver" and arrive as "gold" in the other, and vice versa.[19] Besides savings in freight and insurance there was also the desire for secrecy as to shipments when private and commercial banks were involved and were assuming the risks.

Coverage of all gold movements by the statistics was unquestionably incomplete because of secrecy, the removal of

---

[19] Table 6 includes a separate row for silver. The results are no better for this metal, as further checks have revealed. Nor does a total of gold and silver give better results, which shows the absence of any self-correcting elements in the statistics. Silver is, of course, more in the nature of a commercial commodity than gold. This gives some idea of what to expect from tests of foreign commodity trade statistics.

gold at arrival in port before customs, and so on. There are, furthermore, the not negligible gold movements in the form of gold carried by travelers during the periods of gold coin circulation. While the amounts were large, they were neglected in *all* the statistics and would not, therefore, even if included, have closed the differences in reporting shown in this study. The discovery of the origin and destination of gold shipments probably offers as great an objective difficulty as for all other commodities. In different countries different practices exist as to how to enter amounts of gold ("specie") into the statistics when the gold is reported by a country other than the sending or receiving country. Sometimes gold would travel through several countries in transit status.

Among a host of other difficulties, one, the earmarking of gold, needs attention, for difficulties arise even when the statistics are accurate. The question of accuracy must be directed to the central banks in this case, rather than to the authorities responsible for foreign trade statistics. Earmarking became widespread from the late 1920's on, and central banks do not as a rule say for whom they hold earmarked gold and sometimes do not say whether they hold it at all. There may thus be many changes in the composition of ownership of an otherwise unchanged total held in a given country. This makes a correction of the foreign trade figures impossible.

There remains the question of substitute statistics from which pairwise gold movements might be deduced. On that basis, in turn, inferences about capital movements could be made. This gives an uncomfortably long chain of deduction and there are no substitutes. Statistics of gold movements represent at best only a small part of capital movements. The published central bank figures do not inform us about pairwise movements, nor can it be expected that pairwise gold transactions could still be uncovered from the unpublished records. Furthermore, it is impossible to reconstruct transactions from the records of commercial and private banks which often put the larger part of gold into the open market. For general economic histories, especially those dealing with large international crises, a combination of foreign trade and central bank statistics may roughly suffice; but for purposes of finer detail of economic theory such is not the case. Moreover, a careful test of the accuracy of central bank figures would also be necessary.[20] They are sometimes deliberately falsified by combining data on gold and silver and by reporting bullion gold or foreign coins under "other assets," a common practice in the period between the two World Wars. Finally, there is the general secrecy regarding operations of exchange stabilization funds whose gold operations overshadowed those of the central banks. Such irregular accounting practices were also common in the nineteenth century, but economists have paid only scant attention to them.

Our discussion of gold movements has been in terms of pairwise trade between countries. This is unquestionably the basic information needed when variations in exchange rates are considered and when general trade with another country is studied. One may also be interested in the aggregate position of the balance of payments of a country. In that case, the total net gold movement is of interest. It is clear, however, that this figure is ultimately based upon those pertaining to the pairwise relationships which we have found to be very defective. If it could be proved that the aggregation has some self-correcting feature, such that the errors in the individual components of the aggregate tend to cancel out, the total would be more valuable than the parts. Yet there appears to be nothing that would allow us to draw this comforting conclusion, though it is a frequent argument whenever grave faults in economic statistics are pointed out. No self-correction can be observed.

The net gold position of a country is thus only inadequately known. It is, however, theoretically possible to check the movement data from the changes in the position of the gold stocks in a country. This is not too difficult in those countries where strict controls exist—at least as far as monetary gold is concerned. But it is a virtual impossibility for the period of the classical gold standard, where bullion and gold coins could be

[20] I have also attempted to break up gold transactions of central banks according to countries in order that such time series might be used as substitutes for those derived from foreign trade statistics. This idea was kindly tested for me for 1898 and 1907 by the Bank of England, but the results were entirely negative. They disclosed that private gold shipments were very large, if the customs figures can be accepted. However, even if such series were constructed, they would not form the desired substitute.

in anyone's possession and where neither commercial banks nor the central bank made correct and complete disclosures of their assets, not to mention the movements in and out of industrial gold.

Considerations of this kind are of interest when the gold movements from the United States to Europe during the last few years are studied. The weekly published figures show that the United States has consistently seemed to lose gold in round numbers. One week the gold outflow would be reported as 100 million dollars, the next three weeks it would amount to exactly nothing; in effect a monthly series accurate to one digit results.

Even if the reported figures were accurate, their meaning should be questioned. Gold is purchased, usually in lump-sums, by countries who have built up their dollar balances beyond their requirements. Since most of these countries (including the United Kingdom) report gold flows monthly, gold will tend to be purchased at monthly intervals.

It may therefore be argued that week-to-week changes are really misleading and that a longer time interval should be looked at regarding the significance of gold flows, and that we need not report the figures more than monthly. The weekly reporting which distorts only the short-run picture might therefore be completely harmless. Yet this sidesteps the issue. If a series is reported on a weekly basis, then it should be significant to the best of the knowledge of the compilers, on a weekly basis. If only a monthly series is desired, then only a monthly series should be published. The present state of affairs must leave the analyst of short-term international financial movements with a considerable and unnecessary burden of uncertainty.

(6) *Summary and conclusions.* The regrettable lack of trustworthy gold statistics deprives the study of international trade and business cycles of one of its most important means of analysis. The effects are felt not only in the inability to make reliable correlations between gold movements and other time series,[21] but also in respect to further exploitation of statistics which make essential use of the information on gold move-

[21] When such correlations have been made, they have failed to show any relations that could be interpreted with our present knowledge.

ments. This matter is particularly relevant with respect to balance-of-payment statistics which abound with fanciful estimates covering large percentages of the total balances.

The question arises whether gold movement statistics are better or worse than others, especially in the field of international commodity trade.

What should be done about this situation? It requires a great deal of strength *not* to use ready-made and commonly available statistics, dealing with important events, when there are no substitutes. But great as the temptation may be to continue as if everything were in tolerable shape, a greater service is rendered to economics by insisting that a good theory cannot be built on shaky data.

3. STATISTICS OF FOREIGN COMMODITY TRADE

The gold statistics discussed above *in extenso* are a special case of the far more voluminous figures on foreign commodity trade. The problem arises whether these large aggregates are less subject to doubt, for example, because of compensation of errors (or at least, differences in reports). As will be seen, this is not the case.

In this sector, we rely on the apparently wholly neglected work of S. Zuckermann, who compared, in the manner of Ferraris, the statistics of trade between many pairs of countries for the years 1909–1913,[22] the League of Nations fundamental study on world trade[23] for the period 1928 to 1938, and the United Nations' compilations of trade statistics.

In 1928 it was reported that imports were $35.5 billions and exports $32.6 billions for total world trade (a difference of 8.9 percent). In 1938 it was reported that imports were $24.6 billions and exports were $21.9 billions (a difference of 12.3 percent). Table 7 shows world trade for 1938–1960 (note, however,

[22] S. Zuckermann, *Statistischer Atlas zum Welthandel* (Berlin, 1920). I owe the acquaintance with this work to the late Professor V. Furlan of Basel, Switzerland. (The author of this atlas of world trade is not to be confused with Sir Solly Zuckerman, who in *Foreign Affairs* (January 1962) published the grossest misunderstandings of the theory of games noted so far, while at the same time acknowledging that he did not understand its mathematical and logical content.)

[23] *Network of World Trade*, League of Nations (Geneva, 1942). (This is the work of the late F. Hilgert.)

the countries omitted for lack of comparable data!). It appears that for some years, e.g. 1953 and 1954 (during the Korean War), correspondence was very good, only to drop again. It will be seen from Tables 8 to 13, that for pairs of individual countries correspondences are as a rule very poor, so it remains a puzzle how the aggregate could be better.

The disparities in statistics of importing and exporting countries are due to the inclusion in imports of transport charges between frontiers (or ports) of the importing and exporting

TABLE 7

TOTAL WORLD TRADE

(billion U.S. dollars)

Year	Imports c.i.f.	Exports f.o.b.	M-X	$\frac{M\text{-}X}{X} \times 100$
1938	23.7	21.1	2.6	12.3
1947	50.1	46.9	3.2	6.8
1948	59.7	53.6	6.1	11.4
1949	58.5	53.7	4.8	8.9
1950	59.0	56.3	2.7	4.8
1951	80.9	76.1	4.8	6.3
1952	79.6	72.3	7.3	10.1
1953	75.9	74.1	1.8	2.4
1954	79.2	76.9	2.3	3.0
1955	88.6	83.7	4.9	5.9
1956	97.4	93.0	4.4	4.7
1957	107.2	99.8	7.4	7.4
1958	100.0	95.2	4.8	5.0
1959	105.6	100.9	4.7	4.7
1960	118.3	112.6	5.7	5.1

Excluding Albania, Bulgaria, Mainland China, Czechoslovakia, East Germany (beginning 1948), Hungary, North Korea (beginning 1948), North Viet-Nam (beginning 1955), Poland, Rumania, U.S.S.R. (A set of supplementary Tables is published by the United Nations for the Soviet area.)

SOURCE:

    1953–60 from *Monthly Bulletin of Statistics*, Statistical Office of the United Nations, January 1962, Vol. xvi, No. 1, pp. 86–87.

    1938,

    1947–52 *Yearbook of International Trade Statistics*, Vol. 1, New York, 1960, pp. 12–13.

NOTE: All exports are valued f.o.b.; imports are c.i.f. except for U.S. and Canada, which are f.o.b.

countries, which amounted to about 9 percent of the world's exports in 1928 and 12 percent in 1938 (*Network*, p. 16). In addition, because of the increase in the number of countries, the additional possibilities of difficulties in recording value, of diversion en route, re-export, time lag, differences in classification of commodities, differences in valuation, existence of multiple exchange rates, and differences in quality,[24] it will be more difficult here than in the case of gold (in fact it is impossible) *to separate actual errors in reporting from mere differences in emphasis and definition,* when sets of statistics are compared. The conversion of statistics to a common unit, mostly the United States dollar, though needed, is one of the prime sources of trouble and not permissible when there are no truly convertible currencies. When exchange control and multiple rates exist on either one or both sides of a pair of countries, the quoted figures are mostly meaningless since it is impossible to know at which rate which imports and which exports were computed, and for what reason. All this was commented on briefly above (p. 161), but it is imperative to bring up the issue at this crucial point. The remark applies to the 1930's and to the time after the end of World War II to the present. Even in 1962 there are still many countries which have multiple exchange rates.

When reporting *values*, differences arise due to the factors mentioned above. It is therefore important to point out that enormous discrepancies in foreign trade statistics (sometimes up to 100 percent) also occur when *physical quantities* are considered. This was found to be the case, for example, before

[24] Each of these factors would deserve a lengthy treatment of its own. Space forbids this. But the reader who wishes to study further any of these points will quickly confirm the seriousness of the situation. The book by Allen and Ely, *op. cit.*, contains numerous, excellent contributions which are relevant in this connection. This important work shows many of the tremendous difficulties of obtaining correct foreign trade statistics, but it offers no method for the numerical estimation of the errors. The book contains detailed references to numerous specific studies of these issues, showing the great efforts that have been made over the decades in many countries to arrive at better information and to estimate the value of the data on hand. Of the literature that has followed this book, I especially mention J. E. Ely, "Variations Between U.S. and its Trading Partner Import and Export Statistics," *The American Statistician,* vol. 15, No. 2 (April 1961), pp. 23–26.

World War II for the carload shipments of coal from Czechoslovakia to neighboring Austria. It is well known that the quantities of grain shipped undergo great changes because of destruction en route, etc. But there are also great differences in the reports of shipments of coal and other bulk transports, even when no transit is involved. These differences cannot be explained except as faults of the reporting of one or of both countries or because of different methods of attribution; differences in definition play a minor role with these types of standard and bulky commodities.

Since the price of gold is constant within each of the years investigated (relative to the gross nature of foreign trade statistics given in millions of $, £, etc.) and other charges are minimal, gold value figures are an indication of what can be expected from the comparison of physical quantities. Therefore they have a wider interest here than merely as statistics of *values* of gold shipments.[25] In the following, we restrict ourselves to the statistics of *values*. [26]

In what follows, we deal with the existing statistics, though we have pointed out that arriving at "values" by the different statistical offices is far from being a simple matter. Even when there are no doubts about exchange rates, there is the possibility that the invoices accompanying the commodities are not properly made out, are falsified, that values are hard to attribute to the right categories of commodities, etc., all of which give rise to variations. Often the imported commodities are not followed or preceded by bills and invoices, which is why price estimation plays such a big role in this area of making sta-

[25] It must be observed, however, that another difficulty arises: While there is no doubt what constitutes the commodity "gold," and while the fineness of the bars is attested, gold shippers have or had (during the gold standard) an interest in declaring gold wrongly (e.g., as silver or as mixtures of gold and silver—obtained by adding a small silver coin to the gold bar) in order to keep shipments secret or to save costs and insurance. This is, therefore, also an instance of deliberate lying, a phenomenon discussed in Chapter II, Section 2.

[26] Concerning the influence of fluctuating *exchange rates* upon these values, cf. below, page 177, where also the obscuring influence of exchange controls is noted.

tistical reports. Special experts for valuation have to be called in and trained, and practices vary widely from one country to another, all of which bespeaks of the great uncertainties prevailing in this area.[27]

Before proceeding, we shall point up one of the principal difficulties in foreign trade statistics: *the classification of commodities.* The enormous importance of forming acceptable aggregates in economics was mentioned above (Chapter II, Section 5), but the difficulties are nowhere as clear as in this area, where they are perhaps the main source of the confused state of information. In the previous discussion the chief difficulty alluded to was the identification and classification of commodities (i.e., "is this object a natural fiber, a synthetic fiber, a plastic material; is it spun glass, or is it . . ., etc.?"). Now we have this problem *plus* that of grouping many items into more comprehensive categories. Since literally millions of different things are being produced, of which undoubtedly at least hundreds of thousands cross national borders in trade transactions, it is clear that the grouping problem is a big one. Full detail being out of the question, only a small, comprehensive listing is possible. What the best listing is, how large it should be, what to do when new commodities appear (as is the case with ever increasing frequency), how often to change the listing, etc.—all this has for a long time been of great concern to those in charge of foreign trade statistics.

Numerous international conferences were held to arrive at a Standard International Trade Classification (SITC).[28] The first conference was held as early as 1853 in Brussels; eventually a first international convention was signed in 1913 by 29 countries. An improved minimum list was published by the League of Nations in 1938; it had 17 major sections, divided into 50 chapters, summarizing the 456 items on the list. The current SITC, first published in 1950, has 10 major sections, divided into 52 divisions, subdivided into 150 groups, which in turn are

---

[27] In 1831, values of imports to England were arrived at officially on prices prevailing in 1690! Cf. G. M. Young, *Victorian England, Portrait of an Age* (London, 1936), p. 32.

[28] Cf. the work by Allen and Ely, *op. cit.*

divided into 570 commodity items. According to the United Nations, by 1960 governments of countries accounting for about 80 percent of world trade were compiling trade-by-commodity data according to the 1950 SITC, and the major international agencies had adopted it as a basis for the reporting of trade statistics. The SITC has recently been revised and has 1,312 basic items: 10 sections, 56 divisions, 177 groups, and 625 subgroups, with 257 of the subgroups divided into 944 subsidiary headings.[29] The task is clearly an unending one and will never be settled to every country's satisfaction. Nor will the scientific user ever be accommodated according to his wishes because of the immense expense that would be connected with any rearrangement according to varying scientific needs.

The *de facto* situation is that a few countries report only principal exports (Brazil, Egypt, Indonesia, etc.); the rest report for all groups of the SITC, although some without analyses of provenance and destination. Even among those countries conforming to the overall scheme the differences in classification are enormous. France, for example, has 6,500 classifications, but the United States export list contains less than half this many, only 2,600 items, though obviously U.S. exports do not contain fewer commodities than French exports! In general, large trading nations provide statistical information on two to three thousand items in the export and import trade. For smaller, or less developed countries, the number of commodities runs only to a few hundred, as for Turkey, which has a list of 300. It is obvious that an item exported from the United States to Turkey will be grouped together with many more items (of probably great diversity) than if the same item is exported to France, which indicates the reason for the confusion attendant upon interpreting the "meaning" of such transactions! Considering that there are 104 countries in the United Nations alone, making up a very large network of trade (though not all trade with each other), one gets an idea of the tremendous complexity of the statistics of total world trade.

[29] *Standard International Trade Classification* (*SITC*), Statistical Papers, Series M, No. 10, United Nations, New York, September 1950; and *Standard International Trade Classification, Revised,* Statistical Papers, Series M, No. 34, United Nations, New York, 1961.

In this light one should doubt that the differences shown on Table 7 can actually be as small as reported, especially when the subsequent tables show very large discrepancies for the pairwise trade. Table 7 is only a statement of the difference between imports and exports. It is built up on figures which will be seen to be of very doubtful value. This is demonstrated in Tables 8 to 13. These summarize in part the work done by Zuckermann for the period 1909 to 1913, and by the League of Nations for 1929, 1935, and 1938. The data for more recent years are from various United Nations documents based upon the original sources. The tables compare the trade transactions between pairs of countries A and B as described by the separate statistics of each country. The first column in each case gives the percentage differences between the estimates of A's imports and B's exports; the second column gives the percentage differences between the estimates of A's exports and B's imports; and the last column describes the differences in percentages between the estimates of the balance of trade. (These last are included in order to show how smaller errors in the import and export statistics may be *magnified* in balance of trade statistics. We shall not make full use of these balance of trade data, however, since this would require a separate study.)

Five main cases have to be distinguished:

Case I: Positive values for columns (1) and (2) in all cases. This may indicate that the first country overstates its foreign trade statistics in both directions, or that the second country understates its foreign trade in both directions.

Case II: Positive values for all cases in column (1). Negative values for all cases in column (2). This may indicate that imports are overstated in both countries or that exports are understated in both countries. A possible reason could be that duties and transportation charges are usually paid by the importing country, are sizeable, and have been included in the statistics of the importing nations.

Case III: Negative values for all cases in column (1). Positive values for all cases in column (2). This may indicate that exports are overstated in both countries or that imports are understated in both countries.

Case IV: Negative values for all cases in columns (1) and

The subscripts 1 and 2 denote the country. In Tables 8 to 12, 1 indicates the United States; 2 indicates the other country. In Table 13, 1 refers to the country listed first and 2 to the country listed second.

$$I_1 = \begin{cases} \text{Imports of country 1 according to 1's statistics} \\ \text{Exports of country 2 according to 1's statistics} \end{cases}$$

$$I_2 = \begin{cases} \text{Imports of 2 according to 2} \\ \text{Exports of 1 according to 2} \end{cases}$$

$$E_1 = \begin{cases} \text{Exports of 1 according to 1} \\ \text{Imports of 2 according to 1} \end{cases}$$

$$E_2 = \begin{cases} \text{Exports of 2 according to 2} \\ \text{Imports of 1 according to 2} \end{cases}$$

$b_1 =$ Balance of trade of 1 according to 1

$b_2 =$ Balance of trade of 1 according to 2

SOURCES FOR TABLES 8 TO 13:

Period

A   Zuckermann, S., *Statistischer Atlas zum Welthandel*, Vol. II, (Berlin, 1921).

B   League of Nations, *The Network of World Trade* (Geneva, 1942).

C   *Direction of International Trade* (Joint publication of the UN, IMF, and IBRD), Series T.

TABLE 8

United States-France

COMPARISON OF AMERICAN AND FRENCH STATISTICS
DESCRIBING TRADE WITH EACH OTHER

Year	(1) $\dfrac{I_1-E_2}{I_1}$	(2) $\dfrac{E_1-I_2}{E_1}$	(3) $\dfrac{b_1-b_2}{b_1}$
A. 1909	+30.7%	−11.2%	+972.3%
1910	+27.8	−2.4	+597.4
1911	+39.8	−24.4	−1220.4
1912	+37.8	−10.7	−316.4
1913	+41.3	−12.0	−492.8
Average: 1909–1913	+35.6	−12.2	−1013.1
B. 1928	+25.3	−1.0	−52.2
1935	+15.5	−1.7	−18.6
1938	+9.3	−13.4	−28.8
C. 1948	+15.4	−0.1	−2.4
1952	+5.6	−25.5	−51.8
1956	+4.1	−21.3	−39.8
1960	−1.4	−29.5	−90.9

TABLE 9

United States-Germany

COMPARISON OF AMERICAN AND GERMAN STATISTICS
DESCRIBING TRADE WITH EACH OTHER

	Year	(1) $\dfrac{I_1-E_2}{I_1}$	(2) $\dfrac{E_1-I_2}{E_1}$	(3) $\dfrac{b_1-b_2}{b_1}$
A.	1909	+10.8%	−21.7%	−83.3%
	1910	+9.4	−9.6	−44.1
	1911	+7.9	−8.1	−29.8
	1912	+10.6	−14.4	−46.7
	1913	+7.7	−15.9	−41.9
Average: 1909–1913		+9.0	−14.1	−46.5
B.	1928	+14.6	−3.3	−19.5
	1935	+11.5	−6.5	−107.1
	1938	+4.8	−55.2	−145.2
C.	1948	−4.9	−4.3	−4.3
	1952*	−17.8	−33.9	−48.6
	1956	−0.6	−21.3	−56.4
	1960	**	−33.7	−213.9

* After 1948 figures are trade of German Federal Republic, including the American, British, and French sectors of Berlin.
** Less than 0.1.

TABLE 10

United States-Great Britain

COMPARISON OF AMERICAN AND BRITISH STATISTICS
DESCRIBING TRADE WITH EACH OTHER

	Year	(1) $\dfrac{I_1-E_2}{I_1}$	(2) $\dfrac{E_1-I_2}{E_1}$	(3) $\dfrac{b_1-b_2}{b_1}$
A.	1909	+41.5%	−2.1%	−41.4%
	1910	+43.5	+6.1	−30.1
	1911	+46.4	−0.1	−40.4
	1912	+53.2	+1.0	−54.6
	1913	+47.6	−7.8	−55.4
Average: 1909–1913		+46.7	−0.6	−44.7
B.	1928*	+34.6	−2.2	−27.9
	1935	+26.5	+7.4	−3.2
	1938	+14.4	−5.2	−10.9
C.	1948*	+2.1	−14.7	−28.5
	1952	−4.1	−31.7	−103.2
	1956	+6.1	−25.8	−207.7
	1960	+3.3	−12.7	−50.6

* Periods B and C represent trade of United States and the United Kingdom.

TABLE 11

United States-Canada

COMPARISON OF AMERICAN AND CANADIAN STATISTICS
DESCRIBING TRADE WITH EACH OTHER

Year	$\dfrac{I_1-E_2}{I_1}$ (1)	$\dfrac{E_1-I_2}{E_1}$ (2)	$\dfrac{b_1-b_2}{b_1}$ (3)
A. 1909	−19.3%	−19.1%	−18.8%
1910	−0.8	−40.0	−80.2
1911	−8.6	−19.1	−23.9
1912	−15.6	−17.6	−18.5
1913	−15.0	−1.8	+5.3
Average: 1909–1913	−12.1	−16.9	−19.7
B. 1928	−3.4	+9.6	+24.5
1935	+3.8	+3.1	−2.7
1938	−3.8	+9.6	+27.5
C. 1948	+2.1	+4.8	+17.4
1952	−0.6	−9.1	−61.0
1956	−1.2	−5.5	−17.1
1960	−7.1	−2.2	+16.0

TABLE 12

United States-Belgium

COMPARISON OF AMERICAN AND BELGIAN STATISTICS
DESCRIBING TRADE WITH EACH OTHER

Year	$\dfrac{I_1-E_2}{I_1}$ (1)	$\dfrac{E_1-I_2}{E_1}$ (2)	$\dfrac{b_1-b_2}{b_1}$ (3)
A. 1909	+43.0%	−20.3%	−298.5%
1910	+39.8	−14.5	−1459.7
1911	+41.1	−31.8	−246.4
1912	+34.3	−27.7	−160.6
1913	+50.3	−26.2	−164.1
Average: 1909–1913	+41.6	−24.9	−224.1
B. 1928*	+9.4	+22.8	+50.0
1935	+5.0	+19.0	+50.0
1938	−23.8	−10.4	+5.7
C. 1948*	+4.7	−15.3	−25.8
1952	+1.4	−24.0	−71.4
1956	−0.1	+6.2	+20.6
1960	+1.8	−10.0	+52.5

* Belgium-Luxembourg, 1928–1960.

TABLE 13

Comparison of Averages* in Pairs of Countries for Periods A, B, and C

Pairs of Countries		(1) $\dfrac{I_1-E_2}{I_1}$	(2) $\dfrac{E_1-I_2}{E_1}$	(3) $\dfrac{b_1-b_2}{b_1}$
United States-France	A	+35.6%	−12.2%	−1013.1%
	B	+21.5	−3.6	−38.3
	C	+2.9	−18.3	−33.4
United States-Germany	A	+9.0	−14.1	−46.5
	B	+13.0	−9.1	−33.3
	C	−2.6	−22.6	−44.1
United States-Great Britain	A	+46.7	−0.6	−44.7
	B	+30.4	−1.1	−18.9
	C	+2.6	−19.8	−72.0
United States-Canada	A	−12.1	−16.9	−19.7
	B	−2.5	+8.7	+24.7
	C	−2.3	−3.7	−9.2
United States-Belgium	A	+41.6	−24.9	−224.1
	B	+1.9	+14.2	−36.5
	C	+1.5	−3.2	−12.0
Germany-France	A	−22.4	−20.3	−6.6
	B	+4.1	−3.9	−4100.0
	C	−0.6	0.0	+3.2
Germany-Great Britain	A	+3.6	−10.2	−40.4
	B	+7.5	−3.0	−34.6
	C	−10.1	−4.8	+41.7
Great Britain-France	A	−34.4	−60.0	+10.5
	B	−8.1	−51.2	+41.6
	C	+10.7	+23.8	−61.8
Canada-Great Britain	A	+16.0	+22.7	+41.5
	B	+11.0	+23.8	+32.4
	C	−1.2	−16.8	−35.4
Canada-France	A	+63.4	+12.1	+76.9
	B	+5.1	−95.1	+233.3
	C	+4.6	−2.4	−7.6
Canada-Germany	A	+8.8	−166.7	+68.9
	B	+14.8	−90.8	−220.5
	C	+3.3	−16.8	−43.6
Belgium-France	A	−81.2	+18.3	+1123.0
	B	−45.8	−11.4	−159.3
	C	+7.7	+8.5	+4.7
Belgium-Germany	A	+13.4	+53.9	+145.5
	B	−4.2	+7.8	−525.0
	C	−1.7	+4.5	−25.9
Belgium-Great Britain	A	+34.0	−1.5	−288.0
	B	+20.6	−19.9	−92.9
	C	+21.8	−1.6	+191.2

* Averages were computed from the original trade data.

(2). This may indicate that the second country overstates its foreign trade statistics in both directions or that the first country understates its foreign trade statistics in both directions.

Case V: The third column is chiefly interesting as expressing the balance of trade between the two countries. The signs here indicate that the balance of the second country is larger than the balance of the first, if the sign is *negative.* The converse is the case if the sign is *positive.*

EXAMPLES:

(1) The comparisons of the United States and France (Table 8) are an example of Case II. This may be partly explained by import duties and transportation charges paid by the importer.

(2) The United States-Germany example (Table 9) also belongs, up to 1938, to Case II, probably for similar reasons. However, in both cases the irregularity of the percentage deviations must be noted. This betrays faulty reporting since transportation costs and other charges cannot possibly have varied to this extent. After World War II, Case IV becomes applicable, but it is doubtful that this should be interpreted as a change in making the statistics.

(3) The United States-Great Britain example (Table 10) shows that there were several changes over the period. This does not fit into any of the simple cases discussed above. Here column (1), referring to United States imports and British exports, shows that the United States import figures were higher throughout both periods. Until 1913, the United States had several tariffs on British imports; transportation was mostly in British bottoms. This meant that British exports to the United States were valued at a higher rate by the United States (for they included the tariffs) than by Britain. After 1914, there were smaller differences between the statistics of American imports and of British exports (although American import figures were still higher than British export figures), a fact that may be due to shifting of American imports away from taxable items, to avoid the very high American tariffs.

In column (2) of Table 10 we see no definite tendency. In

more than half of the cases British imports were stated to be higher than American exports. Until 1913, the British had only a small revenue tax. This may account for the slight excess in the British import statistics over American exports. In the later period, 1928–1938, nothing conclusive can be said about the influence of tariffs in producing discrepancies between the two reports. The devaluations of Sterling and the Dollar in 1931 and 1933, respectively, also fall in this period. A noteworthy jump occurs in 1948–1960, when the negative entries in column (2) are multiples of those for the earlier years and the reverse for column (1). It should be noted that the figures in *all* these tables do not record what actually happened, but only examine the character of the statistics. The above changes describe, therefore, quality and recording characteristics, not the simultaneous changes in trade structure, post-war aid, currency troubles, etc. These latter may very well have contributed to the observed variations, but there is not only no need for these effects to have occurred; rather they should not have shown up at all, since the ideal difference for all columns is zero, no matter what the volume, structure, direction, or rate of change of the trade.

(4) In the instance of the United States trade with Canada (Table 11), we have an example of Case IV for the earlier period and something similar to Case III for the second period. For 1909 to 1913, Canada consistently *over*stated both its imports and exports to the United States, as compared with American statements. (Or did the United States consistently *under*state imports?) In 1928, 1935, and 1938, American exports were stated to be larger than Canadian imports. But during these same years American imports were reported as smaller than the corresponding Canadian exports! For 1952, 1956, and 1960, we revert to the pattern of period A. No firm conclusions can be drawn[30] since no definite patterns appear and no other

[30] Canadian wheat exported to Europe via the United States appears to have been a particularly disturbing factor. Though we can mention it and may be told to consider its influence (as the transit trade of any country, e.g., Belgium), the brutal fact still is that the statistics do not agree, that the reader does not know how to disentangle these influences, and if he knew how, would require an incredibly large machinery which no one

knowledge can be brought into play allowing the determination of the errors.

(5) Comparison of American and Belgian statistics (Table 12) indicates an example of Case II for the period 1909–1913. American imports were stated on the average to be about 40 percent higher than Belgian exports. Belgian imports, on the other hand, are stated to be about 25 percent higher on the average than American exports. The large discrepancy in the former case would have to be explained by factors other than tariffs and transportation. In the periods 1928–1938 and 1948–1960, no definite tendency is indicated.

We have mainly discussed discrepancy of signs so far, and have said little about magnitudes. Signs might differ, but the differences in amounts might be slight. But in fact, the quantities are large, sometimes even grotesquely so. A probing into the reasons for such magnitudes would require a detailed study of tariffs and transportation charges[31] in order to state conclusively what part of the differences was due to error in the comparisons examined. It must be emphasized again that these differences due to error would still not yield margins of error for *either* of the statistics concerned. We are only attempting to indicate a *method* whereby statistics could be tested for error, but we do not come to definite conclusions about the *size* of errors, although we feel confident enough to state that they are very large.

In Table 13, a summary is given of the averages found in the previous tables. Also included are averages (but not the basic data) of several other pairs of countries.

---

has at his disposal. Therefore we have here a particularly good illustration that it is one thing to state a probable source of trouble (or error?) and a very different one to assess quantitatively its influence upon the final figure.

[31] The reader is referred to H. F. Karreman, *Methods for Improving World Transportation Accounts, Applied to 1950–1953*, National Bureau of Economic Research, Technical Paper 15, 1961, especially Chapters I and II. This study not only shows the great difficulties of arriving at reliable information but also illustrates the nature of one of the principal gaps in balance of payment statistics of all principal nations. The variations in transportation costs among countries is discussed also in C. Moneta, "The Estimation of Transportation Costs in International Trade," *The Journal of Political Economy*, LXVII (February 1959), pp. 41–58.

An average is taken for each of the three periods for each column in the original tables. Although an average for a single period is not very significant, because the years are scattered, few, and fairly unrelated, it does give some indication of the order of magnitude of divergency. The totals for the three columns show that in some periods there was slightly less discrepancy between estimates than in others. Is this an indication that perhaps international conventions and agreements about uniformity of statistics did have some effect on foreign trade observations, even though they did not eliminate the wide margins? On the other hand, violent fluctuations in exchange rates occurred and exchange controls involving multiple rates were introduced which greatly obscured the valuation of goods moved across national borders. The decreasing importance of import duties and their substitution by complicated licensing systems strengthens the tendencies toward more numerous and probably larger errors in foreign trade statistics.

Examining this table in more detail, we find that there are some pairs of countries that reflect close agreement in their statistics (if we take a divergence of 25 percent in all cases in columns (1) and (2) as a "good" result!): Germany-France, United States-Germany, Canada-Great Britain, United States-Canada, and Germany-Great Britain, with the last two combinations producing the closest agreement. In three of these pairs the countries border on each other or are close to each other. However, proximity has not counted heavily in other pairs of countries, e.g., pairs of European countries such as Belgium-Germany, Belgium-France, and Great Britain-France. Thus, there must be other more important factors to produce these wide discrepancies.

The obviously bad results obtained in the cases of Canada-France, Great Britain-France, Canada-Germany, and Belgium-France are difficult to explain in terms of tariffs and transportation costs alone. It would require a much fuller treatment of this subject to decide whether the discrepancies are significant and due to differences for these more valid reasons, or to errors in the reports of one or both of the parties. The published material of either country does not make this possible. The books are forever closed. However, we can state intuitively and with confidence that discrepancies of the order of 50 to 60 percent are not solely attributable to an inadequate consideration of tariffs and transportation costs.

Although the columns on the balance of trade are included in Tables 8 through 13, we forego a thorough discussion. The reader will have no difficulty interpreting the figures and convincing himself of the highly doubtful value of statements about trade balances. The quantitative differences reported are so large as to limit the use of these statistics severely. They cannot be used for "fine-structured" arguments; they are at best suitable for broad overall statements and observations. The size of foreign trade differs widely from one country to another. Even though we are just discussing the unreliability of foreign trade statistics and shall find similar results regarding national income, there is no doubt that foreign trade is a far larger percentage of the latter in Belgium, Holland, Norway, Germany, Japan, etc., than in the United States. Thus the observations in this section have different relevance for the various types of countries. But for all it can be stated safely that we have here another indication that our picture of the various economies is far more vague and hazy than the pretended sharpness of the figures would make us believe.

It is easy to arrive, if one wishes, at diametrically opposed conclusions, based on "the facts," by merely making a suitable and just as reasonable choice of the statistic.[32] Beyond this, however, it is necessary to understand that the sum total of commodities included in trade statistics, as already stated earlier, is only an arbitrarily cut-off segment of all items making up the balance of payments. This segment of "visible" commodities has only very limited value for the analysis of the foreign trade of a nation, even if the information should be excellent. This does not preclude that commodity by commodity studies have good meaning, provided, of course, that the statistics for individual commodities are reliable in the particular case and circumstance. As was shown, the chances that

---

[32] However, if we had to choose in describing, say, American-Chinese trade, we would probably take the statistics from the former source. We would be governed by a generally higher confidence, although a large error, resting in the United States statistics, would still remain unknown.

this is the case often enough are slim. The *statistical accident* of which aggregate of items is chosen to represent *all* transactions between countries is hardly of much economic significance, although economists usually attribute to this truncated information a deeper economic meaning.

4. Concluding Remarks

Further investigations of this nature must be undertaken to decide whether foreign trade statistics can be trusted in proving fine theoretical points and in formulating policy. Their great role in the estimation of national income is obvious, and their influence upon the construction of adequate input-output tables is also evident.

We have not tested the foreign trade statistics by more elaborate and sophisticated tests, but there is no doubt that the situation is not better; it is bound to be worse. Economists should carefully consider what the implications are: The theory of international trade with all its fine points of delicate changes in the "terms of trade," "comparative costs," etc., rests, *at best,* on this type of information. There is no other information. So do further theorems derived with the aid of these concepts. Comparisons of foreign trade fluctuations with business cycles, exchange rates, etc., by necessity requiring high detail and precision, are likewise adversely affected.

The *balance of payments* is estimated with such figures included in the total, to which are added pure guesses of the most doubtful character. Yet, consider its immense practical significance, involving the gift of billions of dollars to foreign countries on the basis of allegedly scientific, accurate, and reliable information!

We have not even discussed the making of statistics of the "invisible" items in the balance of payments. There the gaps are enormous and the methods for closing them fall far short of the needs. It appears to be *a priori* certain that the "invisible" items cannot be *better* known than the visible ones. Yet statistics of the latter are found to be of poor and uncertain quality, even in their best appearance—gold.

It is perhaps possible to estimate from the movement of the exchange rates (provided there is an absolute free market!)

whether the balance is "active" or "passive." But it would be naive to think that one could determine the movements from the component statistics.[33] Sampling is sometimes used conscientiously to ascertain emigrant remittances, tourist expenditures, medical services used abroad, etc., and this is a sound procedure. Nevertheless the results are in grave doubt, largely because of the lie-component, strongly at work because of fear from income tax involvement. Any one who has ever sat through meetings (as the author has) in which final balance of payment figures for most invisible items were put together, can only marvel at the naiveté with which these products of fantasy, policy, and imagination, combined with figures diligently arrived at, are gravely used in subsequent publications. Even if the practices are fairly good in one country, recall that there are at present 104 United Nations members, and that statistical and political standards differ widely.

Writers on all phases of foreign trade will have to assume the burden of proof that the figures on commodity movements are good enough to warrant the manipulation and the reasoning to which they are customarily subject.

[33] Noteworthy are the recent differences between European observers of the difficulties of the American balance of payments and the U.S. Treasury. In 1961, the Europeans believed that the Treasury (i.e., American statistics) overstated the U.S. deficit, which was promptly denied by the Secretary of the Treasury. This is a nice illustration for the presence of a strong policy-making and political factor in what under other circumstances purports to be a strictly scientific matter.

❧ CHAPTER X ❧

PRICE STATISTICS

1. THE MEASUREMENT OF PRICE

A STUDY of the accuracy of economic observations, however rudimentary, must deal at least briefly with the most basic economic and statistical variable of all, *price*. It would appear that the accessibility and abundance of price data would lead to highly accurate measurement; however, experts in this field can testify that price statistics are exceedingly difficult to construct. Because of the vast complications that price statistics offer, we shall deal with them only briefly and merely point out some of the main difficulties.

The points to be raised in the following discussion are not exhaustive and they are presumably all well known. However, they are only seldom considered and taken into account. Significant contributions in this field are due to F. C. Mills, who has made many valuable studies of the behavior of prices and the difficulties of measurement.[1] Mills has perhaps tried to extract more information from prices than any other contemporary investigator, and he was well aware that the accuracy of his observations and the conclusiveness of the interpretations are not fully established as long as there are no adequate expressions of the limitations of the data. But very little work of this type has been done since Mills wrote.

Virtually all the tendencies that contribute to errors of observations cumulate in price measurements, *viz.*, the desire to hide the true price, the measurement of incompletely described phenomena, difficulties of definition and of classification, changes in quality, pseudo-accuracy in the description of ir-

---

[1] Cf., especially, "Price Statistics," *Encyclopedia of the Social Sciences,* vol. 12, pp. 381–5, 1934; *The Behavior of Prices,* National Bureau of Economic Research (New York, 1927); and *Price-Quantity Interactions in Business Cycles,* National Bureau of Economic Research, (New York, 1946).

relevant parts of the price, etc. Many efforts have been made and are being made to improve price statistics, and, as a consequence, we are better informed in this field than in many others. The state of this information is partly dependent upon the competitive situation under which many prices are formed. As a consequence, prices are best known in the largest market of all, the stock market. There, as a rule, anonymity of buyer and seller prevails, the turnover is well known, and the securities traded are homogeneous (for the same company).[2] Even in this large market the reported prices often differ from one source to another, and whether that be the case or not there are several prices to choose from: opening, lowest, highest, closing prices, etc., which makes it clear that prices, as are all economic data, are statistical variables and only as such enter whatever indexes are being designed.

With the increasing role of monopoly and similar forms of market organizations the likelihood that the "quoted" prices, which very likely are used for many complicated indexes, are identical with the *effective* (not necessarily the "posted") prices has considerably decreased. Aside from this, the growth of enterprise and the complicated nature of most commodities with many shades of quality (even for staples like grains, cotton, etc.) make for a *multiplicity of prices* that often diverge widely from each other. From these prices, representatives are picked to enter indexes that influence policy decisions, etc. Wage rates are also prices and they are notoriously difficult to determine accurately, partly because of their connection with "produc-

[2] It is rather perplexing that the stock market is not studied more thoroughly by economists. Take almost any economic textbook, or special treatises on prices, and you will look in vain for a detailed account of the stock market and for a general theory of its operations as a significant component of a general theory of price. However, there are innumerable assertions in the literature regarding the observation of many different, often obscure, trends and cycles, alleged regularities, etc. Regarding the existence of alleged cycles of stock prices, cf. C. W. J. Granger and O. Morgenstern, *Spectral Analysis of New York Stock Market Prices*, Econometric Research Program, Princeton University, Research Memorandum 45, 28 September 1962, published in *Kyklos*, vol. XVI, Jan. 1963, pp. 1–27. This investigation shows conclusively that stock market prices in New York do not follow any cyclical pattern of the conventional kinds, but are mostly random fluctuations superimposed upon very long term upward or downward movements.

tivity," and partly because of the difficulty of ascertaining wages in many important fields of employment.

Prices (when they are not *fees*) are the result of voluntary transactions and can therefore be ascertained separately from the seller and from the buyer. The information obtained from both sources should be identical; but this is seldom the case. Moreover, the same goods are, as a rule, sold in many different units and at different times, so that the individual, historical transaction loses in importance, and repeated observations can easily be made. This is an important factor working toward high accuracy, especially when the goods transacted are each time of identical quality. However, when monopolistic conditions prevail, other features become more important. Then *secrecy of the true price paid* is often a primary concern of both buyers and sellers because of the private rebates and the individual treatment of customers. Even when several firms charge the same (or different) prices for identical commodities the true price (or price-differences) may not be revealed because of side-payments, kickbacks, etc., which are frequent occurrences. To this must be added that discriminatory treatment occurs most easily when firms are producing a great variety of commodities (e.g., steel, of which there are reportedly more than 10,000 different kinds, most having somewhat different prices from each other), and when there are great variations in the quantities bought per customer. Thus, large automobile producers will obtain a very different price of "steel" (with different range and frequency of fluctuation) than regional, small builders buying their "steel." A measure of "the" price of steel is, therefore, difficult to construct. The quotation of a single number gives only very limited information and may, for many purposes, be quite meaningless. Which particular "steel" to pick is a sampling problem. Furthermore, the significance of secret rebates and of special arrangements due to the size of sale—the "shaving" of prices—varies greatly with the business cycle. They shrink when business is improving, and increase when it deteriorates.[3] However, the pattern is not definitely known nor is it necessarily the same for all in-

---

[3] This is described in some detail in my "Free and Fixed Prices in the Depression," *Harvard Business Review*, vol. 10 (1931), pp. 62–68.

dustries and all countries where secret rebates occur. And that is the case everywhere.

So far, we have assumed that a *price* is adequately described by *a simple monetary expression*. If this were the case, the previous difficulties might all be overcome without too much trouble, and a quantitative notion of "error" could be evolved. The real difficulties, however, lie elsewhere. They concern the definition of "price." Economists tend to limit themselves to the consideration of the *amount of money paid in the transaction as a complete expression of the price.* However, there are some non-monetary components of price, such as quality of service rendered in conjunction with the sale, which could be translated into monetary equivalents, but which often differ from one purchaser to another. Furthermore, they are virtually impossible to ascertain by the mere observation of the "money-price" even if one could find those true, actual money prices which are so often shrouded in secrecy. A firm may be accommodated in the manner of payment, in the type and place of delivery, in the burden of insurance charges, etc.; these factors could be translated into money terms. However, they are either not considered in determining the price statistic or are, indeed, inaccessible, even should a technique exist for representing such information in terms of "price." Differences of this sort, especially due to variations in treatment according to quantities purchased, are reported to amount sometimes to 100 percent of list prices. In some industries it is customary in times of depressed business to accommodate customers by labeling certain standard products, say polyethylene, as "off grade," while in fact it is of the required grade. This is equivalent to a price reduction, not affecting the list price, which falsifies simultaneously price and production statistics. Variations in the monetary expression of a price therefore show only very imperfectly what changes really occurred. In particular, it is known that "the" money price is often left entirely unchanged when there is a serious competitive struggle among a few producers, because it is far more convenient for future operations and more effective for the present to vary the other components of the price.[4]

[4] The scalar notion of price now generally used has to be replaced by a vectorial one, i.e., "price" is not only a certain amount of money (scalar)

Buyers may not easily respond to changes in the money price, but rather to the variations in the other components. This has far-reaching consequences for the statistical determination of demand curves, "elasticity" of demand, and the like.

To give a concrete example of the complexities of price data, I quote from Reavis Cox: ". . . a price of, say, iron ore becomes not merely $4.60 a ton but $4.60 per gross long ton of 2,240 pounds of Mesaba Bessemer ore containing exactly 51.5 percent of iron and 0.045 percent of phosphorus, with specified premiums for ore with a higher iron content or a lower phosphorus content and with specified discounts for ore with a lower iron content or a higher phosphorus content; samples to be drawn and analyzed on a dry basis by a specified chemist at Cleveland, the cost being divided equally between seller and buyer; 48,000 tons to be delivered at the rate of approximately 8,000 tons per month during April–September, inclusive, on board freight cars of the New York Central Railroad at Cleveland, Ohio; the purchaser to pay all charges involved in moving ore from the rail of the lake steamer to the freight car and other port changes, such as unloading, dockage, storage, reloading, switching and handling; ore to be weighed on railroad scale weights at Cleveland; payment to be made in legal tender or bank checks of the buyer to the Cleveland agent of the mining company on the 15th of each month for all ore received during the preceding month."[5]

---

but money paid at a given moment in time, over time in certain installments, etc. (vector). Similar considerations apply to "money"; but we shall not dwell upon this further, except to point out that there exist great and most interesting possibilities in this area for advances in economic theory. It is noteworthy that there does not seem to exist one single publication describing and analyzing a vectorial notion of price. Cf. the recent important work by Wilhelm Krelle, *Preistheorie*, (J. C. B. Mohr: Tübingen, 1961), an 800 page monograph in which neither rebates nor vectorial prices are discussed. In my *International Financial Transactions, op. cit.*, I have repeatedly shown how various rates of interest have to be viewed as vectors, rather than scalars (as they are otherwise always treated in the literature). Cf. pp. 162–164; 442–448 of my book, *International Financial Transactions, op. cit.*

[5] "Non-price Competition and the Measurement of Prices," *The Journal of Marketing*, vol. x (April 1946), p. 376. This study is a model for detailed investigations into the nature of prices. Economic theory would benefit greatly from extensive descriptions of this kind.

It is this type of description which is needed—especially for textbooks on price theory!—in order to show what a "price" really is like. What Cox describes for iron ore could, of course, be duplicated, *mutatis mutandis*, for coal, paper, steel—in fact for almost any commodity. Even the security markets have rules about settlement dates, sequence of fulfillment of orders, etc. But the more perfect the market, i.e., the larger it is in respect to the individual transaction, and when the commodity is strictly homogeneous, the less important will be the side conditions. This situation is only rarely to be found in reality.

An indication of the complex role of price can be obtained by considering "discount houses" and ordinary stores. The price the discount house charges for, say, an appliance includes little more than the commodity itself; the higher price charged by the ordinary store for an identical commodity really covers such additional items as transportation, delivery, guarantees, free servicing, choice of color, etc.

A price of particular interest is the wage. On the proper determination of wage rates, wage payments, and labor cost depend some of the most important economic measurements such as income. On it also depend countless policy decisions, for example, in situations where productivity is involved; or when it is asserted (or denied) that there exists a wage-push inflation, etc. Yet wages are not easily ascertained. It is possible to measure money flows to wage earners with the usual error components, which are small in large corporate organizations (especially where electronic data processing is used), but large when the business units are small. These payments take into consideration time worked, overtime, premiums, etc., and are therefore not simple entities. The wage costs (to the company) cannot be easily inferred from these cash payments since they include such fringe benefits as company contributions to pension funds, housing, paid vacations, the value of tenure coupled with automatic increases, etc.[6] As these factors become more important the comparisons (overtime, or among countries with different such practices) of mere money wage

---

[6] It is clearly not easy to compare the wage income of a worker in a country who receives a certain amount of money and nothing else with that of girl workers in Japanese electronics companies who are housed free

rates tend to be of increasingly doubtful value. It would be a different matter if a vectorial concept and expression could be used as mentioned above.

2. PRICE INDEX NUMBERS

Partly because it is so difficult to list prices adequately, and partly because there are so many prices, their presentation by *index numbers* has assumed a great role. These index numbers are freely quoted and interpreted. In the manner referred to elsewhere in this work, changes of indexes are taken to be significant—even when they occur in the last of several decimal digits—although they are neither exhaustive descriptions nor can they be so accurately recorded as to warrant such descriptive detail. Despite the wide use of index numbers, the emphasis of the work in this particular field of statistics has been for the most part on the theory and methodology of index numbers as mathematical constructions.[7] The accuracy of the original price and quantity data entering the indexes has not been treated as exhaustively, in spite of the progress made by various government bureaus specializing in index number construction.

In addition to the overriding question of the objective accuracy of data, there is the conceptual problem of arriving at a principle for the calculation of an index when the data are already given. For example, in the concept of a cost-of-living index, consumer preferences are an essential ingredient; thus, the outstanding problem is to have a principle of calculation that makes just recognition of that.

The cost of living, for a current date relative to a base date, may be conceived of as the minimum cost required at the

---

in dormitories and receive as part of their compensation gratis instruction in flower arranging (as is actually the case). Working conditions (light, ventilation, distance of place of work, etc.) are always a part of the working contract and hence influence the "wage."

[7] Irving Fisher's great book, *The Making of Index Numbers* (Houghton Mifflin, Boston, 3rd ed., rev. 1927), was designed to establish standards of accurate measurement for judging different types of indexes. Cf. also Bruce D. Mudgett, *Index Numbers* (John Wiley, New York, 1951), which is aimed at improvements in practical index number construction. See also footnote 8 following, referring to the recent fundamental work by S. N. Afriat.

current prices of commodities, for obtaining a composition of amounts of commodities not inferior in preference to the composition obtained at the base date. The only way the preferences can be known is by their effects, as recorded in expenditure data. So an appropriate principle has to be found for combining such data, to obtain an index which makes full recognition of the evidence on preferences.

Many algebraical formulae have been proposed. Indeed, several hundred of them are listed in Irving Fisher's book alone. But no single one has been distinguished as finally appropriate. Moreover, even why the index should be given by an algebraic formula at all has never been clarified. There might well be other ways of combining the data which is required to answer the problem.

Recently, S. N. Afriat[8] has arrived at a method of constructing index numbers of a more general combinatorial character, involving the solution of systems of linear inequalities. He has also investigated an algebraical approach, in the context of this more general one, and has obtained results which clarify the possibilities of using an algebraical formula.

The importance of such a conceptual inquiry is intensified by the ever-increasing importance of a cost-of-living index in economic practices, such as sometimes making changes in wage rates dependent upon changes in the price level, etc. How important these indexes are in the United States economy may be indicated by the facts that (1) in 1958 about 4 million workers were covered by wage escalation clauses in collective bargaining contracts involving 1,000 workers or more, and (2) a change of 1 point in the Parity Index can mean a change in support outlay of millions of dollars.[9]

In spite of the widespread use of government price indexes,

[8] Cf. S. N. Afriat, "The Cost-of-Living Index: Algebraic Theory," Econometric Research Program, Research Memorandum No. 24 (Princeton University, March 1961); "The Cost-of-Living Index: Combinatorial Theory," Research Memorandum No. 27 (Princeton University, April 1961); and "Preference Scales and Expenditure Systems," *Econometrica,* vol. 30 (April 1962), pp. 305–323.

[9] J. W. Garbarino, "Wage Escalation and 'Wage Inflation,'" *1959 Proceedings of the Business and Economic Statistics Section,* American Statistical Association, Washington, D.C., p. 140; and B. R. Stauber, "Critical Problems in Index Number Construction," *ibid.,* p. 184.

there has been little work done in attempting to determine the error inherent in these indexes. The Bureau of Labor Statistics does not publish descriptions about the construction of its indexes in a thorough, technical way in any of its publications, so that nowhere is it possible even for a trained statistician to formulate with any precision an estimate of the error attached to these important measures.[10]

The mounting problems concerning the government price indexes finally led the Bureau of the Budget to request the National Bureau of Economic Research in 1959 to form a Price Statistics Committee to review and appraise the main price series compiled by the government—the Consumer Price Index (CPI), the Wholesale Price Index, and the Indexes of Prices Received and Paid by Farmers—and to make recommendations for their improvement.[11] The most important single recommendation of the Committee (though hardly a surprising one, indeed a trivial one!) was that the Bureau of Labor Statistics publish periodically a full description of the methods by which each of the major price indexes is constructed.[12] While "full description" is not attainable, they suggested that at least full monographs, equal in scope to those describing the national income accounts, be published after every significant revision of methods or results. This will be of little value, however, for the routine user of these indexes, for whom they are essentially designed.

The Committee also suggested that for all indexes, schedules of periodical revisions of weights be adopted; probability sampling be used, so that the precision of the index could be

---

[10] An excellent study of a major component of the Consumer Price Index by William H. Kruskal and Lester G. Telser, for example, met with limited success apparently just for this reason. Even with considerable cooperation from the Bureau of Labor Statistics, they could not obtain the kind of technical information which would lead to measuring the accuracy of that index. This was especially clear in the case of sampling error, which should be a minor concern. See "Food Prices and the Bureau of Labor Statistics," *The Journal of Business of the University of Chicago,* xxxiii (July 1960), 259–79.

[11] U.S. Congress, Joint Economic Committee, *Government Price Statistics,* Hearings, 87th Congress, 1st Session, January 24, 1961.

[12] In fact, the same obvious demand was made in a far more general context and with much less effort involved, in the first edition of the present work (1950). No doubt it was not an original idea then either!

measured; new commodities be introduced more promptly; and that research divisions be established in the price collection agencies whose major function should be the development of methods for coping with quality changes. As for the Consumer Price Index, the Committee further recommended that this index be extended to include single persons as well as families and should cover rural nonfarm as well as urban workers; a more comprehensive index should be made for the entire population, not only for the wage and salary earners. Because of some of these problems, it was suggested that the official published price indexes be reported in terms of full percentage points rather than in tenths of percentage points as is now done —again a simple conclusion that is in agreement with the more general comments made above (p. 63).

The principle is constantly violated by the Bureau of Labor Statistics and, as a consequence, by the leading newspapers. It it grotesque to see *The New York Times*, for example, often reporting on its front page that "consumer prices" have "risen" or "fallen" by 1/10 of 1 percent without any qualifying word about the significance of this change in a mere index of doubtful validity. The temptation to take index numbers, whether of prices, production, or anything else, at face value is, of course, enormous. How could it be that a number that has been ground out after so many steps, operations, computations, etc., all based on a great deal of theory, should *not* be correct and free from error, or in other words not be significant to the last digit to which it is given? But the idea that as complex a phenomenon as the change in a "price level," itself a heroic theoretical abstraction, could at present be measured to such a degree of accuracy is nevertheless simply absurd. So are the "inferences" that the country undergoes inflation or the reverse, as the case may be.[13]

[13] It is astonishing that in the United States changes in stock market prices are not only reported, but also *interpreted*, in absolute terms. For example, financial papers will report that the prices of a number of stocks rose, say, $1.00, neglecting the percentage significance of this change or throwing the burden of the correct interpretation upon the reader. Such restrictive reporting is as misleading as is the "conclusion" (cf. page 64) that by virtue of such price changes the aggregate "value" of all stocks has changed by the amount of the price change per stock times the number of shares outstanding.

3.   ERRORS AND INDEX NUMBERS

A closer look at just one aspect of the many problems in this area will indicate both the nature of the difficulties and the possible reasons for the lack of a concrete measure of error. Some of the data used in computing the indexes are ordinarily derived almost entirely from a highly complex network of samples. While it is natural to ask, therefore, how far the observed values can be expected to deviate from a "complete population" index, in order to have the sampling precision of the index, in numerical terms, such measures of precision are not available for any of the currently prepared price indexes. The Bureau of Labor Statistics has taken the position that this type of error is probably small in relation to systematic error (e.g., the error due to the constantly changing universe of commodities available to the consumer) because parts of the index structure depend on judgment and are "therefore" not capable of qualification of errors. Some of the investigations of the Committee suggested that for the overall index the procedural error may dominate the sampling error, but in their opinion, this does not mean that sampling error can be ignored. Empirical studies of procedural error are almost as lacking as those of sampling error. In answer to criticism on this point, the Bureau of Labor Statistics has pointed out, as already mentioned above, that they are not trying to measure the *level* of prices, but rather their *change*.[14] But it would seem that this would make an estimate of sampling error even more essential since, in this case, it is likely that this kind of error will be more important than the procedural error.

It should be pointed out that while the Price Statistics Committee offers an extensive program for the Bureau of Labor Statistics, the adoption of these recommendations is not necessarily imminent. First, an increase in the accuracy of data often may demand additional expenditures for the collection of the data, and the Bureau of Labor Statistics must get its funds from Congress. Second, there is some reluctance on the part of the

[14] This position has been taken by Ewan Clague, Commissioner of Labor Statistics, in a "Comment" on the Kruskal-Telser article, *op. cit.*, pp. 280–284.

Bureau of Labor Statistics to accept any methodological changes in the indexes for the reason that such changes would be too difficult to explain to the primarily non-technical users of the index.[15] (But even the currently used index construction and the theory behind the present index formulae are totally out of reach for the "non-technical" user. Hence, there is no sound reason why a better procedure should not be used as soon as it becomes available.)

This dilemma occurs virtually everywhere, especially when indexes, capacities, and all manners of technical measurements are involved. There is only one way out; that is to proceed in the technically best manner, making no concessions and relying on the fact that part of the public will catch up eventually. Twenty-five years ago notions such as a safe radiation level, cholesterol counts, etc., were also uncommon; yet today they have penetrated deeply into daily life.

Finally, here as for some other kinds of statistics presented in this part of our study, the revision and correction policies of the data collection agency have important consequences. Because the indexes have become institutionalized, the Bureau of Labor Statistics does not issue preliminary consumers' price indexes, but errors are corrected in the index for the month in which they are discovered, unless the error in a major component, city or the United States index, exceeds a certain magnitude. The Committee feels "that the agencies can serve the legitimate demands of wage, contract, and parity escalation without being in such a straitjacket."[16] Preliminary indexes could be used as the basis of contractual and legislative uses, with final indexes published later if necessary. Changes based on outside information could then be incorporated into the revision.

It is clear to anyone who has followed the making of index numbers in different countries and over a great variety of time periods that we are here confronted with a *political* as well as an economic problem. For example, when wage increases are dependent on a certain index, it is to the interests of employers

---

[15] S. A. Jaffe, "The Consumer Price Index—Technical Questions and Practical Answers," 1959 *Proceedings of the Business and Economic Statistics Section, op. cit.,* p. 192.

[16] *Government Price Statistics, op. cit.,* p. 48.

and wage earners to insist that certain commodities be included, others be excluded, in the index. This may all be veiled under pseudo-scientific argument. The economist will do well to guard against an interpretation of "data" which are often anything but economic measurements; rather they are tools in a continuing struggle for power.

It should be noted that two important segments of economic activity, Government and direct construction costs, are not included in either the Consumer Price Index or the Wholesale Price Index. Both of these are, however, included in an index known as the Gross National Product Deflator; this index is the link between gross national product in "current dollars" and in "constant dollars." The deflator is considered to be the most widely representative price index available for the economy as a whole.[17]

Because most of the individual prices which go to make the gross national product deflator are taken from sources which include components of the Consumer Price Index and Wholesale Price Index, it is subject to the same qualifications regarding differences in quality, frequency of appearance of new products, etc. Two additional difficulties resulting from the inclusion of Government and construction sectors both lend an upward bias to the deflator. The price index which is applied to the government sector measures the change in the cost of inputs, i.e., the level of wages and salaries of government employees; it does not attempt to measure the imputed prices of government "output." Thus no account is taken of the (presumably rising) productivity of government employees. The index of new construction is based largely on data provided by private trade organizations, with the concomitant uncertainty regarding reliability. It is likely that here, too, productivity gains will not be fully reflected, due to heavy reliance on wage rates (given material costs) in determining construction costs.

Even from our necessarily limited discussion of price, it would be safe to say that a remark made elsewhere in this study is again in order: entirely new ideas are required so that nu-

[17] See U.S. Congress, Joint Economic Committee, *Staff Report on Employment Growth and Price Levels* (Washington, Government Printing Office, 1959), p. 108.

merical, comprehensive expressions of the limitations and errors of the observations can be found. Without such numerical values, the statistics of prices as conceived today must, by necessity, remain exceedingly limited in value, if not frequently misleading. This is of particular importance in those numerous cases where prices are multiplied by quantities of goods in order to obtain expressions of the alleged value of transactions that cannot be determined directly.

Without the notion of price there would be no economic science. The concept is of absolutely central significance. It is not as easy and trivial a concept as it appears to be at first sight. A satisfactory measurement of price is, as a consequence, a difficult undertaking, and it is not surprising that price statistics, abundant as they are, have to be approached with utmost caution.

It will require the concentration of the minds of many men to make the most basic economic concept and its statistical equivalent fully meaningful for economic research.

❧ CHAPTER XI ❧

MINING STATISTICS

1. INTRODUCTION

MINERAL industries have in recent years, according to official statistics, accounted for less than 2 percent of national income and of gainful employment. However, in 1957, the mining industries supplied 34 percent of all raw materials produced, compared with 59 percent for agricultural materials and 7 percent for forest, fishery, and wildlife. The share of the mining industries in total primary production has doubled in the past half-century.[1]

Raw materials are, of course, essential for the peacetime operation of manufacturing industries and for the continued growth of the economy. Moreover, much of the material is critical and strategic for national security, as is demonstrated by the huge stockpiling activity of the United States government.[2] Despite the growth of domestic production, the United States has, in less than fifty years, moved from a position of self-sufficiency in raw materials to one of increasing dependence on foreign suppliers; today about 35 to 40 percent of the free world's output of basic materials flows into the United States. Important problems for national policy arise.[3]

[1] U.S. Bureau of the Census, *U.S. Census of Mineral Industries: 1958,* General Summary Report MIC 58 (1)–1, Preliminary, Washington, D.C., U.S. Government Printing Office, 1961.

[2] Compare the following: "Programming the Supply of Strategic Materials," *Research Memorandum No. 2,* Econometric Research Program, Princeton University (September 1957); "Econometric Analysis of the United States Manganese Problem," *Research Memorandum No. 3, ibid.* (October 1958); "Econometric Analysis of the United States Manganese Problem, Final Report, Part I," *Research Memorandum No. 14, ibid.* (March 1960); Herman F. Karreman, "Programming the Supply of a Strategic Material, Part I, A Nonstochastic Model," *Naval Research Logistics Quarterly,* Vol. 7, No. 3 (September 1960); Herman F. Karreman, "A Stochastic Model for Programming the Supply of a Strategic Material," in *Mathematical Programming, Proceedings of a Symposium,* Robert L. Graves and Philip Wolfe, eds. (McGraw-Hill, 1963).

[3] Percy W. Bidwell, *Raw Materials, A Study of American Policy* (New York, Harper and Brothers, 1958).

2. THE EXTENT OF THE COVERAGE

Data on the mineral industries are available from two sources: first, the *Census of Mineral Industries,* which is conducted by the Bureau of the Census of the Department of Commerce; second, the *Minerals Yearbook,* prepared by the Bureau of Mines of the Department of the Interior. Data are available from the Bureau of the Census on the quantity and value of ore produced, value of shipments, minerals received for preparation, supplies, fuel, and electrical energy, and value added by mining.[4] The Bureau of Mines conducts canvasses to obtain data on the quantity and value of production and/or shipments.[5] For major minerals the data are available monthly or quarterly.

Between these two sources coverage of the mining industry is considered fairly complete.[6] The Census itself gives some discussion of the extent of the coverage. The 1958 Census was based on reports from about 32,000 mining companies. In addition to exclusions due to the cutoff of small establishments, some production is excluded on account of the method of classification. "In general, it is believed that the 1958 mineral census reports provided essentially complete coverage of production and development operations."[7] For the crude petroleum and natural gas industry, coverage was probably somewhat less complete. Only about 97 percent of the total shipments of oil and probably about 97 percent of the total shipments of gas were covered. These figures were 96 and 95 percent, respectively, in the 1954 Census. The undercoverage, while more significant for some states, appears to have reduced the overall

[4] Such censuses were conducted in 1850, 1860, 1870, 1880, 1889, 1902, 1909, 1919, 1929, 1935, 1939, 1954, and 1958; present legislation calls for another census in 1963 and every 5 years thereafter.

[5] An extensive and definitive discussion and critique of the statistics produced by the Bureau of Mines was prepared by a committee of the American Statistical Association. See *Statistical Operations of the Bureau of Mines,* American Statistical Association, July 1952.

[6] *Output, Input and Productivity Measurement,* National Bureau of Economic Research, *Studies in Income and Wealth,* Vol. 25 (Princeton University Press, 1961), p. 151.

[7] *Census of Mineral Industries, 1958, op. cit.,* p. 5.

minerals census coverage of value of shipments by only one percent.

3. RELIABILITY OF THE ESTIMATES

Although the coverage of the mining statistics is fairly wide, major difficulties exist regarding their reliability. The overriding problem is that the estimates published by the Bureau of the Census are not exactly reconcilable with those of the Bureau of Mines (see Table 14 below). Differences in the two sets of figures occur for numerous reasons. First, the Census figures are based on an industrial classification, whereas Bureau of Mines data are classified by product produced. A certain amount of mining output occurs in non-mining industries which was not included in the 1954 Census, but instead shows up largely in manufacturing. The Bureau of Mines, however, did include such production.

A second reason for discrepancy between Bureau of Census and Bureau of Mines figures is the difference in measurement stage (Table 14, columns 1 and 4). For example, the Bureau of Mines measures cement production on shipments from mills, whereas the Bureau of Census uses gross shipments. Third, there are some differences on what is included for a particular commodity. For example, for bituminous coal, the Bureau of Mines excludes from its statistics mines producing less than 1,000 tons, while the Census excludes only establishments for which neither value of shipments nor expenses for production, development, and maintenance work exceeded $500. Finally, differences will arise simply because of the questionnaire methods used by the two agencies. The voluntary nature of much of the reporting procedure will complicate the already inevitable fact that the same producer may give different responses to the same question to different interrogators on different days.

Table 14 compares Bureau of Mines mineral production data on a commodity basis for 1954 with those presented in the 1954 *Census of Mineral Industries.* The individual comparisons are designed to provide users of the statistics of these agencies with a rough measure of the extent to which their coverage matches.

The percent differences for quantity and value series are due to the several factors mentioned above. These factors are more

TABLE 14

COMPARISON FOR SELECTED SERIES OF THE BUREAU OF MINES AND BUREAU OF CENSUS
MINERAL PRODUCTION DATA FOR 1954

COMMODITY DATA—CONTINENTAL U.S.

Mineral	Bureau of Mines			Bureau of the Census			Percent Difference in Quantity col. (2)–(5)	Percent Difference in Quantity col. (3)–(6)
	Measurement Stage	Quantity (000 short tons unless otherwise stated)	Value ($ thousand)	Measurement Stage	Quantity (000 short tons unless otherwise stated)	Value ($ thousand)		
	(1)	(2)	(3)	(4)	(5)	(6)	(7)	(8)
Mineral Fuels								
Bituminous coal	Production	386,797	1,752,847	Net Production	387,186	1,774,400	–0.1	–1.2
Pennsylvania anthracite	"	29,083	247,870	"	29,255	250,699	–0.6	–1.1
Natural gas (bil. cu. ft.)	Marketed Production	8,743	882,501	Marketed Production	8,315	978,712	+5.1	–9.8
Crude petroleum (mil. 42-gal. barrels)	Production	2,315	6,424,930	Production	2,221	6,156,659	+4.2	+4.4
Natural gasoline and cycle products (mil. gal.)	"	5,385	402,418	Net Production	5,391	397,745	–0.1	+1.2

(*Cont.*)

TABLE 14 (*Cont.*)

Comparison for Selected Series of the Bureau of Mines and Bureau of Census Mineral Production Data for 1954

COMMODITY DATA—CONTINENTAL U.S.

Mineral	Bureau of Mines			Bureau of the Census			Percent Difference in Quantity col. (2)–(5)	Percent Difference in Quantity col. (3)–(6)
	Measurement Stage	Quantity (000 short tons unless otherwise stated)	Value ($ thousand)	Measurement Stage	Quantity (000 short tons unless otherwise stated)	Value ($ thousand)		
Nonmetals (except fuels)								
Cement (000 376-lb. barrels)	Shipments from Mills	274,703	763,413	Gross Shipments	280,400	779,932	–2.0	–2.1
Sand and Gravel	Sold or Used	549,401	496,672	Sold or Used	428,599	445,075	+28.2	+11.6
Metals								
Copper	Production	835,468	492,927	Production	835,340	—	*	—
Iron ore (000 long tons, gross weight)	Shipments	76,126	525,818	Net Shipments	76,999	537,688	–1.1	–2.2

SOURCE: U.S. Department of Interior, Bureau of Mines, *Mineral Yearbook, 1957*, Vol. I, p. 134.
* Less than 0.1%.

important for some minerals than for others; hence larger discrepancies. For example, the large difference for sand and gravel, where 4 percent of the operations were out of the primary industry, can be explained partly by the fact that Census classifies by industry and Mines by commodity.

Although, in most cases, the differences do not exceed 10 percent, it should be emphasized that this uncertainty is by no means insignificant.

In order to reduce the incomparability of the mineral statistics and to avoid duplication of effort, there has been increased cooperation between the Bureau of the Census and the Bureau of Mines in the last 20 years. This cooperation has taken the form of 1) collection, editing, and processing of certain groups of schedules by the Bureau of Mines, and 2) provision for interagency comparisons by means of tielines on individual forms in some of the areas where each agency collected its data on a separate form.

With regard to the 1954 Census, the Bureau of Mines acted as collection agent for about one-third of the establishment reports, including almost all companies having only one establishment in the metal mining and coal areas, and about one-half of such companies in the non-metallic minerals (except fuels) industries. The Bureau of the Census collected all reports for multi-establishment companies and all reports for the crude petroleum and natural gas, stone, clay, and some other non-metallic mineral industries. Joint surveys were used for several products, including iron and manganese ores, copper, lead, zinc, gold, silver, and nickel, and much of the coal industry.

It must be emphasized that in many areas each agency used its own form with no tieline provisions. Each prepared its own tabulations in accordance with its own needs and responsibilities. This fact plus the often discussed drawbacks of all data collected by means of questionnaire should serve as sufficient warning for the user of mining statistics.

4. Conclusion

In this chapter we have pointed out differences in mineral statistics estimates prepared by two government agencies, the

Bureau of Mines and the Bureau of the Census. The existence of discrepancies in the two series of estimates should caution the users of such statistics to be exceedingly careful in knowing the background of the estimates he selects. The differences, although under 10 percent for most minerals, reflect harshly on the fact that the figures in the body of the table are given to seven (!) significant digits. It is at best exceedingly unlikely that such accurate measurement is ever possible. Neither is it clear what purposes of government or economics are served to produce an (alleged) accuracy of up to one in two million, an accuracy that would by far exceed many of the best measurements in the natural sciences.

❧ CHAPTER XII ❧

AGRICULTURAL STATISTICS

1. SIGNIFICANCE OF AGRICULTURAL STATISTICS

AGRICULTURE'S contribution to gross national product has declined to a relatively small share. Gross farm product and net farm income now stand at only about 4–5 percent of the corresponding national aggregates.[1] But changes in farm conditions continue to exert a strong influence on economic developments in particular sectors of the nonfarm economy. Agriculture is a great user of certain kinds of resources and is a major contributor to commodity production, especially food processing and textiles. Developments in this area affect important economic variables such as consumer prices, Federal budget estimates, and U.S. merchandise exports.[2] The portion of the total Federal budget spent on agriculture and agricultural resources in 1960 was approximately 6 percent, about two-thirds of which was for price supports and other programs to stabilize farm prices and farm income.

A measure of the importance of agricultural statistics is indicated by the government's expenditure on its statistical programs. Of the 44 million dollars the government spent in 1961 on current statistical programs (not including special programs, e.g., censuses), the largest share, approximately 13 million dollars, was appropriated to the Department of Agriculture.

---

[1] Percentages such as these and others quoted elsewhere in this study are computed from sets of data where each set is afflicted with unknown and unspecified errors. Strictly speaking, we should not have given the above figures (which are sometimes even presented to two decimals). But it will be clear to the reader, at this point, that we use them only as a rough approximation for the undeniable fact that agriculture's share in total output is very small—a sign of economic progress of a formerly predominantly agricultural country. In underdeveloped countries the percentage may exceed 70 or 80.

[2] Boris C. Swerling, *Agriculture and Recent Economic Conditions: Experience and Perspective,* Federal Reserve Bank of San Francisco, August 1959.

For these reasons, and because two agencies of the government, the Department of Agriculture and the Bureau of the Census, to a certain extent make independent estimates of some of the important series, we will examine these statistics.

2. HISTORY OF THE ESTIMATES

The Federal Government assumed an early responsibility for the development and transmission of new agricultural technology. The reason in earlier times was that agriculture was an important part of the American economy, and the small farm units were in no position to finance their own research facilities. Interest in estimating agricultural production grew during the New Deal era when agricultural regulation was expanding rapidly. At present, this great and continuing activity on the part of the government is a reflection both of the needs of the massive support programs and of its aim generally to provide fundamental guides for the efficient use of agricultural resources.

The first agricultural census was made in 1840 at the same time as the Sixth Decennial Census of Population; from 1850 until 1920 it was taken every 10 years. With increased application of scientific findings and the growing use of mechanization in agriculture, farming practices were changing so rapidly that facts collected at 10-year intervals were no longer adequate, and beginning with 1920 a national agricultural census has been taken every 5 years. The latest census, for 1959 (which is, at the present writing, available only for counties), was the 17th nationwide agricultural census.

At about the same time that the first agricultural census was made, statistical work was undertaken by the government which eventually was to become the responsibility of the Department of Agriculture. In an attempt to improve the farmer's bargaining position vis-à-vis the persons to whom they sold, Congress authorized the Patent Office in 1839 to spend $1,000 for the distribution of seeds and the collection of agricultural statistics. Annual estimates of the production of about a dozen major crops for each year from 1841 to 1845 were published; they were discontinued after 1845. The Department of Agriculture was established by Congress in 1862, and was specifically authorized to collect statistics. By 1867, the program was well under way and, since that time, continuous series of agricultural estimates on acreage, yield, and production of major crops and numbers of major species of livestock have been available.[3]

3. THE ESTIMATES

The data on agriculture may be broken down into three main types: (a) actual enumerations for some statistics relating to foreign trade and government programs, e.g., numbers and amounts of loans made to farmers and amounts of loans made by the Commodity Credit Corporation; (b) estimations of the U.S. Department of Agriculture; (c) Bureau of the Census data. We will be concerned with some of the series published by these two agencies.

Since there are at least two government agencies definitely concerned with providing information on agriculture in overlapping areas, some comparisons can be made between their reports. The Bureau of the Census makes counts of agricultural production and acreage every five years, and the Department of Agriculture regularly estimates production and acreage by various methods. The comparisons, however, will not directly provide estimates of the error of Department of Agriculture and Bureau of the Census statistics, since there is some interaction between the two agencies in producing their data, and the various series are not entirely independent of each other. But some comparisons can be made which should provide clues about the margins of error attached to these statistics.[4]

---

[3] United States Department of Agriculture, *The Agricultural Estimating and Reporting Services of the United States Department of Agriculture* (Miscellaneous Publication No. 703), December 1949, p. 2.

[4] We note here a fact which is true for almost all of the statistical activities of the government at the present time: A great effort is being made to improve the statistics. There is also a general move to combine activities of various agencies within a department. For example, the Department of Agriculture has recently announced a plan to reorganize its economics research and statistical reporting functions. These activities, previously assigned to the Agricultural Marketing Service, Agricultural Research Service, and Foreign Agricultural Service, are being brought together to form an Economics Research Service and a Statistical Reporting Service under a Director of Agricultural Economics. It is disappointing, however, that a parallel effort is not usually made in the presentation or explanation of the details of the estimating procedures.

The statistics published by the two government agencies are collected in various ways. First we discuss briefly the methods used by the Bureau of the Census; then, before we show some comparative tables, we will discuss the methods presently used by the Department of Agriculture.

(a) *The Bureau of the Census.* The 1959 Census of Agriculture used 30,000 enumerators. About 2 weeks before the start of the enumeration, agriculture questionnaires were mailed to most households in rural areas. These questionnaires were to be filled in and given to the enumerators. The actual enumeration started at dates varying from October 7 to November 19, 1959. The dates were based upon regional variation in harvesting seasons and on weather conditions, so that the enumeration would be late enough to follow the harvesting of the bulk of important crops. Sampling was used for enumeration and tabulation of data. The sampled items relate to sales of dairy products and sales of livestock, use of fertilizer and lime, farm expenditures, land-use practices, farm labor, equipment and facilities, rental agreements, farm values, and farm mortgage debt. The same sample of farms was used for tabulations involving "type of farm," "economic class of farm," and some tabulations involving "size of farm" and "color and tenure of operator." The sample used for the 1959 Census consisted of all farms with a total area of 1,000 or more acres with estimated sales of $100,000 or more in 1959, and approximately 20 percent of all other farms. The sample was adjusted to improve the reliability of the estimates and also to reduce enumerator bias for that part of the sample which included farms of less than 1,000 acres and with estimated sales of less than $100,000. The adjustment was essentially a stratification of the farms in the sample by size of farm. The estimated totals for all farms are subject to sampling errors. The sampling errors for different sample sizes are shown in the census volumes, and are approximate measures of the sampling reliability of the estimates for numbers of farms reporting and for item totals. While these measures indicate the general level of sampling reliability of the estimates, they do not completely reflect errors arising from sources other than sampling, principally errors in the original data reported by farmers. Errors arising from sources other than sampling may, in some instances, be relatively more important than sampling variation, especially for county totals.

The data obtained from the various censuses of agriculture are not strictly comparable for all items. For example, differences from one census to another in the time of enumeration, the wording of the questions, and the definition of a farm cause some lack of comparability. The census definition of a farm has changed. For the 1959 Census, the definition was based primarily on a combination of "acres in the place" and the estimated value of agricultural products sold. Places of less than 10 acres in 1959 were counted as farms if the estimated sales of agricultural products for the year amounted to at least $250. In both the 1950 and 1954 censuses, places of 3 or more acres were counted as farms if the annual value of agricultural products, whether for home use or for sale but exclusive of home-garden products, amounted to $150 or more. The decrease in the number of farms in 1959, as compared with all prior censuses, resulted partly from the change in farm definition. The fact that sales of agricultural products in 1959 were used as a criterion resulted in the exclusion of some places that would have qualified as farms had the value of agricultural products alone been considered. The increase in the acreage minimum also had an effect.[5]

(b) *The U.S. Department of Agriculture.* The other important collector of agricultural statistics is the United States Department of Agriculture, which provides current estimates of state and national totals and averages. Generally, the estimates of the Department of Agriculture are based on bench mark data supplied by the censuses of agriculture taken every 5 years and on sample data supplied by farmers and by people who do business with farmers, together with check data from other sources. Since they are estimates, they are subject to revisions as more data become available from commercial and government sources. The census data, since they do not become available for a year or more after the year to which they relate, are used for bench marks in future years and in revising historical estimates.

---

[5] U.S. Bureau of the Census, *U.S. Census of Agriculture: 1959,* Vol. I, *Counties,* Part 8, New Jersey, Washington, D.C., 1961.

A major reform of the Agricultural Estimates Division, one of the more important data collecting agencies of the Department of Agriculture, is at present under way. For a century, the government has been making estimates of crops and livestock. In 1912, the Crop Reporting Board, which is now under supervision of the administrator of the Agricultural Marketing Service, began its forecasts of the production of important crops prior to harvest. Up to now crop forecasters have relied almost entirely on answers to questionnaires mailed voluntarily by farmers and other rural reporters who work largely on the basis of past production from a well-known field plus the general appearance of the current crops on that field. Only about one-fourth of the one million monthly questionnaires are filled out and returned. Inevitably, considerable uncertainty prevails.

The new efforts consist of dispatching government agents, for the first time, to make an actual count and to measure some of the nation's crops. The Department hopes in this way to reduce the sampling error from about 15 percent to 1.6 percent of reality. The new "objective yield" method is more costly and more complex but the increased accuracy should make it worthwhile over time. This information is the basis of the monthly crop production forecasts of the Crop Reporting Board. The government's crop forecasts form the basis for business decisions involving the marketing and processing of $34 billion worth of farm commodities annually. For example, railroads plan movements of thousands of freight cars, traders buy and sell in major markets, and processors and manufacturers plan production. Farmers can gear production and marketing activities more rationally.[6]

The difficulties of crop forecasts are, of course, not restricted to the United States. Russian projections, for example, are notoriously poor. The frequently reported variations in actual crop reports differ widely from each other and usually are at

---

[6] *Wall Street Journal*, August 7, 1961. Some details of the various statistical series published by the Department of Agriculture have been published in "Agriculture Handbook No. 118," *Major Statistical Series of the U.S. Department of Agriculture*, 9 volumes published in 1957 and the 10th in 1960. A more detailed explanation of the methods used for certain major series is found in USDA, *The Agricultural Estimating and Reporting Services . . . , op. cit.*

great variance with earlier crop estimates. Similar observations apply to most other countries.[7]

4. MEASUREMENT OF ACCURACY

Geoffrey Moore, in his excellent article on the "Accuracy of Government Statistics,"[8] has used the study of revisions of agricultural statistics in his analysis of errors. He cites as an example a case in agricultural production in which a preliminary estimate of the potato crop was radically changed by revisions. He exhibits Department of Agriculture estimates for the census years 1919 and 1924. In 1919 the preliminary estimate for that year's crop was 358 million bushels. In 1920 this was revised to about 356 million, and in 1921, after the census figures were published, the potato crop was stated to be 323 million bushels. The Census figure was 290 million bushels, and subsequently the 1919 crop was estimated by Agriculture to be about 298 million bushels. The 1924 crop estimates underwent similar changes; Agriculture stated the crop to be over 450 million bushels, Census then published a figure close to 350 million bushels, and subsequently Agriculture revised its estimates for 1924 to about 380 million bushels.[9]

Moore then examines the level of confidence with which one could state an estimate in this field on the basis of past experience. With regard to 1930 data on the potato crop, he writes:

"One could be certain that the preliminary estimate for the 1929 crop was not accurate to thousands of bushels, probably not even millions of bushels. An error in the neighborhood of 10% would not be at all unlikely. The subsequent history of the

[7] Reference should be made to a very interesting attempt to discuss crop statistics by showing "the importance of the individual withholding crop intentions information from the group (of all farmers) as part of his optimal strategy" (cf. S. Moglewer, "A Game Theory Model for Agricultural Crop Selection," *Econometrica*, Vol. 30 (April 1962), pp. 253–266. The author, however, does not investigate the effect of the withholding on the reported crop statistics.

[8] *Harvard Business Review*, xxv (Spring, 1947), pp. 306–317.

[9] Revisions up and down, year after year, for the same statistics are common, of course, in most areas. Some of special interest are discussed below for national income. (See Chapter XIV, especially Table 23.)

1929 crop estimate is indicated . . . . First it was raised 2 million bushels, then lowered 30 million, then lowered another million, then boosted 5 million, and recently raised another million. It now stands at 333,392,000. Disregarding the 0's, the only digit remaining of the six given in the original estimate is the first, the figure 3!

"It may be surprising to some that the size of the potato crop depends so much on which Yearbook of Agriculture the figure comes from. But this case is not in the least unusual. The same thing happens in non-Census as well as Census years, and it is just as true of other crops as of potatoes, and likewise of industrial production, employment, and most other estimates. It is almost a statistical axiom that no revision is ever final. Not all revisions turn out to be improvements either."[10]

An interesting case in the light of the preceding is the story about world rice production. *The Economist* reports: "Estimates of world rice production made by the U.S. Office of Foreign Agricultural Relations show quite an encouraging picture. Output has been steadily rising during the past three seasons; it is now 2 percent higher than before the war, and the new season's crop may be just as large." Here we have an impossibly "accurate" statistic (for the whole world![11]) gravely interpreted by a leading economic journal as highly significant. And what applies to rice, in this instance, can be repeated *mutatis mutandis* for other crops.[12] We observed elsewhere that political and economic decisions are often based on this type of "information" and interpretation.

Our study will follow the lines of Dr. Moore's. First, we make a comparison of the most preliminary estimates published by the Department of Agriculture and the Bureau of the Census data for census years. This will indicate the range of variation between the two sets of statistics when the least amount of cooperation between the two agencies has taken place. That is, at this stage, the Agriculture estimate is unaffected by the

---

[10] *Harvard Business Review, op. cit.,* pp. 314–316.

[11] London, October 22, 1949, p. 910.

[12] Consider the accuracy of, e.g., Chinese, Burmese, Siamese, . . . , farmers' reports added together in order to get a world total!

current census since it appears before publication of Bureau of Census data. Second, the final revision of the Agriculture estimate, and the discrepancy between it and the Census figures should, aside from differences in classifications, provide indications of the error in the latter. Third, examination of the revisions in the Agriculture figures may indicate the measure of uncertainty of these estimates. These revisions are the result of further studies of the Department of Agriculture toward increasing accuracy, where one of their aims would be to reconcile their work with that of the Bureau of the Census.[13]

The tables presented below show preliminary versus final estimates of acreage harvested and production. We use them to show discrepancies, but these do not necessarily indicate the magnitude of error. The classifications of crops are technical but the explanatory information provided in the underlying sources is lacking in detail. Therefore, no attempt was made to estimate what part of the discrepancies was due, say, to definitional differences or differences in dating. The presentation we use shows only a measure of difference. Each statistic itself, of course, has its own, possibly very sizeable, error which cannot be disclosed by this procedure. In order to estimate it, entirely different studies are necessary which, if at all possible, are beyond the scope of this book or of any individual program.

Table 15 (A) compares the estimates of acreage harvested made by the Bureau of the Census and the Department of Agriculture for two census years, 1949 and 1954. Because some of the census does not include all states, we expect the Census figures to be smaller than the Agriculture figures, which is usually the case. Column 3 gives the percent differences between Census figures and preliminary Agriculture figures; column 5 gives these percent differences using final Agriculture figures. As is clear from column 5, the differences between the Bureau of the Census and the final Department of Agriculture

---

[13] Census data are not revised to bring them into line with other indications, according to the Department of Agriculture, despite the difficulties of obtaining a complete enumeration. The reason given is that any effort to make such revisions would produce estimates—as if a "complete" enumeration were something else! One is always dealing with statistical variables, a fact that cannot be emphasized enough.

figures range from 0.1 percent for soybeans to 26.4 percent for potatoes. The magnitude of the latter figure is probably due to the exclusion of many farms with small production on the part of the Census Bureau.[14]

Comparing the final estimate of Agriculture with Census figures (column 5), rather than comparing the preliminary estimate with Census figures (column 3) reduces the difference only negligibly. This casts some doubt on the improvement in accuracy made by the Department of Agriculture revisions.

One reason for compiling the table for both 1949 and 1954 was to see if the relative differences would be the same for the various items for the two years. Although the differences shown in both columns 3 and 5 are in general smaller for 1954 than for 1949, there seems to be little identifiable relationship among the specific crops.

Table 15 (B) is set up in the same manner as Table 15 (A) and shows the estimates of production of the various crops for the same two years. Although the range is smaller, from 1.2 percent to 16.8 percent, half of the values differ by more than 8 percent. Again, simple observation of the figures indicates no apparent trend in the percentage columns. The five intervening years have not brought an appreciable improvement. Though this is neither a very long time interval nor a very large sample of crops, it nevertheless seems to be another indication that even in countries which spend a great deal of money and competent effort on statistical data, more recent statistics are not automatically better or more reliable than earlier ones. And, at any rate, even if the future should bring significant improvements, the economist will always have to work with long time series which means that he will have to fall back on the above information. No future improvement changes the earlier data. Whether the differences shown in these tables are "large" or not can only be decided from the basis of the *use* to which they are put. If growth rates or any other rates of change are important,

---

[14] The acreage figures for Irish potatoes for 1949 and 1954 are the lowest for any census, but except for stating the exclusions in these years (see *Notes* to Table 15 for exact figures), there is no other explanation in the census volume.

TABLE 15

Comparison of Bureau of the Census and Department of Agriculture Series on Some Principal Crops: 1949 and 1954

A. Acres Harvested (in thousands of acres)

Crop	(1) Census[1]	(2) Prelim. USDA	(3) % Diff. (1)−(2)/(1)	(4) Final USDA	(5) % Diff. (1)−(4)/(1)	(6) % Diff. (2)−(4)/(2)
1949						
Corn (for grain)	75,133	78,833	−4.9	79,198	−5.4	−0.5
Sorghums (for grain and seed)	6,325	6,612	−4.5	6,612	−4.5	0.0
Wheat	71,163	76,751	−7.9	76,559	−7.6	+0.3
Barley	9,180	9,879	−7.6	9,857	−7.4	+0.2
Oats	35,344	40,560	−14.8	40,440	−14.4	+0.3
Rice	1,819	1,821	−0.1	1,840	−1.2	−1.0
Soybeans (for beans)	10,148	9,912	+2.3	10,156	−0.1	−2.5
Alfalfa	16,412	17,288	−5.3	17,341	−5.7	−0.3
Cotton	26,599	27,230	−2.4	27,230	−2.4	0.0
Irish potatoes	1,514[2]	1,901	−25.6	1,913	−26.4	−0.6
Tobacco	1,532	1,630	−6.4	1,631	−6.5	−0.1
1954						
Corn (for grain)	66,793	69,084	−3.4	68,668	−2.8	+0.6
Sorghums (for grain and seed)	11,304	10,764	+4.8	11,702	−3.5	−8.7
Wheat	51,362	53,712	−4.6	54,356	−5.8	−1.2
Barley	12,556	12,994	−3.5	13,370	−6.5	−2.9
Oats	37,921	42,151	−11.2	40,551	−6.9	+3.8
Rice	2,498	2,405	+3.7	2,550	−2.1	−6.0
Soybeans (for beans)	16,444	17,037	−3.6	17,047	−3.7	−0.1
Alfalfa	26,008	22,996	+11.6	26,576	−2.2	−15.6
Cotton	18,858	19,251	−2.1	19,251	−2.1	0.0
Irish potatoes	1,211	1,408	−16.3	1,413	−16.7	−0.4
Tobacco	1,557	1,666	−7.0	1,668	−7.1	−0.1

Sources: col. (1), 1949 and 1954, *United States Census of Agriculture: 1954*, Vol. II, General Report, Washington, D.C., 1956.

col. (2), 1949, *Agricultural Statistics, 1950*, U.S. Department of Agriculture, Washington, 1950.

col. (4), 1949, *Agricultural Statistics, 1951*, *ibid.*, 1951.

col. (2), 1954, *Agricultural Statistics, 1955*, *ibid.*, 1956.

col. (4), 1954, *Agricultural Statistics, 1956*, *ibid.*, 1957.

Notes: USDA estimates based on census benchmark data and sample data supplied by farmers or businesses dealing with farmers. Most census figures exclude some states. We show the originally given seven "significant" digits as they appear in the sources quoted.

[1] Drought conditions existed in 1954 in parts of the Great Plains and the South. In the drought area, in some cases farm operators and census enumerators may have reported as harvested the entire acreage in the crop, even though only part of the acreage on the farm was actually harvested.

[2] For 1954, Census does not include acreage for farms with less than 20 bushels or 10 bags harvested; for 1949, acreage for farms with less than 15 bushels or 10 bags harvested.

(*Cont.*)

TABLE 15 (Cont.)

B. Production

Crop	Units	(1) Census[1]	(2) Prelim. USDA	(3) % Diff. (1)−(2) / (1)	(4) Final USDA	(5) % Diff. (1)−(4) / (1)	(6) % Diff. (2)−(4) / (2)
1949							
Corn (for grain)	bu.	2,778,190	3,108,812	−11.9	3,114,726	−12.1	−0.2
Sorghums (for grain and seed)	bu.	140,835[3]	152,630	−8.4	152,630	−8.4	0.0
Wheat	bu.	1,006,559	1,146,463	−13.9	1,141,188	−13.4	+0.5
Barley	bu.	220,963	238,104	−7.8	236,737	−7.1	+0.6
Oats	bu.	1,136,642	1,322,924	−16.4	1,329,473	−17.0	−0.5
Rice	bags	40,244[4]	40,113	+0.3	40,747	−1.2	−1.6
Soybeans (for beans)	bu.	212,440	222,305	−4.6	230,897	−8.7	−3.9
Alfalfa	tons	32,254	38,546	−9.3	38,645	−9.6	−0.3
Cotton	bales	15,419[5]	16,128	−4.6	16,128	−4.6	0.0
Irish potatoes	cwt.	219,802[6]	241,177	−9.7	246,939	−12.3	−2.4
Tobacco	lbs.	1,769,769	1,970,376	−11.3	1,972,541	−11.5	−0.1
1954							
Corn (for grain)	bu.	2,612,911	2,652,426	−1.5	2,707,913	−3.6	−2.1
Sorghums (for grain and seed)	bu.	224,014[3]	204,087	+8.9	235,295	−5.0	−15.3
Wheat	bu.	908,928	969,781	−6.7	983,900	−8.2	−1.5
Barley	bu.	354,716	370,126	−4.3	379,254	−6.9	−2.5
Oats	bu.	1,314,142	1,499,579	−14.1	1,409,601	−7.3	+6.0
Rice	bags	65,284[4]	58,853	+9.9	64,193	+1.7	−9.1
Soybeans (for beans)	bu.	323,965	342,795	−5.8	341,075	−5.3	+0.5
Alfalfa	tons	54,914	49,328	+10.2	56,364	−2.6	−14.3
Cotton	bales	12,921[5]	13,679	−5.9	13,696	−6.0	−0.1
Irish potatoes	cwt.	204,113[6]	213,619	−4.7	219,547	−7.6	−2.8
Tobacco	lbs.	1,921,526	2,236,408	−16.4	2,243,735	−16.8	−0.3

[3] Census does not include sorghums for syrup; U.S.D.A. does.

[4] Census figure (in 1,000 bu.) converted to comparable units to USDA figures (in 100 lb. bags) by multiplying census figures of 89,437 (1949) and 145,076 (1954) by .45 (conversion factor from *Agricultural Statistics*: 1 bu. equals 45 lbs., approximately).

[5] Census of Agriculture figures in running bales averaging approximately 480 lbs. USDA estimates are 500-lb. gross weight bales.

[6] Census production (in bushels) converted to USDA units (1,000 cwt.) using 60 lb. per bu. as a basis of connecting 100-lb. bags to bushels (conversion factor from U.S. Census, 1954).

these differences are very large and uncomfortable. (Cf. Chapter XV below, dealing with growth rates in general.) This remark applies, of course, to any series.

The Department of Agriculture claims that when the differences are considerable between the Bureau of the Census totals and the Department's final estimates, checks generally show that the estimates are based on more nearly complete information about some items on the part of the Department. For example, for tobacco (a difference of 16.8 percent in 1954 and always large), the Department considers its estimate of production more precise—given for the whole United States down to the last single pound!—because the estimates are revised in line with actual production as shown independently by Internal Revenue records and State records of tobacco sales. The Department of Agriculture also cites in this connection sugar beets, sugar cane, peanuts, and rice. It would be difficult to evaluate this claim. It is true that many of the specific questions asked in the agricultural censuses are based on incomplete counts, e.g., those restricted to important producing states, or coming from samples. On the other hand, the Department of Agriculture's own estimates may also exclude some areas. The discrepancies arising on this score, however, may be more interesting for smaller geographic areas than for the nation.

We have not included a discussion of the value or number of livestock on farms, although both government agencies publish such series. The Bureau of the Census regularly reports the number and value of various classes of livestock, but the successive enumerations have occurred at various times of the year and the data are not really comparable. The Department of Agriculture estimates always relate to January. The Department makes allowances for possible incompleteness of the census and for changes in livestock numbers between January 1 and the date of the census enumeration in order to establish a bench mark estimate for January 1.

It should be noted that in these statistics entirely unnecessary, meaningless, and expensive detail is carried. Seven "significant" figures are commonplace, although no conceivable use can be made of such detail even if it should be possible to obtain it accurately—a very remote chance, indeed an impossibility.

We conclude this section with a statement made by the Federal Statistics Users' Conference:

"Despite the variety and amount of statistical information relating to American agriculture there is a growing concern about its adequacy for the need of present-day public and private policy decisions.

"Agriculture as an industry has changed radically in the past 25 years. Rural society is changing, too. Yet for the most part, available information continues to portray American agriculture in terms which were more applicable a generation or more ago than they are today.

"The use of direct measurements and sample surveys in making crop and livestock estimates, a development which is only now getting underway, is an encouraging step forward. It is to be hoped that this improvement program will be expanded systematically and that its objectives will include the development of estimates at intervals consistent with present-day production practices. As the use of these techniques is expanded geographically to include the whole country, it should become possible to employ them as a valuable and flexible tool for obtaining a variety of kinds of needed information not now available.

"But the use of modern techniques is not enough. There is also a need to change the way of looking at American agriculture. Less attention should be given to averages. More attention should be given to developing current information by economic class of farm and by kinds of commercial farms. Such a framework would provide more meaningful information than does the present system which produces primarily per farm or per capita data."[15]

[15] "A Long Range Program for the Improvement of Federal Statistics," Federal Statistics Users' Conference, Washington, 1961, p. 12.

CHAPTER XIII

EMPLOYMENT AND UNEMPLOYMENT STATISTICS

1. SIGNIFICANCE OF UNEMPLOYMENT DATA

THE success or failure of a government's economic policy is often measured by the number of involuntary unemployed existing in a country. "Full employment" is a national goal in most advanced nations. But as soon as one tries to discover when that desired condition has been reached, considerable difficulties are encountered. They are conceptual as well as statistical.

First, it is known that there is always some "unemployment" which may not be truly involuntary, because labor shifts from one place to another, young people enter the labor force, others more or less gradually slip from it because of age, ill health, emigration, death. These transitions take time for purely technological reasons, such as slow transmission and dissemination of knowledge, time needed to move to other places of employment etc. This is then the so-called "frictional" unemployment which is at some level unrelated to the state of the economy. There is also possibly a great deal of "hidden unemployment," e.g., when persons becoming unemployed in industry go back to farms for varying periods of time. There is a shift in occupations, for example when skilled workers are displaced by machines and now have to find employment at lesser skills. Numerous further complications arise making the very definition of unemployment uncertain. Consequently we shall not be surprised that reliable unemployment statistics are very difficult to make.

Second, because of the high political significance of unemployment figures, this area is charged with emotions, insinuations, assertions etc. Depending on the political position of the parties concerned, facts are produced and debated, and the separation of truth from fabrication is difficult. This applies in particular to times of great stress, of political upheavals and changes in the form of government. Some countries, such as the Soviet Union, flatly assert that they never have unemployment, this allegedly being impossible because of their political system. Others, such as Nazi Germany, "reduced" unemployment by drafting men into the army and thereby changing the statistics to their liking. In still other countries, more subtle procedures are used in order to show that unemployment allegedly is what one would like it to be. Frequently different estimates are simultaneously presented to the confused public. Sometimes contradictory estimates are arrived at honestly by the legitimate use of varying statistical procedures. In this case, differences in the final series show how difficult it is to arrive at convincingly good statistics in a field which offers so many obstacles for adequate description even when political machinations are absent.

In the following, we are only concerned with the last case. But the reader should be aware that this is a very severe limitation in judging the quality of figures on unemployment with which he may find himself confronted, especially when dealing with periods of great crises—precisely when the issue is most important. From the figures alone it is not possible to discern what method was used to get the statistic.

This chapter will deal almost exclusively with United States statistics. The procedures for determining employment and unemployment differ so widely from one country to another that it would lead too far to discuss more than one country. Though we believe United States statistics in general to be at least as good as those of other countries—and generally better—this is not necessarily true for the present instance. The reason is that various other nations have had a longer experience with unemployment insurance and subsidies, have older and more encompassing labor unions, as well as many regulations concerning work, licenses etc., all of which has contributed to the makeup of unemployment statistics. American time series tend to be of more uneven quality, recent data generally being substantially better than those of even two decades ago. But it should be remembered that the economist needs long, homogeneous time series in order to be able to study a given field and that economic time series often are subject to strong trends. Time series are needed when historical comparisons are made, and also for the computation of rates of change. The value of the latter is singularly sensitive to the quality of the data, as Chapter XV will show for the case of Gross National Product.

Differences among nations show up very clearly in the employment field. There are enormous variations in skills, working conditions, capital equipment, individual savings, education, etc. so that unemployment will mean very different things. Though these factors are mostly connected with interpretation of the data—which normally has not concerned us much in this book—they nevertheless point to the inherent difficulties in international comparisons of unemployment statistics.

A particular difference is that in some countries *complete counts* are made (e.g., with the aid of registrations, through labor unions, statistics of unemployment subsidies and the like). In the United States, sampling procedures are used primarily, a method that is very powerful when properly handled. This is, indeed, the case, but we shall see that in a large population sampling with living beings having attributes that are difficult to describe and often not wanted by those questioned, is a far more complicated matter than, say, sampling for quality control of goods manufactured.

In the following sections we will discuss two different concepts of error applicable to employment statistics: (a) inaccuracies in a measure given its definition, and (b) divergencies between two or more measures which are often related for purposes of economic analyses but are based on differing definitions. The latter concept will be referred to as "divergency" or "discrepancy" and will be emphasized in section 3; the former will be denoted by "error" or "inaccuracy" and will be treated in section 4.

American labor force statistics, in particular the monthly survey conducted by the Bureau of the Census, generally rank among the superior economic series compiled anywhere. This is largely due to the continuing re-evaluation of the data by those responsible for their collection and use.

Although the evidence below may appear to contradict this statement, this seeming paradox is readily explained when we consider that no aggregate statistics can serve *all* purposes similarly well. Many of the criticisms that have been directed against the labor force statistics are admittedly or implicitly concerned with their divergence from measures that would be called for by different concepts. But the very fact that these labor force series are subject to critical evaluation speaks for the fact that the materials needed for judgment have indeed been compiled.

2. PRINCIPAL EMPLOYMENT SERIES[1]

Most information on employment and unemployment in the United States comes from four major sources—the Bureau of the Census, the Bureau of Labor Statistics (BLS), the Bureau of Employment Security (BES), and the United States Department of Agriculture (USDA). Since 1959, the data from the first three agencies have been summarized in a single publication, *Monthly Report of Labor Force* (MRLF), issued by the Bureau of Labor Statistics.[2] Total farm employment is estimated and published by the Department of Agriculture.

(a) The *Census-MRLF* estimates are the only source providing employment and unemployment information for the entire population. The data are based on a geographically stratified random sample of about 35,000 households. These households are randomly chosen from sampling cells which have themselves been chosen according to a multi-stage cluster sampling procedure involving the use of probabilities proportional to size, from over 300 geographical areas.[3] The sample is taken in the middle of each month to maximize comparability with other monthly series.

---

[1] The following (Sections 2–4) is largely based on a special survey by G. J. Stolnitz: *Evaluation of the Accuracy of U.S. Employment and Unemployment Statistics,* Econometric Research Program, Princeton University, July 1962.

[2] This volume combines two earlier publications, *Current Population Reports, Labor Force, Series P–57* (Bureau of the Census) and *Employment, Hours and Earnings* (BLS) with data on insured unemployment (BES).

[3] At present, the sample is spread over 330 sample areas covering every state and the District of Columbia. There are 42,000 habitations designated. Each month, about 35,000 households with 80,000 inhabitants 14 years old and over are interviewed. About 1500 households which should be interviewed are not because no-one is available, e.g., due to temporary absence, or failure to be found at home by interviewers. The other designated units not interviewed include such things as vacancy, demolition of

The major aggregates covered by the Census-MRLF compilations are size of labor force (total and civilian), number of employed in agriculture, number of employed in nonagricultural industries, number of unemployed and number of persons not in the labor force. The sum of the employed and unemployed equals, by definition, the size of the civilian labor force. Adding the Armed Forces to this number yields total labor force.

Information is also provided on a large and growing number of sub-categories within the civilian labor force total. Examples are the distributions of the employed and unemployed by sex, age, color, and by industry and occupation, the number of part-time workers and reasons for working part-time, and the characteristics of the long-term unemployed.

The Census Bureau attempts to identify persons as belonging or not belonging to the labor force according to the "degree of their attachment" to the labor markets. The basic guideline for including someone in the labor force is that he or she be working or looking for work. There are, to be sure, modifications to this basic maxim in practice. Thus, the so-called "inactive unemployed" include persons not at work but also not seeking work because they were temporarily ill or believed they could not find employment in their line of work or in their community. Any such person is to be included among the unemployed and hence in the labor force.[4] Additional conventions of the Census

residence, and occupation by persons with residence elsewhere. These unavoidable failures to carry out the sample design strictly are typical of the problems encountered by even the most carefully conducted collections of data. They are not the fault of the Census Bureau, and they do not add in any significant manner to the uncertainty surrounding the data. Cf. U.S. Bureau of the Census, *Current Population Reports, Series P–23*, no. 5, May 9, 1958 (Washington, D.C.). This publication gives a detailed outline of the survey design.

[4] The actual method of obtaining this information is rather arbitrary. Interviewers are instructed not to ask whether these were in fact the reasons for not seeking work; only if such information is volunteered is the interviewed person classified as in the labor force (and hence unemployed). The Bureau's justification for this procedure is that it serves as the best screening device so far available for distinguishing between those seriously desiring work and those with more cursory, ambivalent or even whimsical interest in the labor market. Observe that the distinction is made not by the investigator but by the many people questioned, which is an invitation for error but one as difficult to discover as to avoid.

Bureau are that the number employed includes persons who have jobs or businesses but were not actually at work during the survey week because of illness, bad weather, or industrial disputes. Seasonal workers in their "off" season during the survey period are not reported as outside the labor force. Unpaid family workers are included among the employed only if they have worked 15 hours or more.

(b) The Bureau of Labor Statistics estimates of wage and salary (payroll) workers is the oldest continuous labor force series for the United States. A variety of measures on employment, hours, and earnings are derived from sample inquiries. In contrast to the Census series, the BLS data are based on reports of establishments rather than households. The BLS sample embraces all nonagricultural industries; reports are presently being received from about 180,000 establishments, with an aggregate payroll of some twenty-five million workers. The BLS sample utilizes a cutoff procedure, whereas the Census uses a stratified random sample covering the whole population.

It appears from this fact alone that the Census series is the superior series, as the random sampling procedure usually gives the truest picture of the population.

Unlike the Census, the BLS employment totals exclude the self-employed, unpaid family workers, persons in domestic service, and those with a job but temporarily not on payroll because of vacation, sick leave, strikes, or various similar reasons. On the other hand, the BLS data include a person with multiple jobs as often as he or she appears on an establishment payroll; the Census data avoids such duplicated counts.

(c) The Bureau of Employment Security publishes monthly data on employment and unemployment for those individuals who are covered by Federal, State, and Railroad Unemployment Insurance laws.[5] Like the BLS, the BES employment series diverges from that of the Census by excluding the agricultural sector, the self-employed and domestic service workers

[5] Inclusion of federal employees began in 1955; as a result there is a substantial discontinuity in the total covered employed series (though little in total covered unemployment).

in private homes. In addition, it excludes most workers in firms with less than four employees and those in non-profit organizations. The BES unemployment figures tend to be lower than those of the Census for all of these reasons and also because of the exclusion of unemployed persons in covered industries who have not filed reports or are ineligible for benefits.

In addition to these definitional differences which stem from the extent of coverage of the unemployment insurance laws, the BES data are essentially based on complete counts, and hence are presumably not subject to sampling variability.

(d) The United States Department of Agriculture series on total farm employment is based on monthly national samples of twenty to twenty-five thousand farm establishments.

The USDA census diverges from that of the Census in that the former is based on establishment reports and therefore includes persons whose occupation is nonagricultural but who also do some work on a farm; the Census system of classification would place all such persons in nonagricultural employment. Similar persons working on more than one farm are double-counted by the USDA but not by the Census Bureau, but conversely those employed in clerical occupations on farms are excluded from the USDA series but appear in the Census agricultural totals. All this makes for divergencies.

3. Divergencies among Principal Labor Force Series

Not unlike the situation already discussed for mining and agricultural statistics, the disparities between related yet divergent labor force series have occasioned considerable confusion in both public and professional circles. These disparities must receive continued close examination if distorting or misleading interpretation is to be avoided.[6]

Tables 16, 17, and 18 present data (with latest revisions) covering the postwar period, for the series discussed in the pre-

---

[6] A recent swell of controversy concerning the adequacy of existing labor force concepts and measurement procedures has led to the presidential appointment of a Committee to Appraise Employment and Unemployment Statistics. Cf. Section 5, page 234.

TABLE 16

Non-Agricultural Employment Principal Series; Levels
and Changes; Monthly Averages 1946–1961

(in millions)

	Non-Agricultural Employment			Year to Year Changes			% Differences	
	Census MRLF (1)	BLS (2)	BES (3)	Census MRLF (4)	BLS (5)	BES (6)	BLS-Census (7)	BES-Census (8)
1946	46.9	41.7	31.9				−11.1	−32.0
1947	49.6	43.9	33.9	2.7	2.2	2.0	−11.5	−31.7
1948	51.2	44.9	34.6	1.6	1.0	.7	−12.3	−32.4
1949	50.4	43.8	33.1	−0.8	−1.1	−1.5	−13.1	−34.5
1950	52.3	45.2	34.3	1.9	1.4	1.2	−13.6	−34.5
1951	53.7	47.8	36.3	1.4	2.6	2.0	−11.0	−32.4
1952	54.2	48.8	37.0	.5	1.0	.7	−10.0	−31.7
1953	55.4	50.2	38.1	1.2	1.4	1.1	−9.4	−31.2
1954	54.4	49.0	36.6	−1.0	−1.2	−1.5	−10.0	−32.7
1955	56.2	50.7	40.0	1.8	1.7	3.4	−9.8	−28.8
1956	58.1	52.4	42.6	1.9	1.7	2.6	−9.8	−26.7
1957	58.8	52.9	43.4	.7	.5	.8	−10.0	−26.2
1958	58.1	51.4	44.4	−0.7	−1.5	1.0	−11.5	−23.6
1959	59.7	53.4	45.8	1.6	2.0	1.4	−10.6	−23.3
1960	61.0	54.3	46.4	1.3	.9	.6	−11.0	−23.8
1961	61.3	54.1[p]	45.3[q]	.3	−0.2	−0.9	−11.7	−26.1

[p] Preliminary. [q] 6 months average.

Sources: Column 1—*Business Statistics*, 1961 edition, p. 61.

Column 2—BLS, *Employment and Earnings Statistics for the United States*, 1909–1960, Bulletin 1312, 1961, p. 2.

Column 3—*Employment and Wages*, 2nd Quarter, 1961, inside cover page.

Column 7— $\dfrac{\text{Column (2)—Column (1)}}{\text{Column (1)}} \times 100.$

Column 8— $\dfrac{\text{Column (3)—Column (1)}}{\text{Column (1)}} \times 100.$

ceding section.[7] The statistical differences which may result from variations in labor force concepts and coverage (even when these differences are partially offsetting or involve "marginal" categories) are apparent from the tables.

[7] The problems presented by continual revisions cannot be overemphasized. The difficulties here are similar to those confronting the user of national income statistics and are discussed and illustrated at some length in Chapter XIV.

TABLE 17

AGRICULTURAL EMPLOYMENT PRINCIPAL SERIES; LEVELS AND CHANGES 1946–1961
(in millions)

	Agricultural Employment		Changes according to		% Difference
	Census-MRLF (1)	USDA (2)	Census-MRLF (3)	USDA (4)	$\dfrac{\text{Col (2)}-\text{Col (1)}}{\text{Col (1)}} \times 100$ (5)
Monthly Averages					
1946	8.3	10.3			24.0
1947	8.3	10.4	0.0	0.1	25.3
1948	8.0	10.4	−0.3	0.0	30.0
1949	8.0	10.0	0.0	−0.4	25.0
1950	7.5	9.3	−0.5	−0.7	24.0
1951	7.0	9.0	−0.5	−0.3	28.6
1952	6.8	8.7	−0.2	−0.3	27.9
1953	6.6	8.6	−0.2	−0.1	30.3
1954	6.5	8.5	−0.1	−0.1	30.8
1955	6.7	8.2	0.2	−0.3	22.4
1956	6.6	7.9	−0.1	−0.3	19.7
1957	6.2	7.6	−0.4	−0.3	22.6
1958	5.8	7.5	−0.4	−0.1	29.3
1959	5.8	7.4	0.0	−0.1	27.6
1960	5.7	7.1	−0.1	−0.3	24.6
1961	5.5	7.0	−0.2	−0.1	27.3

SOURCE: Column (1)—*Business Statistics,* 1961 edition, p. 61.
Column (2)—Farm Labor, January 1957, p. 9.
January 1959, p. 7.
January 1960, p. 7.
January 1961, p. 7.
January 1962, p. 7.

Tables 16, 17, and 18 give the data for nonagricultural and agricultural employment 1946–1961, and the principal unemployment series for the same periods. Earlier data are shown below in Tables 20 and 21. Only the data since 1946 attain a degree of reliability compared with statistics in other fields. It is necessary to consider both employment and unemployment, since there is obvious interest in evaluating the latter which can only be done in terms of the former.

Since the tables offer no difficulty, only a few comments are necessary. The three counts of nonagricultural employment differ widely by four to eighteen million people. The differences

TABLE 18

UNEMPLOYMENT PRINCIPAL SERIES; LEVELS AND CHANGES 1946–1961
(in millions)

	Unemployment		Changes According to		% Difference
	Census-MRLF (1)	BES (2)	Census-MRLF (3)	BES (4)	$\dfrac{\text{Col }(2)-\text{Col }(1)}{\text{Col }(1)} \times 100$ (5)
Monthly Averages					
1946	2.3	2.8			21.7
1947	2.4	1.8	0.1	−1.0	−25.0
1948	2.3	1.5	−0.1	−0.3	−34.8
1949	3.7	2.5	1.4	1.0	−32.4
1950	3.4	1.6	−0.3	−0.9	−52.9
1951	2.1	1.0	−1.3	−0.6	−52.4
1952	1.9	1.1	−0.2	0.1	−42.1
1953	1.9	1.1	0.0	0.0	−42.1
1954	3.6	2.0	1.7	0.9	−44.4
1955	2.9	1.4	−0.7	−0.6	−51.7
1956	2.8	1.3	−0.1	−0.1	−53.6
1957	2.9	1.6	0.1	0.3	−44.8
1958	4.7	2.8	1.8	1.2	−40.4
1959	3.8	1.9	−0.9	−0.9	−50.0
1960	3.9	2.1	0.1	0.2	−46.2
1961	4.8	2.5	0.9	0.4	−47.9

SOURCE: Column (1)—*Business Statistics*, 1961 edition, p. 61.
Column (2)—*Business Statistics*, 1961 edition, p. 80.

fluctuate from year to year but there is apparently neither a trend nor an easily distinguishable cycle. The differences between the Census and the BES figures appear to have decreased since about 1956, but they are still very large, i.e. over 20%. For agricultural employment the figures from the Department of Agriculture are consistently higher than those of the Census, the differences averaging about 25%.

The two unemployment series shown in Table 18 receive the closest attention of all labor force compilations for policy purposes. Yet the discrepancies are enormous; they have averaged 50% of the average of the two series, with the BES series being lower in every year but 1946. Obviously, considerable caution must be exercised in using these series. The exact definition upon which each is based must always be borne in mind. It is frequently argued that the effects of divergent definitions may be much less significant when discussing period-to-period changes than when considering absolute magnitudes[8] and that variations are all one needs to know even for policy purposes. The problem therefore is whether or not the changes are consistent in regard to their changes, i.e., whether the different series move in the same direction from year to year. Our conclusions are discouraging.

As can be seen from Tables 16, 17, and 18, the corresponding employment and unemployment series differ from each other in *direction* of movement on several occasions. For example, non-agricultural employment fell from 1957 to 1958 on both Census and BLS basis, but rose *significantly* on the BES definition. Thus, if only the BES series were consulted, the existence of a recession would not become apparent as far as employment is concerned; if all three are used it is not clear through which phase of the business cycle the economy is passing.[9]

Criticism of the concepts underlying the major employment series has been almost continuous, and is especially severe during recessionary periods. The controversy during the 1960–1961 recession points up some of the uncertainties and indicates how groups with different political viewpoints can get "conclusions" in support of their individual cases.

One point of view maintains that the Census definitions and survey procedures lead to exaggerated measures of unemployment by including in the labor force large numbers of housewives living with their husbands, as well as teen-agers and persons over 65. The argument is that such persons have only marginal attachment to the labor force and should not be grouped with the "hard core" unemployed (males over age 20 and unattached females aged 20 to 44) in assessing the unemployment situation and in prescribing economic policies. United States unemployment rates cannot be directly com-

[8] See in particular Chapter XIV on national income. This point is also made by P. Simpson in his review of the first edition of this book. (*American Economic Review*, September 1951, pp. 695–696.)

[9] Monthly data reveal that the changes are even less consistent. One month movements are largely random and cannot be taken at face value, nor expected to be consistent whether the changes are in the same direction or not.

pared with those abroad, which are usually based on unemployment insurance counts and appear to be much lower than they would be if they were based on American definitions. Advocates of this line of argument, who may be called fiscal conservatives, will understate the unemployment problem so that they can recommend preferred fiscal and monetary policies.

On the other hand labor organizations argue that American data substantially understate unemployment by including all part-time workers among the employed though they are willing but unable to obtain full-time employment. Also, it is claimed that the present procedure of counting "inactive unemployed" in the labor force only when they volunteer information about the reason for their being unemployed leads to an underestimate of the size of the labor force and hence of the number of unemployed. If unemployment is actually underestimated, monetary and fiscal policies would be prescribed quite different from those of the other group.

A recent example of some of the difficulties in using unemployment statistics pertains to the problem of seasonal adjustment, and has been pointed out by P. A. Samuelson.[10] Samuelson notes that the official method of seasonal adjustment utilized by the Bureau of Labor Statistics applies the adjustment to the percentages of unemployed directly. The "residual" method applies seasonal adjustment to both the unemployment and labor force raw data and then performs the division. The two methods may yield very different results. The official method showed no fall in the unemployment rate from February to October 1961 (6.8 percent in each month), whereas the residual method showed a fall from 7.1 percent to 6.4 percent in this period. Looking at the former series, many economists claimed that the unemployment rate did not fall despite the business expansion apparent in the other indicators. Yet another method yielded entirely different results perfectly consistent with a cyclical decline in unemployment![10a]

[10] Letter to *The New York Times,* November 12, 1961.

[10a] It might be noted that the residual method has not been found superior to other methods. The principal difficulties in connection with seasonal adjustment arise not from the failure to use the best methods available, but from the failure to develop better methods than those known at present. Cf. The Report of the President's Committee to Appraise Employ-

The trickiness of drawing conclusions about "real" changes in series that have been seasonally corrected was simply illustrated already more than twenty-five years ago. Then I observed at the Austrian Institute for Business Cycle Research that the series of unemployed, which was steadily rising from year to year, when seasonally corrected by the widely used Persons' link relative method, was simply inverted. That is, when the uncorrected figures were going down, the "corrected" figures would rise and *vice versa*—a gradually weakening seasonal component still being in evidence. This was an obviously absurd result, but some time had to pass before the phenomenon could be noted and assessed. In the meantime, interpretations of the alleged occurrence were attempted but it was, of course, impossible to find an acceptable economic interpretation. As a consequence, Persons' method was rejected and A. Wald developed his ingenious new method that was henceforth used.[11]

4. ERRORS IN EMPLOYMENT STATISTICS

The Census-MRLF employment series are prepared with evident statistical sophistication. First-class descriptions of the methods involved in collecting the data and their sources of error are available, so that users of these statistics can discover their quality. This is in contrast to most of the statistics discussed in this book. Employment statistics, as a result, offer an opportunity to examine the quality of well-prepared economic statistics. Our discussion is based primarily on a paper by Gertrude Bancroft[12] of the Bureau of the Census and the official description of the statistics,[13] both outstanding examples of how makers of statistics can explain their figures clearly.

---

ment and Unemployment Statistics, *Measuring Employment and Unemployment* (Washington, 1962). I am indebted to Professor F. F. Stephan for emphasizing this point in discussing these questions.

[11] A. Wald, *Berechnung und Ausschaltung von Saisonschwankungen* (Vienna, 1936). I should like to note, on this occasion, that Wald was thus started in the field of statistics to which he made so many notable contributions.

[12] Gertrude Bancroft, "Current Unemployment Statistics of the Census Bureau and Some Alternatives," National Bureau of Economic Research, *The Measurement and Behavior of Unemployment* (Princeton, 1957).

[13] U.S. Bureau of the Census, Current Population Reports, Series P–23, no. 5, May 9, 1958.

Since the Census-MRLF series are based on samples, the data are necessarily subject to sampling variability. While for most categories, error from this source is small, for some categories with relatively few members, it may become large. Sampling errors may arise both from the sampling of areas and from the sampling of individuals in areas. Only taking a larger sample could reduce this error.

Response variability is a prime source of possible error. The person answering the questions may not have precise knowledge about the activities of other members of the household or they may not understand the questions. Interviewers may not always ask the questions properly or they may misinterpret or misrecord the answers, despite their training and quality control checks of their work. Another interviewer might obtain different results. Four indications of the nature of this error are available:

(a) While response errors may cancel out, it is quite possible that they lead to bias in the figures. Studies were conducted in 1946 to 1950 to check the effects of different questions and question sequences. It was found that considerable variability arose in the number of people seeking employment and whether they were included in the labor force. We have already commented (cf. page 220) on the survey's method of finding the "fringe" unemployed. Even in the framework of questions asked and definitions used, this category might well be an important source of variability due to the interviewers, since the method of questioning may produce varying results in areas where different questions lead to substantially different replies.

(b) Early in 1954, a substantial change was made in the current survey sample design. The method of selecting units was altered and the number of households interviewed was increased. In connection with the sample change-over, very careful attention was given to training new staff while training of old staff seems to have been skimpy. The new sample estimates of employment agreed very closely with the old, but the estimates of unemployment were very different. By the old sample, unemployment was 3.8% of the labor force, by the new, 4.9%. This was a far larger difference than could be accounted for by sampling variability. While the difference may be largely attributable to the changing of staff, and demonstrates the effect of relaxation of survey controls and standards, and while variability of estimates using the same staff would be much smaller, the episode demonstrates clearly both the truth that different interviewers arrive at different results and that bias is introduced into the data by interviewers.[14]

(c) A third example is provided by contrasts between decennial census returns, compiled by hurriedly and only partially trained enumerators who have been engaged for a single short-period survey, and the results of the monthly samples, compiled by a more or less permanent crops of interviewers, who have been performing a recurring survey operation under supervision and on-the-job training. The census returns for employment and unemployment were substantially below the comparable monthly survey results, and the reported rate of unemployment especially was lower to a very much larger extent than could be accounted for by sampling variability. In 1950, for people enumerated at the same date, matched returns show that in *half* the cases the two sets of interviewers classified differently! It is believed that superior training of the sample-survey interviewers made the sample figures more reliable than the census figures.

(d) Recent information on enumeration errors is afforded by the reinterviews program conducted by the Bureau of the Census. Every month, reinterviews are carried out for a sub-sample of about 1 in 14 of the Census-MRLF sample households. The sub-samples provide a check of each enumerator's work about three times a year and are used both to identify

---

[14] Incidentally, this episode also shows what peculiar things occur in economic statistics. In view of the evidence that quality of enumeration had been deteriorating before January 1954, the Bureau of the Census published revised monthly estimates for September through December, 1953. The adjustments were apparently derived by starting with the January, 1954 differences between old and new surveys, merely scaling these down by interpolation to zero over the preceding four-month period. The revised estimates of unemployment differ from the original ones by about 20 percent for December, 15 percent for November, 10 percent for October, and 5 percent for September. This indicates a frequent phenomenon in economic statistics, how data may become "finalized" by means of adjustments which are themselves open to considerable doubt.

sources of errors and to reduce their frequency. The reinterviews are conducted by supervisors or other well-trained personnel.

Data on such errors have not customarily been published by the Bureau of the Census, but information was made available in early 1962 on the occasion of the special review of labor-force data undertaken by the President's Committee to Appraise Employment and Unemployment Statistics. Table 19 presents some of the findings. The percent net difference is the change in the number of persons in a category as a result of reinterviewing relative to the reinterview number. The index of gross differences for each category is the ratio of those persons added to the category plus those subtracted from it relative to the reinterview number in the category. It indicates the total misreporting in relation to a category in the interviews. A few of these findings indicate enumeration variability. After screening out apparent differences by rechecking with respondents, it was found that of those persons reported as being employed, about 98% had been so recorded in the first interview. The number of persons reported as being employed increased about 1% in reinterviewing. About 88% of the people reported as being unemployed in the reinterviewing had been so reported on first interviews, while the number reported as being unemployed was almost 4% lower in the first interviews. Thus, even as good a survey as that of the Census-MRLF may seriously understate certain categories for reasons of enumeration errors alone.

One of the great difficulties of the survey is that the definitions are not always easy to apply. Borderline cases occur which do not fit properly in a particular category. Problems of application of definitions may be a source of error in the statistics, and may in some categories bias the results significantly.

Publications of the Census-MRLF employment data include estimates of the standard errors of the figures arising from sampling and response variability and estimates of the standard errors attaching to month-to-month changes have been reported. The Census has estimated that the errors in month-to-month changes are less than would occur if each month's sample were independent of previous ones. The errors in month-to-

TABLE 19

Employment status, sex	(1) Percent identically reported	(2) Percent net difference	(3) Index of gross differences
Both Sexes			
Labor force	98.1	1.1	2.7
Employed	98.2	.9	2.6
Agriculture	94.7	1.8	8.8
Non-Agriculture	98.3	.8	2.5
Full time	98.6	−.6	3.5
Part time	89.0	6.7	15.2
Unemployed	87.7	3.8	20.8
Not in labor force	98.9	−1.4	3.5
Males			
Labor force	99.0	.5	1.4
Employed	99.0	.4	1.6
Agriculture	96.1	.6	7.2
Non-Agriculture	98.9	.4	1.8
Full time	98.9	−.5	2.8
Part time	88.4	6.3	16.9
Unemployed	90.1	2.5	17.3
Not in labor force	97.9	−2.1	6.2
Females			
Labor force	96.3	2.2	5.1
Employed	96.7	2.0	4.6
Agriculture	89.1	6.5	15.2
Non-Agriculture	97.2	1.7	3.9
Full time	97.9	−.8	5.1
Part time	89.6	7.1	13.7
Unemployed	83.7	6.1	26.5
Not in labor force	99.2	−1.2	2.8

NOTE: All figures refer to differences "after reconciliation," i.e., after screening out apparent differences by checking for real differences with respondents. In any category let N_1 be the number in first interview, N_2 the number in second, and N the number identically reported in both.

Column 1 reports $N/N_2 \times 100$

Column 2 reports $(N_2-N_1)/N_2 \times 100$

Column 3 reports $(N_1 + N_2-2N)/N_2 \times 100$.

SOURCE: U.S. Bureau of the Census, *Supplementary Statement No. 4 to Committee to Appraise Employment and Unemployment Statistics*, February 13, 1962, Tables 1, 3A.

month changes are usually smaller (in absolute terms), or of the same size as those in the figures themselves. (Errors for differences between figures more than one month apart are not computed.) The commendable and rare practice of publishing standard errors allows users of the statistics to assess better the significance of the figures.

In general, the standard errors of the statistics are small. For instance, the standard error of the number employed is only about one-third of 1%.[15] However, for the smaller categories and, of course, for small changes, they become substantial. For example, for unemployment, the standard error of one hundred thousand is, on a figure of unemployment of four million, 2½%. Roughly, the unemployment percentage figure would be subject to a standard error of about .15, i.e., a standard error of about 3% of an unemployment rate of 5%. On the average, in one case out of twenty, errors in month-to-month changes of the unemployment rate will exceed three-tenths of a percentage point. These are still small errors, but it is not unusual to find statements based on the implicit assumption that the figures are even a great deal more accurate than is the case.

There are other sources of error in the labor force statistics. We mention three: (1) failure to obtain responses from a small proportion of designated sampling units (cf. footnote 3); (2) the population estimates used in the estimation procedure to weight the sample returns so as to bring the sample into close conformity with known distributions of population characteristics.[16] This technique may well improve the reliability of estimates. However, errors may be introduced through independent population estimates if there are errors in the decennial census reports or in the interpolations made during the periods

[15] It should hardly be necessary to point out that the error in the number of employed is not the same thing as the error in the number of unemployed, nor in the unemployment rate, but C. Clark in his review of the first edition of this book (*Econometrica*, vol. 20, no. 1, January 1952, pp. 105–106) made this mistake when he concluded from the estimate of error in the number of employed of 6 percent, then cited, that ". . . in some year for which unemployment was estimated at 10 percent of the labor force, there may in fact have been a situation of virtually full employment without our knowing it." Such a conclusion was wholly unwarranted both by the nature of the estimates of error and by our discussion.

[16] Cf. *Current Population Reports*, Series P–23, no. 5, pp. 7–8.

between censuses which are then carried over to the weights used in making population estimates on the basis of the sample results; (3) as occurs with all statistics, processing errors may occur in the handling of the data despite the quality control program of the Census Bureau, though it is probable that errors arising from this source are negligible.

5. REPORT OF THE PRESIDENT'S COMMITTEE

After most of this chapter had been prepared, the report of the President's Committee to Appraise Employment and Unemployment Statistics, *Measuring Employment and Unemployment* (Washington, 1962) appeared. This report contains a detailed, well-balanced appraisal of the presently available statistics. Among other things, it describes and evaluates the definitions and concepts used, the various series available, the consistency shown by the various series, the statistical procedures and the problems of sampling reliability, and seasonal adjustment, even employing spectral analysis for this part of the evaluation.

The Committee made a number of conclusions and recommendations, especially for research into aspects of labor force statistics. By and large, the Committee approved the concepts and procedures of the household survey, though believing there might still be room for improvement, and that more detail should be acquired about characteristics of some categories. The Committee was "convinced that the technical procedures utilized to provide employment and unemployment statistics are reasonably appropriate, given the practical circumstances under which the data are produced." Recommendations, however, were made for strengthening the employer survey and to enlarge the household survey sample over the next ten years tenfold to improve the accuracy of the statistics, especially in connection with smaller categories and changes in figures over time. The increasing demand for greater detail and separate geographic area tabulations was the principal reason for the Committee's recommendation. However, such an increase would also improve the accuracy of the statistics substantially and it is difficult to know whether the latter was not also a strong secondary motive in the extraordinary, tenfold, increase in the sample. Expansion taking the form of supplementary surveys and the development of a second panel to be used for special studies and for checking the main survey were endorsed. Bold research with seasonal adjustment problems was recommended and is certainly necessary.

The Committee's report forms a very valuable addition to the material available on employment statistics and is a fine example of the sort of appraisal that needs to be made if users of economic statistics are to be sufficiently informed to make worthwhile use of statistics.

6. HISTORICAL NOTE

The series discussed in this chapter do not go back much before the Second World War, with the exception of the Bureau of Labor Statistics series which, in various forms, have somewhat longer coverage. Prior to 1940, a variety of private estimates were available. Some of the more widely cited ones are reproduced in Table 20 from a compilation presented in Woytinsky.[17] The spread in estimates tells its own story—there is no reliable time series of employment data extending into the 1930's. Yet one should note again the five digit "accuracy."

A recent attempt by S. Lebergott to derive an American unemployment series since 1900 yields numerous interesting contrasts with the results of the well-known series derived much earlier by the National Industrial Conference Board and by Paul Douglas.[18] The three series, shown in Table 21 for 1900 to 1930, are sufficient added indication of the obstacles confronting historical investigations of the United States labor force, even in the fairly recent past. In particular, the annual percentage changes implied by the alternative series often differ by enormous margins. If we assume that Lebergott's estimates

[17] W. S. Woytinsky and Associates, *Employment and Wages in the United States* (New York: The Twentieth Century Fund, 1953), p. 716.

[18] Cf. S. Lebergott, "Estimates of Unemployment in the United States," in National Bureau of Economic Research, *The Measurement and Behavior of Unemployment* (Princeton, 1957).

TABLE 20

Estimates of Unemployment, 1929–1940
(in thousands)

Year (1)	American Federation of Labor (2)	Congress of Industrial Organizations (3)	National Industrial Conference Board (4)	Robert Nathan (5)	Alexander Hamilton Institute (6)	Labor Research Association[a] (7)	Cleveland Trust (8)	National Research League[b] (9)	Daniel Carson (10)
1929	1,864	1,831	429	1,752	3,456	—	—	1,250	1,910
1930	4,735	4,710	2,896	4,646	6,929	—	4,124	—	4,825
1931	8,568	8,322	7,037	8,118	10,939	—	8,777	9,800	8,725
1932	12,870	12,120	11,385	11,639	14,727	16,783	13,416	12,880	13,100
1933	13,271	12,643	11,842	11,942	14,394	16,138	14,098	16,750	13,700
1934	11,424	10,845	9,761	9,998	12,419	16,824	12,130	15,110	12,115
1935	10,652	10,050	9,092	9,102	11,629	16,658	—	14,950	11,240
1936	9,395	8,756	7,386	7,723	10,009	14,751	—	—	10,000
1937	8,282	8,109	6,403	6,856	8,366	14,825	—	—	9,235
1938	10,836	11,030	9,796	9,865	11,934	16,368	—	—	—
1939	9,979	10,813	8,786	9,835	10,696	—	—	—	—
1940	9,104	10,276	7,607	9,552	9,379	—	—	—	—

NOTES: [a] Estimates as of November, except 1938, which is as of April.
[b] Estimates as of January, except 1929, which is as of September.

SOURCE: W. S. Woytinsky and Associates, *Employment and Wages in the United States* (New York: The Twentieth Century Fund, 1953), p. 716.

TABLE 21

THREE SERIES OF AVERAGE ANNUAL UNEMPLOYMENT
ESTIMATES, 1900 TO 1930

(in millions)

Year (1)	Lebergott (2)	National Industrial Conference Board (3)	Douglas (4)
1900	1.4	1.6	.8
1901	.7	1.7	.6
1902	.8	.5	.6
1903	.8	1.5	.6
1904	1.5	1.4	.9
1905	1.0	.6	.6
1906	.3	−.1	.6
1907	.6	.8	.7
1908	3.0	2.3	1.7
1909	1.9	.7	.9
1910	2.2	.6	.8
1911	2.3	1.6	1.0
1912	2.0	.9	.8
1913	1.7	1.0	.9
1914	3.1	2.2	1.9
1915	3.8	2.4	1.8
1916	1.9	.2	.8
1917	1.9	−1.9	.8
1918	.6	−3.1	.7
1919	1.0	−.9	.9
1920	1.7	.6	.9
1921	5.0	4.8	2.9
1922	3.2	2.9	2.3
1923	1.4	.7	1.0
1924	2.4	2.0	1.5
1925	1.8	.8	1.1
1926	.9	.5	1.0
1927	1.9	1.6	
1928	2.1	1.9	
1929	1.6	.4	
1930	4.3	2.9	

NOTE: Negative values in NICB series arise from estimating unemployment as a residual. Series by Douglas covers manufacturing, mining, transportation and construction.

SOURCE: S. Lebergott, "Annual Estimates of Unemployment in the United States, 1900–1954," in National Bureau of Economic Research, *The Measurement and Behavior of Unemployment* (Princeton: Princeton University Press, 1957), p. 218.

are approximately accurate, at least the details of our "history of cycles" would have to be substantially rewritten.

7. DETERMINING "FULL EMPLOYMENT" FIGURES

The great political significance of labor statistics has at least two indications. There is first the obvious one, i.e., the directly accessible fact that unemployed are sometimes numerous; in times of great crises they and their misery are the strongest, most visible sign of a deficiency of the economic system. Sometimes there are hardly any persons out of work, there is a "labor shortage." It shows up in the fact that for jobs there are no applicants, i.e., that for many occupations there are more jobs available then men willing to take them. The second, more indirect indication is the variation of the percentage of unemployed in the total labor force, a figure that is carefully watched, argued about and made the subject of policy measures. The success of a policy of full employment—in some countries, such as the United States, a formal obligation of the Government—is measured by this figure.

There is no need to discuss the directly apparent aspects of unemployment; that shall be left to the sociologists, who at any rate have problems of accuracy far in excess of those of the economists—and have faced up to them even less. But there remains the issue of the reliability of the percentage which determines "full employment." However good the unemployment statistics are, they do contain errors. The sampling procedure is good, but errors must needs persist.

The data of the actual numbers employed are unquestionably also subject to doubt. The numbers given for both employed and unemployed, obtained by using weights derived from the decennial census, are subject to considerable error. Lest this be doubted, the reader is reminded of the deficiencies in counting total populations. These specific counts, conducted at great expense and with great competence, have erred, involving (in the United States) several millions of persons, most of them in the labor force age group (cf. above and Chapter XIV, p. 258, and the literature quoted there). It is notorious that population counts in other countries—and *a fortiori* counts of the working force—are seldom better than in the United States.

In many underdeveloped countries, including China, they are at best educated guesses. While this will not affect ratios of figures derived from samples directly, it still leaves considerable uncertainties in other aspects of the figures.

But even in the United States and in Western European countries, such percentages are computed by dividing one indeterminate number by another indeterminate number. Both numbers have a variance, a distribution; both are statistical variables; so their division produces again a statistical variable (cf. the discussion in Chapter VII). The idea that a precisely stated percentage, computed no matter for which country, has any similarly precise meaning has to be rejected. The same is the case with the comparison of successively computed percentages. Only very limited value can be attributed to observed variations, as is explained in more detail below when growth rates are discussed (Chapter XV) and their great limitations are shown.

Current usage does not view the percentage of unemployed in this manner. The Government and its critics are both guilty of an exaggerated interpretation of data, making their own existence both more difficult or easier as the particular, supposed development might happen to go. In addition, in publications on economics by professional writers the same addiction to these numbers prevails which are used as if they represented faultless measurements of a precision and reliability which would be the envy of most other sciences.

It is not uncommon, indeed it is frequent, to find the government making strong statements about developments in unemployment over periods as short as *one* (!) month. The nation's largest or most important newspapers play up a "drop" in the unemployment rate, say from 5.8% to 5.5% as a highly significant event and the Secretary of Labor will not hesitate to make speeches on that occasion.[19] All this is done on the basis of "seasonal correction" and dealing with figures given to four "significant" digits. It is, of course, clear that statements of this kind are completely devoid of the meaning attributed to them.

---

[19] Cf., for example, the report in *The New York Times* or the *Wall Street Journal* on November 1, 1962.

8. INTERNATIONAL COMPARISONS

The very importance attached to unemployment rates carries over to the question of their international comparability. If comparisons could be made with confidence, we would possess an important measure for describing the relative state of different economies.

Considerations in the preceding chapters, as well as the more specific study in Section 8 of Chapter XIV below, show that international comparisons are always difficult. The study of foreign trade has proved this in particular, dealing with an area where they ought to be easy to make. The strong political undertones in any discussion of unemployment and the wide differences in the structure of the labor markets in various countries make it *a priori* likely that unemployment figures cannot be compared easily. But numerous adjustments, seemingly harmless and merely statistical, are made and the conclusion is arrived at that even unemployment rates can be put on a comparable basis, though countries differ as widely as the United States and Italy. This is the opinion of the above-mentioned President's Committee which is based on a detailed study of international comparability prepared for it by the Bureau of Labor Statistics.

How such optimistic views can be maintained is difficult to see when even for the United States divergent series are presented and the United States sample is found to be inadequate by the same commission to the extent that its tenfold (!) increase is recommended in order to give us more trustworthy information of much greater detail than we now possess. The entire discussion of unemployment rates for different countries is carried on as if the figures for the number of unemployed and those for the labor force were entirely free from error. Yet this is not the case. The errors in different countries vary for each of the two components and again from country to country. Hence the ratios have widely varying properties that are completely neglected in stating that the rate is, say 6.9% for the United States and 0.9% for France, be they "adjusted" or not. Even if there were no such uncertainties there still remains the fundamental fact that being unemployed means very different things in different countries.

The point is not to compare some dubious and primitive statistical ratios but to compare complex economic phenomena in a meaningful manner.

❧ CHAPTER XIV ☙

NATIONAL INCOME STATISTICS

1. INTRODUCTION

"The official national income estimates prepared by the . . . Department of Commerce . . . have become widely accepted in this country and abroad by professional and lay users alike. The publication of new estimates is front page news . . . and the business and financial world eagerly awaits their arrival. Such a reception of a body of economic data is almost unprecedented—it can be explained only on the basis that income and product accounts help satisfy the urgent need for informative statistical data on current economic developments. . . . The wide use of the accounts places a serious obligation on national income analysts both inside and outside the government. The concepts, methodology and estimates underlying the estimates affect their meaning and their movements, and deficiencies in any one of these elements can lead to misleading results."[1]

IN THIS CHAPTER we shall examine the question of the accuracy of the national income estimates. Many of our comments also apply to aggregative measures in general, although we shall be specifically dealing with the difficulties confronted in the estimation of national income.

Our concern will be primarily with data for the United States, because they are plentiful; and American writers have been pioneers in the establishment of national income statistics. The problems can be most clearly seen in examining American statistics. Later, in Section (8), we shall also refer to British data and their errors. There the situation is similar: great efforts, important contributions, eminent authors involved. Yet there are like results: great errors, many revisions of estimates, lack of convergence of the revisions. Space forbids going into the study of the statistics of additional countries. But it is safe to say that it would be only by extraordinary circumstances that the efforts in other countries were more successful. In fact, it is clear that

---

[1] *A Critique of the United States Income and Product Accounts,* Studies in Income and Wealth, Vol. 22, National Bureau of Economic Research (Princeton, 1958), p. 3.

if the United States and the United Kingdom cannot produce better national income statistics than they do, those of others will, in general, not even come near their quality. This is certainly true of the underdeveloped regions of the world, which, though not containing the largest parts of the world's incomes, do comprise the greatest number of people. It is simply technically impossible for national income statistics of Africa, South and Central America, and Asia to be *better* than those of the United States and the United Kingdom. Even if a few were in some specific sense of the same quality, that would neither satisfy nor affect the specific problems of their comparability (see below, Section 9).

In recent years, the trend in economics has been toward the collection of vast aggregates of data. These aggregates present large problems in estimation,[2] for they require data on parts of the economy which are not fully explored and about which there is still little precise information. Therefore all sorts of ingenious (and often inexact) devices are employed for arriving at estimates of these relatively unknown components. As a result of these uncertainties, the aggregates are frequently of dubious accuracy. All this is mitigated only by a general hope— seldom specified and never proved—that errors in components will cancel out and that we would get an acceptable total. Whether the errors are "large" or not depends, of course, on the uses to which the statistics are to be put, as will be mentioned more specifically below.

2. Concepts of National Income

In the notion of a "national income," most difficulties of economics culminate. The "Wealth of Nations" has been the prime

[2] In view of the often immense practical-political consequences of showing one rather than another figure for national income, in order to arrive at a "suitable" number the use of deceptive and political methods similar to those mentioned in Part I is not unheard of. So the national income of Japan was *negotiated* between the Japanese Government and the American Occupation Forces shortly after the last war, as reported by M. Bronfenbrenner in his review of the first edition of this book (cf. *Land Economics*, February 1952, p. 82). The reason was, of course, that the amount agreed upon influenced the size of economic assistance by the United States. Have these figures entered later econometric research? What other, similar, instances could be mentioned?

concern of economists as long as there has been any systematic writing in economics, and so it will be for the future. Neither the conceptual nor the statistical problems in this field have been resolved to anyone's satisfaction, though a great deal of progress has been made in both respects. The two areas are interdependent, since nothing can be measured for which there exist no good concepts, and concepts, no matter how precise, are of little practical value if the corresponding measurements cannot be performed. The literature in this field is immense and comprises most of the famous names of the discipline. It is clearly impossible to survey it, or even to list the most important works.[3] We shall limit ourselves to a brief discussion of those principal points that are of direct relevance for the evaluation of errors of measurement and reliability of basic data. Besides S. Kuznets, at least the names of M. A. Copeland, M. Gilbert, G. Jaszi, and I. Kravis should be mentioned for this country. All have in various ways beneficially influenced the National Income Division of the Department of Commerce, the basic source of all American figures.

In the following, no attempt is made even to list all conceptual difficulties. Instead, only those are mentioned in which problems of errors arise strongly. Some of these problems are discussed elsewhere in this study (e.g., regarding the volume

[3] Apart from early classical works and the literature associated with I. Fisher, A. C. Pigou, V. Pareto, and others, there are the efforts of the National Bureau of Economic Research, where S. Kuznets has been, and still is, one of the prime movers. A survey, still of value, is Kuznets' "National Income," *Encyclopedia of the Social Sciences* (1933), reprinted in *Readings in the Theory of Income Distribution* (American Economic Association, 1946), where there is found an extensive Bibliography. Particular mention is deserved by the important and massive work of Paul Studenski, *The Income of Nations, Theory, Measurement, and Analysis: Past and Present* (New York, 1958). The book contains vast amounts of valuable information about the history, methods, and results of income measurements. The question of accuracy for different methods and countries is discussed on pp. 254–264. For the rest we refer to the more than 25 volumes, *Studies in Income and Wealth* (National Bureau of Economic Research). This large number speaks tellingly of the effort that has been made in the United States alone. Similar efforts have been made in Great Britain and other countries, where gradually more means are being put to the task as the economies expand, new scholarly talent becomes available, and the uses increase to which governments and private interests try to put these statistics.

and value of agricultural or mining output, or regarding the reliability of price statistics, etc.), but even for these our mention is only of an illustrative nature.

We can limit ourselves to the few following comments on concepts because we assume the reader to be reasonably well acquainted with the manner in which the Gross National Product is obtained, and how it differs from Net National Product, National Income, Personal Income, etc. But in order to have the respective relationships and magnitudes before us, Table 22 shows the composition of Gross National Product for 1961.

(a) *Imputation of value,* perhaps *the* classical problem of economic theory, had not been resolved until in the theory of games a satisfactory solution was found.[4] In the present case,

TABLE 22

COMPOSITION OF GROSS NATIONAL PRODUCT, 1961
($ billion)

*Gross national product**		518.7
Less:	Capital consumption allowances	45.3
Equals:	*Net national product*	473.4
Less:	Indirect business tax and nontax liability	48.2
	Business transfer payments	2.1
	Statistical discrepancy	–3.1
Plus:	Subsidies minus current surplus of government enterprise	1.7
Equals:	*National income*	427.8
Less:	Corporate profits and inventory valuation adjustment	45.5
	Contributions for social insurance	21.6
	Excess of wage accruals over disbursements	0.0
Plus:	Government transfer payments to persons	31.3
	Net interest paid by government	7.3
	Dividends	15.0
	Business transfer payments	2.1
Equals:	*Personal income*	416.4
Less:	Personal tax and nontax payments	52.8
Equals:	*Disposable personal income*	363.6
Less:	Personal consumption expenditures	338.1
Equals:	*Personal savings*	25.6

SOURCE: *Survey of Current Business,* July 1962, pp. 6–8.
* Individual items may not add to totals due to rounding.

[4] By means of the characteristic function of an *n*-person game, expressing the non-additivity of the phenomenon of value. From there it is, of course, still a long way to the statistics of national income!

the problem is to assign to goods and services produced a measure largely derived from money flows. But if money does not flow, this does not mean that income which is not being recorded is not being generated. This is an old problem. A classical illustration is that of persons living in houses they own themselves. If these same houses were owned by others, rent would have to be paid (in money, goods, or services), thereby swelling the national product. To avoid this, a value has to be imputed to owner-occupancy. This is, obviously, a tricky affair, with less certain results than finding out about rent payments made in money. These estimates are uncertain and many arbitrary decisions have to be made. To speak here of "accuracy" is difficult, since alternative records and procedures do not exist; the question is primarily one of procedure. Other items have to be treated similarly, e.g., unmarketed food consumed on farms. This item should show a sharp decrease (a) with a falling farm population and (b) with agricultural production geared for sale and farmers buying larger parts of their food in stores. At earlier times (and now still in other countries) this would have been quite different. To the extent that the National Income Division uses a limited welfare concept, i.e., imputes only for a few such cases, it depresses the total. The more price- and market-oriented a country is, the smaller is the imputation problem; on the other hand, in the United States most people live in owner occupied houses for which "rent" is a very uncertain figure. The less developed a country is, the larger looms the imputation problem. In those (underdeveloped) countries statistics in general are of poorer quality, thus compounding the problem.

Difficulties of this type are quite common; they become especially important when comparisons over time or among differently organized countries are to be made. Trivial as it may seem, the disappearance of domestic help increases the imputation problem. Insofar as domestic help is replaced by housewives' labor which does not involve money payments, national income will be depressed. Of course, if the domestic help released enters the industrial labor force, national income will rise again, perhaps even above its former level. Obviously, there will be errors in both counts, and their nature and distribution will remain obscure. There are countless other illustrations.

(b) The treatment of *government services* involves another characteristic difficulty. National income is a monetary magnitude; for the private sector, the pricing mechanism is a suitable mechanism by which to value the final amount of goods and services. For the government sector, the pricing mechanism often offers no clue about the *value* of final output. For example, how should the contribution to the national product made by expenditures on national defense, on highways, or on schools, etc., be evaluated? A related problem is the question of the "intermediate output" of the government. It is sometimes argued that part of the government output should not be treated as final, since it has utility only insofar as it affects the private sector—e.g., government highway building derives much of its value from the use that business makes of roads, say in the distribution of goods. It forms the overhead of society's capital. If this were somehow valued, there would be the additional problem of depreciation of this capital investment. These problems are familiar from Capital Theory and the Theory of Public Finance where the role of "social" capital has always been one still awaiting resolution.

Defense expenditures pose another difficulty because they raise the question: Is there any positive utility gained from national defense? Those who accept the welfare concept of the treatment of government in the national accounts believe that national defense does not add to the standard of living. Such expenditures would therefore merely represent a kind of intermediate expenditure, necessary to provide the conditions in which the private sector can adequately function. Under the welfare concept, therefore, the output of the governmental sector should not be valued at factor cost as is the current practice; rather that proportion which does not go toward increasing the standard of living should be considered as intermediate and therefore not be included. In general, the National Income Division totally rejects this viewpoint and argues that government output should best be valued at *factor cost*. Kuznets, on the other hand, is much closer to "welfare concepts" and therefore believes that some provision for double counting should be made.[5]

(c) The main problem in getting from gross national product to national income is posed by the *depreciation allowances*. (The other element, indirect taxes, is determined with relative accuracy.) Estimates of depreciation are made by corporations themselves, guided by the rather unrealistic assumptions underlying the tax laws and their own often inappropriate ideas (e.g., lack of understanding of the process of inflation). It would be difficult to argue that such methods as "double declining balance" and "sum of the years digits," lifo and fifo, present a realistic appraisal of the depreciation of capital that actually takes place in the economy in a given time interval. The effects of price changes on profits and depreciation estimates are a further problem.

Another main conceptual difficulty which leads to problems in making the actual estimates is the valuation of services performed by financial intermediaries and the imputed interest that arises therefrom.

This list could be lengthened greatly. What has been said suffices, however, to show that conceptual differences held among statisticians at different times and in different countries are bound to have decisive influence upon these statistics. Depending on the choice of one concept rather than of another, the phenomena thus defined have their own error characteristics.

Given these difficulties, it is easy to understand that conceptual changes are frequent. They account for many of the almost continuous revisions, some of them very substantial, as inspection of Table 23 will show. One must also ask whether it is the constantly changing nature of the economy that calls for these conceptual revisions or whether they are an expression of our inability to settle conceptual issues.

[5] S. Kuznets, "Discussion of the New Department of Commerce Income Series, National Income: A New Version," *Review of Economics and Statistics*, xxx, August 1948, pp. 151–179. See also Volume 22 of the National Bureau of Economic Research Series, *Studies in Income and Wealth*, for an explanation and justification of Kuznets' definition of government output as tax revenues minus transfers.

TABLE 23

U.S. National Income Revisions

(As reported in *Survey of Current Business*)

($ billions)

	1947	1948	1949	1950	1951	1952	1953	1954	1955	1956	1957	1958	1959	1960	1961
Feb. '48	202.6														
July '48	*202.5														
Feb. '49	202.5	224.4													
July '49	*201.7	*226.2													
Feb. '50	201.7	226.2	221.5												
July '50	*198.7	*223.5	*216.8												
Feb. '51	198.7	223.5	216.8	235.6											
July '51	198.7	223.5	*216.7	*239.0											
*1951	198.7	223.5	216.7	239.0											
Feb. '52	198.7	223.5	216.7	239.0	275.8										
July '52	198.7	223.5	*216.3	*239.2	*277.6										
Feb. '53	198.7	223.5	216.3	239.2	277.6	290.4									
July '53	198.7	223.5	216.3	*240.6	*278.4	*291.6									
Feb. '54	198.7	223.5	216.3	240.6	278.4	291.6	307.7								
July '54	*197.2	*221.6	*216.2	*240.0	*277.0	*291.0	*305.0								
Feb. '55	197.2	221.6	216.2	240.0	277.0	291.0	305.0	300.0							
July '55	197.2	221.6	216.2	240.0	277.0	*289.6	*303.6	299.7							

(*Cont.*)

TABLE 23 (*Cont.*)

U.S. NATIONAL INCOME REVISIONS

(As reported in *Survey of Current Business*)

($ billions)

	1947	1948	1949	1950	1951	1952	1953	1954	1955	1956	1957	1958	1959	1960	1961
Feb. '56	197.2	221.6	216.2	240.0	277.0	*289.5	303.6	299.7	322.3						
July '56	197.2	221.6	216.2	240.0	277.0	*290.2	*302.1	*298.3	*324.0						
Feb. '57	197.2	221.6	216.2	240.0	277.0	290.2	302.1	298.3	324.0	342.4					
July '57	197.2	221.6	216.2	240.0	277.0	290.2	302.1	*299.0	*324.1	*343.6					
Feb. '58	197.2	221.6	216.2	240.0	277.0	290.2	302.1	299.0	324.1	343.6	358.0				
***July '58	*198.2	*223.5	*217.7	*241.9	*279.3	*292.2	*305.6	*301.8	*330.2	*349.4	*364.0				
Feb. '59	198.2	223.5	217.7	241.9	279.3	292.2	305.6	301.8	330.2	349.4	364.0	360.5			
July '59	198.2	223.5	217.7	241.9	279.3	292.2	305.6	301.8	330.2	*350.8	*366.5	*366.2			
Feb. '60	198.2	223.5	217.7	241.9	279.3	292.2	305.6	301.8	330.2	350.8	366.5	366.2	398.5		
July '60	198.2	223.5	217.7	241.9	279.3	292.2	305.6	301.8	330.2	350.8	*366.9	*367.7	*399.6		
Feb. '61	198.2	223.5	217.7	241.9	279.3	292.2	305.6	301.8	330.2	350.8	366.9	367.7	399.6	417.1	
July '61	198.2	223.5	217.7	241.9	279.3	292.2	305.6	301.8	330.2	350.8	366.9	*367.4	399.6	417.1	
Apr. '62	198.2	223.5	217.7	241.9	279.3	292.2	305.6	301.8	330.2	350.8	366.9	367.4	399.6	417.1	430.2

* Indicates change.

** 1951 Supplement to *Survey of Current Business*.

*** Major revision in 1958.

3. Types of Errors

There are three principal types of error in the statistics of national income. *First,* there are the errors introduced in the basic data of production or expenditure for the separate industries and other economic activities. These data may arise from sampling investigations—in which case there would be the usual statistical sampling errors—or from mass enumeration. There will be difficulties in taking the proper count. Studies of the accuracy of foreign trade, mining, and agriculture give an idea of the substantial magnitude of the errors to be expected in these components.

Second, error may be produced independently of enumeration or sampling difficulties. These errors result from the effort to fit the available statistics to the conceptual framework of the aggregate. The accuracy and the success of an estimate is conditioned by the quality and quantity of the primary data. In some cases, the existing data are not collected in a form directly suitable for use in estimating gross national product or one of its component items. For example, the Census Bureau's industrial enumerations and sample surveys do not provide adequate information on industry purchases of intermediate goods which must be netted from industry sales figures for gross national product purposes.[6] Most of the national income and product estimates are based on government-produced statistics, which must be assembled and adjusted to build up the income and output measures. For example, some data that become available from government agencies are a by-product of their administrative functions.[7] This is frequently a very strong reason to suspect the quality of data obtained in this manner.

Third, since not all basic data are available, another type of error is introduced in trying to fill in the gaps for those industries and years where estimates are not known. Methods such as interpolation, extrapolation, use of imputed weights, in-

[6] U.S. Department of Commerce, Office of Business Economics, *U.S. Income and Output,* A Supplement to the *Survey of Current Business* (Washington, 1958), p. 66. (This will hereafter be cited as *U.S. Income and Output.*)

[7] *U.S. Income and Output,* p. 70.

serted trends, and "blowing up" of sample data are used in order to fill in missing data which introduce uncertainties of their own. Such gaps are particularly noteworthy for underdeveloped countries which produce only partial statistics or for countries such as the Soviet Union where statistics of certain sectors are withheld for political and other reasons or could not be obtained because of the effects of war and revolution. This third source of error is, therefore, of great significance in international comparisons of national incomes and figures derived from them, such as growth rates, investment rates, etc.

4. MEASUREMENT OF ERROR

These three basic possibilities for error are present to a greater or lesser extent in each of the components. National income is a total of composites which differ in reliability from sector to sector and year to year, and hence the error of the composite is a "complex amalgam of errors in the parts whose magnitude is not easily determined."[8] The National Income Division of the Department of Commerce provides no measure of the possible error, taking the position that "meaningful mathematical measures of reliability cannot be calculated for national income statistics; only a frank evaluation of the sources and methods underlying them can provide the understanding which is needed for their effective use in economic analysis."[9] Any quantitative estimate is left to the user of the statistics based on his knowledge of the sources and methods as provided by the U.S. Income and Output and 1954 National Income supplements. The national income is built up of so many cells, and since there may be several types of error operating in each cell (for each cell may be the composite of many series), a variety of procedures must be used in compressing the economic activities of the nation into the accounting framework.

We have seen that conceptual differences play an important role in casting doubt upon the accuracy of any one statistic over

[8] S. Kuznets, "Discussion of the New Department of Commerce Income Series, National Income: A New Version," *op. cit.*

[9] *U.S. Income and Output*, p. 48.

the others that are available and over the previous unrevised estimates. However, as yet, no one has arrived at a measure of the margins of errors which are inherent in the estimates of national income. These margins could only be stated by the agencies that collect the basic data or the compilers of the aggregates. Since most of these groups either seem to have ignored the problem, or simply refuse to deal with it systematically, it becomes impossible for the user to determine with what confidence he may employ the data. The fact that little or nothing is said about accuracy[10] is more dangerous than if the margins of error were frankly stated to be very high. This is particularly important in view of the great and increasing importance attached to national income figures in policy making.

To throw the burden of estimating the errors and the reliability upon the user, though exceedingly convenient for the maker, is a totally inadmissible procedure. How can the individual user be expected to accomplish something where the government with its vast resources fails? This kind of evasion is also frequently encountered, as we have seen, in other fields of government statistics. It either shows that one is lacking in clear ideas and procedures or does not dare to use them since they would show up the tremendous limitations of the figures which the government itself uses freely in the pursuit of its business. It certainly demonstrates that those who attempt to place the burden of proof on the reader or user have only an inadequate idea of proper scientific procedure.[11]

---

[10] British authorities, in charge of putting together national income statistics, have officially classified categories of quality (cf. below, section 8). On the other hand, as I am reliably informed by Erwin von Beckerath, the German Government has expressly forbidden that errors of components of national income statistics be indicated by the government agencies responsible for producing these data!

[11] We might, at this point, recall the discussion of autocorrelation of errors (Part I). It is frequently maintained that national income statistics may be subject to a very considerable bias or that errors in these statistics are highly autocorrelated. Though this may well be true, there can be little doubt that national income statistics are subject to considerable margins of error which do not have this convenient property, and these errors must render small changes in the figures meaningless.

5. DIRECT ESTIMATES OF ERROR BY EXPERT JUDGMENT

The most important study on margins of error in national income estimates that has been made so far is by Simon Kuznets.[12] It has pointed the way for future work. Kuznets considered the aggregate national income as composed of 520 cells (40 industries, 13 income and employment categories). Then he and two of his co-workers attempted to classify each of these entries according to its margin of error. The possible margins of error were grouped into four categories:

I.	5–10%	with average of	7.5%
II.	11–20%	"	"	" 15%
III.	21–40%	"	"	" 30%
IV.	41–80%	"	"	" 60%

and for each cell each of these three investigators made independent classifications. An average was taken of their judgments[13] and the deviation between them was noted. As a result a measure was obtained of the general magnitude of errors in each of the component estimates of national income as well as of the aggregate itself. (Estimates were judged both directly and by their component parts and the error for the direct estimate was in most cases noted to be lower because of cancellations.) From this classification, Kuznets distinguished three groups of industries according to the relative margins of error judged to be present in their estimates. *First*, with a margin of error well below 15 percent (in categories I and II above), were the basic manufacturing industries and public utilities—electric light and power, steam railroads, street railways, telephone, telegraph; *second*, with margins of error of about 15 percent but well below 30 percent, were agriculture, mining, manufactured gas, pipe

---

[12] S. Kuznets, *National Income and Its Composition*, National Bureau of Economic Research, 1942, Vol. II, Chapter 12.

[13] On the use of *judgment* in statistics and the construction of judgment indexes, cf. John W. Tukey, "Future of Data Analysis," Statistical Techniques Research Group, Section of Mathematical Statistics, Department of Mathematics, Princeton University, July 1961. Cf. also D. R. Cox, "The Use of a Concomitant Variable in Selecting an Experimental Design," *Biometrika*, 44 (1957), pp. 150–158, for the use of judgment indexes as competitors for covariance.

lines, trade, banking, insurance, and government—industries for which information is extensive but not complete; and *third* were industries with an error margin of about 30 percent and higher—construction, water transportation, real estate, direct service industries, and the miscellaneous division. Kuznets' estimates of these margins of error in the period 1919–1935 are shown in Table 24, which also compares his results with the average importance of each industrial division in the period 1919–1938. (Note that even so meticulous an investigator as Kuznets computes a mean of pure guesses to two decimals.)

In the examination of margins of error in estimates of number of employed and engaged, the same grouping of industries was noted.[14] However, in this case the total margin, which was found to be 16 percent, was expected to be an exaggeration, since it was judged by parts and therefore did not permit cancellations to take place.

The weighted margin of error for the estimate of national income was found to be about 20 percent by this method of averaging "expert guesses" of the components, and summing. However, Kuznets felt that this figure was exaggerated, that if interest and dividends were included in nationwide estimates of income, and if entrepreneurial withdrawals were combined with entrepreneurial net savings, there would be substantial cancellation in the error margins assigned to each component separately. Also, if the statistics of employee compensation were examined for the nationwide total, their error factor would be considerably reduced. As a result, Kuznets infers that an *average margin of error for national income estimates of about 10 percent* would be reasonable.[15]

Although Kuznets' evaluations are little more than "informed opinions," which are based on studies of the errors involved in interpolation and extrapolation, comparisons with estimates from other sources, and revisions of official data from time to time, they provide a method of finding margins of error in this

---

[14] S. Kuznets, *National Income and Its Composition,* pp. 501–537.

[15] A very well known and highly informed American statistician has recently stated that a ± 20 percent error in U.S. national income statistics is not implausible. Unfortunately, the text of his speech has not yet been released for publication.

TABLE 24

NET INCOME ORIGINATING, MARGIN OF ERROR BY INDUSTRIAL DIVISION, 1919–1935 AND RELATIVE IMPORTANCE OF DIVISION, 1919–1938

| | MARGIN OF ERROR | | | | |
| | Directly Estimated | | Estimated by Parts | | |
Industrial Division	Mean	Relative Deviation*	Mean	Relative Deviation	Percent of National Income
Group I					
Electric light and power	11.43	32	12.36	34	1.4
Manufacturing, total	9.45	36	9.76	17	21.0
Steam railroads, pullman and express	7.50	0	7.50	0	5.4
Street railways	10.98	29	11.06	30	0.74
Telephone	7.50	0	7.50	0	0.94
Telegraph	7.50	0	7.50	5	0.16
Group total					29.64
Group II					
Agriculture	12.40	40	24.32	99	9.6
Mining, total	13.10	45	17.94	29	2.2
Manufactured gas	17.90	27	20.32	30	0.25
Pipe lines	15.00	35	12.99	37	0.20
Trade	20.50	62	24.82	31	13.5
Banking	15.63	11	15.25	12	1.4
Insurance	14.80	2	17.56	5	1.6
Government, total	17.66	18	29.31	39	11.6
Group total					40.35
Group III					
Construction	26.91	12	28.36	8	3.8
Water transportation	27.27	14	26.26	17	0.73
Real estate	36.78	35	38.33	25	8.9
Service, total	27.27	14	39.10	9	12.6
Miscellaneous	54.56	14	49.36	12	4.0
Group total					30.03

* The relative deviation is $\frac{\sigma}{x} \times 100$.

SOURCE: S. Kuznets, *National Income and its Composition*, pp. 513–4; 166–7.

field where none has existed before. Since the data in national income studies are "partly a by-product of administrative activity, partly a result of direct observation of complex phenomena without controls designed to reduce the variations observed, the best that we can do is to express an opinion in quantitative form."[16]

Kuznets' observations are of critical importance. The judgments and very carefully considered estimates of this eminent authority, in a field which he has helped so much to develop, touch on a class of economic statistics that are in wide use and employed for the most diverse purposes. The almost religious attention paid to "GNP"—it being continually used and quoted in the teaching of economics as well as in Government and in the business community—would lead one to expect that criticism would be reacted to sharply. This has not been the case. The textbooks on national income and macroeconomics show little if any evidence of awareness of these difficulties and limitations. The trade journals likewise go on accepting the statistics at face value and do not seem to be conscious of their severe limitations. This is a thoroughly unsatisfactory state.

The method described above may be very useful in future work in estimating margins of error. This is of particular interest for input-output tables which are, fundamentally, also accounts of national income. Input-output tables do, however, involve even finer measurements. If they could be fully justified, they would give more information directly useful for economics than the also highly desirable national income figures.

It behooves us to pause in order to see what even a 5 percent difference in national income means. Taking the United States and assuming a gross national product of about 550 billion dollars, this error equals ±30 billion dollars. This is more than twice the best annual sales of General Motors, the country's (and the world's) largest industrial corporation. It is far more than the total annual production of the entire electronics industry in the United States. Yet we have seen that a 10 percent error is even more reasonable: but that amounts to a plus or minus variation exceeding the entire defense budget of the nation, or it is about three times the total exports of the United States! The possible differences are, of course, not concentrated

[16] S. Kuznets, *National Income and Its Composition*, p. 535.

in the manner of these illustrations; instead they are scattered in an unknown way throughout all activities producing the national income. On the other hand, the reader, like everyone else, has probably become conditioned to accept economic data as being so highly accurate that even a mere 1–2 percent *variation* of national income is considered significant enough for making statements about "true" variations in the state of the economy. Yet 1–2 percent in gross national product are 5–10 billion dollars, and even that is an amount which few would judge irrelevant for the economy of the United States. On the contrary, these are amounts now used in order to estimate and predict the future performance of the entire economy and to justify far-reaching policy measures.

If it seems unreasonable to accept errors illustrated by such absolute magnitudes, the answer is that, as always, the burden of proof is on those who wish to continue using these (or any other) data in the traditional manner. Illustrations of the above kind are apparently needed, in order to stress the seriousness of the situation and to caution against the uncritical practices of the day, the mere mentioning of the percentages not having made the necessary impression. One should also recall the fact that the population census of 1950 for the United States failed to account[17] for the presence of approximately 5,000,000 persons. That is equivalent to the United States *not* possessing cities of the size of Chicago plus Detroit, which should certainly make some difference! And certainly the presence or absence of 5,000,000 people should make some difference in personal disposable income, or in gross national product, even if some of those omitted were children or infirm!

If, on the other hand, confidence in the published figures be maintained, i.e., the existence of errors or at least of errors of the above magnitudes be denied, then the procedures and methods of evaluating the statistics which have led to the above mentioned error estimates have to be rejected. That, too, would be a very serious matter, since it would be tantamount

[17] Cf. A. Coale and M. Zelnik, A *Study of White Births and Birth Rates in the United States, 1855–1934, and of Completeness of Enumeration in Decennial Censuses, 1880–1960.* (Scheduled for publication in 1963.)

to questioning large parts of present statistical theory. In the area of economic statistics, some problems have arisen that are, as yet, not even dealt with adequately in current statistical methodology.

The decision whether to accept the official figures or the error estimates is ultimately a matter of intuition. If the error estimates were to run as high as 50 percent, we would probably reject the method of arriving at such estimates. But is this point already reached at 5 or even 10 percent? This is most doubtful, and we will therefore have to accept living with data which are widely thought to be much better. In particular, we will have to accept the meaning of errors of this magnitude in the calculation of growth rates (cf. the following chapter).

To summarize: The rudimentary information obtained so far about errors in national income statistics shows that these important statistics are in especial need of decisive improvement. In particular, it should be stressed that the present exaggerated practical applications must be avoided. It is not unusual, for example, to consider changes in the national income figures of plus or minus one-tenth of one percent (or even less!) as significant for either theory or policy. In the face of the facts such procedure is completely void of meaning.

It is distressing to see that even the high-placed Council of Economic Advisors to the President engages in the practice of taking the figures for gross national product and national income at face value. In its entire history it appears never to have investigated their accuracy, and as a consequence draws wholly unwarranted "conclusions" from alleged one percent changes of these great aggregates. The same applies to their treatment of growth rates.

6. INCOME VS. PRODUCT

Gross national product totals are derived in two separate ways. One method is to sum the income of all the factors of production, i.e., employee compensation, profits, rent, net interest, and add indirect taxes, capital consumption allowances, and several minor items. Gross national product may be viewed also as the sum total of all expenditures paid out, and in this case it is the sum of expenditures for consumption, private domestic investment, government expenditures, and net foreign investment. If the counting were accurate, the income and product sides would exactly agree, as the sum of all incomes paid out in a given period must be equal to the sum total of all income received in that period. However, since in fact the two sides never balance exactly, there is a reconciling item termed "statistical discrepancy" which appears as an item in the national income accounts (by convention it is entered on the debit side). If the procedure of obtaining estimates of income and product is free from bias, the statistical discrepancy obtained from estimating income and product over the years should behave like a random error of measurement. In a study made a few years ago, the statistical properties of this discrepancy were examined. "Since the GNP estimates are built up from generally independent sources, the discrepancy may be taken to represent the net result of the numerous forces which introduce errors in the estimates of the detailed components on each side of the accounts."[18] However, while the discrepancy indicates that the totals do contain errors, it is taken by the National Income Division of the Department of Commerce to indicate a lack of consistency between the two sides and not as an absolute measure of the errors therein. If the National Income Division finds that the discrepancy is large or erratic in movement, the estimate is reexamined and attempts are made to trace and eliminate the source of the difference as far as possible.[19] But even though improvements may be made, a residual discrepancy remains. Gartaganis and Goldberger did find some indication of patterns of temporal interdependence in the estimates in some cases, particularly in the pre-1954 estimates.

[18] A. J. Gartaganis and A. S. Goldberger, "A Note on the Statistical Discrepancy in the National Accounts," *Econometrica*, Vol. 23, No. 2 (April 1955), pp. 166–173.

[19] For example, see the description of the revision of consumer expenditures in 1954 by the Department of Commerce, made when the discrepancy turned out to be a positive figure. The reexamination resulted in a scaling down of the initial calculation of consumer expenditures by 1½ percent of the 1954 total, or by $3½ billion. *U.S. Income and Output,* pp. 74–75.

7. Absolute Size of the Estimates, Relative Changes and Revisions

The problem of the accuracy of national income statistics may be viewed from two aspects. First, how good are the totals, i.e., what is the probability that the real national income figure falls within, say, plus or minus twenty billion dollars of the published estimate? Second, and more importantly from a practical point of view, is the question of the reliability of changes in direction (flow) of the various national income series from year to year or quarter to quarter.

(a) *Absolute magnitude.* The absolute size of national income depends primarily on the conceptual foundations of the measure (besides the effects of the problems due to sampling, interpolation, etc., alluded to above). We have mentioned above the complicated conceptual problems of imputation, measurement of the government's contribution to national income, inventory and depreciation treatment. We emphasize again that statistical measurement is only one part of the problem of the accuracy of national income statistics; conceptual difficulties prove to be no less plaguing.

The National Income Division laid the foundations for the present national income estimates in 1947, when revisions were made for the period 1929–1946, incorporating the conceptual framework and statistical methodology which were established in 1947. In Table 25(A.) we see the magnitude of adjustments in the revision of national income estimates in 1947. On the average, the total revision for this period is ±7.1 percent (this is for the entire period; we have chosen only a few years as illustrative) and the average statistical revision is ±1 percent. Changes due to differences in concept account for the major part of the revision,[20] but it can be seen that in some cases the statistical revision was of some importance. In 1946 there was a 4.2 percent increase over the earlier estimate, due to statistical revision, and in 1932 there was a decrease of 2 percent. On the other hand, revision due to changes in concept pro-

---

[20] This statement is, of course, only plausible under the assumption that the basic underlying figures which enter into different conceptual frameworks, are usable. Whether this is the case or not is a separate question.

TABLE 25

COMPARISON OF ESTIMATES OF NATIONAL INCOME

A. *Reconciliation of New and Old Series of National Income: 1947 Adjustments[1] 1929–1946 ($ billions)*

1929–1934	1929	1930	1931	1932	1933	1934
National income (new)	87.4	75.0	58.9	41.7	39.6	48.6
National income (old)	83.3	68.9	54.5	40.0	42.3	49.5
Total revision	+4.1	+6.1	+4.4	+1.7	−2.7	−0.9
Amount of revision due to concept changes	+4.4	+6.7	+5.1	+2.5	−2.1	−0.6
Statistical revision	−0.3	−0.6	−0.7	−0.8	−0.6	−0.3
Total revision as % of old series	+4.9	+8.9	+8.1	+4.3	−6.4	−1.8
Revision due to concept changes as % of old series*	+5.3	+9.7	+9.4	+6.3	−5.0	−1.2
Statistical revision as % of old series*	−0.4	−0.9	−1.3	−2.0	−1.4	−0.6

1935–1940	1935	1936	1937	1938	1939	1940
National income (new)	56.8	64.7	73.6	67.4	72.5	81.3
National income (old)	55.7	64.9	71.5	64.2	70.8	77.6
Total revision	+1.1	−0.2	+2.1	+3.2	+1.7	+3.7
Amount of revision due to concept changes	+1.3	+0.2	+2.3	+3.1	+1.3	+3.6
Statistical revision	−0.2	−0.4	−0.2	+0.1	+0.4	+0.1
Total revision as % of old series	+2.0	−0.3	+2.9	+5.0	+2.4	+4.8
Revision due to concept changes as % of old series*	+2.3	+0.3	+3.2	+4.8	+1.8	+4.6
Statistical revision as % of old series*	−0.4	−0.6	−0.3	+0.2	+0.6	+0.1

1941–1946	1941	1942	1943	1944	1945	1946
National income (new)	103.8	136.5	168.3	182.3	182.8	178.2
National income (old)	96.9	122.2	149.4	160.7	161.0	165.0
Total revision	+6.9	+14.3	+18.9	+21.6	+21.8	+13.2
Amount of revision due to concept changes	+6.1	+13.2	+17.4	+21.1	+19.5	+6.3
Statistical revision	+0.8	+1.1	+1.5	+0.5	+2.3	+6.9
Total revision as % of old series	+7.1	+11.7	+12.7	+13.4	+13.5	+8.0
Revision due to concept changes as % of old series*	+6.3	+10.8	+11.6	+13.1	+12.1	+3.8
Statistical revision as % of old series*	+0.8	+0.9	+1.0	+0.3	+1.4	+4.2

(*Cont.*)

TABLE 25 (Cont.)

COMPARISON OF ESTIMATES OF NATIONAL INCOME

B. *Preliminary Estimates and Latest Revisions of National Income*
1947–1960 ($ billions)

1947–1950	1947	1948	1949	1950
National income (revised)[2]	198.2	223.5	217.7	241.9
National income (preliminary)[3]	202.6	224.4	221.5	235.6
Difference (bil. $)	−4.4	−0.9	−3.8	+6.3
Difference as % of preliminary series	−2.2%	−0.4%	−1.7%	+2.7%

1951–1954	1951	1952	1953	1954
National income (revised)[2]	279.3	292.2	305.6	301.8
National income (preliminary)[3]	275.8	290.4	307.7	300.0
Difference (bil. $)	+3.5	+1.8	−2.1	+1.8
Difference as % of preliminary series	+1.3%	+0.6%	−0.7%	+0.6%

1955–1958	1955	1956	1957	1958
National income (revised)[2]	330.2	350.8	366.9	367.4
National income (preliminary)[3]	322.3	342.4	358.0	360.5
Difference (bil. $)	+7.9	+8.4	+8.9	+6.9
Difference as % of preliminary series	+2.5%	+2.5%	+2.5%	+1.9%

1959–1960	1959	1960		
National income (revised)[2]	399.6	417.1		
National income (preliminary)[3]	398.5	417.1		
Difference (bil. $)	+1.1	0.0		
Difference as % of preliminary series	+0.3%	0.0%		

* These figures may not add up to the total revision because of rounding.
SOURCES:
[1] U.S. Department of Commerce, "National Income and Product Statistics of the United States," Supplement to *Survey of Current Business*, 27: 14, July, 1947.
[2] National income (revised) from *Survey of Current Business*, July, 1961.
[3] National income (preliminary) from *Survey of Current Business*, Annual Review numbers, every February issue from 1948 to 1961.

duced changes of 13.1 percent (in 1944) and an average revision over the period of 6.2 percent. We can thus conclude that even though the revisions here are largely due to changes in concept, they do reflect the considerable measure of uncertainty which even their makers attach to these statistics. This is particularly noteworthy regarding the revisions in the 1940's, which are larger than earlier ones. Compared with much smaller earlier revisions, this shows that it is not generally true that more recent statistics are subject to less doubt than earlier ones (assuming that these revisions themselves can inspire confidence).

The years 1947–1960 show that the process of correction continues and that both positive and negative changes are required. In Table 25(B.) we show the differences between the preliminary and the latest estimates of national income in this period. The largest absolute change is for 1957, with +8.9 billion (2.5%), incidentally a rather critical year for the currently used procedures in determining business cycle turning points. If the change finally approaches zero (for 1960) this should not be taken as a contradiction to the last sentence in the preceding paragraph. The reason for the small percentage changes of the last 2–3 years is simply that it sometimes takes ten years before the final figure is arrived at, as may be seen from Table 23 where the consecutive corrections are listed.

The problems of revision which are so important in these measures, although of course affecting the absolute size of the magnitude of the various income and product series, will be discussed in the next section. There we shall deal, first, with United States data and practices, and second, with the experience in the United Kingdom, in order to show that the problem presents itself everywhere when national income statistics and similar accounts are being put together.

Revisions of previously reported figures may derive from conceptual changes (but there have been no significant alterations in concept since the major revision of 1947), from later or more reliable bench marks, and from better statistics or advanced methods of processing.[21]

(b) *Relative changes and revisions.* The fact that the estimates of the absolute level of national income may leave us with doubts as to their reliability does not necessarily mean that the *flow* figures or changes from period to period are subject to the same magnitude of error. For example, the conceptual difficulties of imputation would present no problem when calculating *short-run* changes if they are consistently handled; it is only as a consequence of a change in a procedure

[21] *A Critique of the United States Income and Product Accounts, op. cit.,* p. 291.

or concept that the flow figures would suffer. However, this does not mean that the user of the statistics on change has reliable estimates of movements in the national income series. Even if we consider only the revisions which are regularly being made, the figures are always of a tentative nature.

We will discuss the problem of revision and changes in the quarterly estimates published by the National Income Division. Few series are more widely used in analyzing the nation's economy than the quarterly estimates of national income and gross national product (and the monthly series on personal income).[22]

There are three basic criteria by which to judge the reliability of quarter-to-quarter changes of the national income series. The *first* is the extent and nature of "bias," i.e., the extent to which the initial estimates tend to be too high or too low on the average. It is necessary to point out that by measuring the amount of bias using the final estimate as reference, there is the implicit assumption that the final revised estimates are "correct." Only for purposes of comparison can the final estimates be considered correct in the sense of being at least the most correct figures available. In other words, it is usually considered that progressive revisions get us closer and closer to the actual truth. The *second* is a measure of the extent of the average revision, i.e., a measure of the firmness of a given quarter-to-quarter percentage movement. *Third,* one may consider the proportion of the times the first estimates of change fail to give the "correct" *direction* of movement.[23] But what is

---

[22] Throughout this section we do not mean to imply that users of any of the series under discussion, gross national product, national income, etc., would confine themselves to any one estimate as an all-purpose indicator of the state of the economy. Judgment as to direction or magnitude of change in the economy, or in any part of it, should rest on a number of indicators, e.g., the Federal Reserve Board index of production, employment rate, steel production, etc. Of course, each of these pieces of information is subject to its unknown errors and there is no guarantee that they would, in general, cancel each other out.

[23] Arnold Zellner follows much the same lines in a study of the provisional and revised quarterly estimates of gross national product and its components in the period 1947 to 1955. One of his most striking findings was that: ". . . whereas provisional estimates of GNP disagreed with revised estimates only in 5 cases, these occurred at the lower turning points of the 1948–9 and 1953–4 recessions." (And this was all before deflation

the "correct" direction when successive revisions of the figures for the *same* year sometimes are positive, sometimes negative *in succession,* as has repeatedly been the case? The latest figure for a given year is not always the final figure even for several years after the given date. Hence there is not necessarily a value towards which the successive, repeated corrections clearly converge. Only if this were known to be the case could one speak of "correct" directions, and if one could be sure of this, the limiting value could easily be computed.

Table 23 shows the repeated revisions of United States National Income since 1947, and Figure 9 represents some implications. We see that, as already mentioned, revisions of the originally given figure sometimes still come after *ten* years! We also note that there seems to be no tendency for the number of revisions to decrease significantly. It is, of course, desirable that revisions be made when new information becomes available. But their frequency and long delays betray an uncertainty —no doubt justified—permeating the whole field, which is in striking contrast with the wide-spread *immediate* use of the first given figure and the assumption that it is significant to one billion dollars or less. We dispense with a more detailed description of this table since it offers no difficulties. But we emphasize again that each consecutive figure, i.e., revision for the same year, is afflicted with its own error and that the mere fact of a revision as such offers no guarantee whatsoever that the error has thereby been reduced. Neither is the converse the case: a lack of revision does not necessarily imply that the given figure is good (that is particularly to be borne in mind when judging *components* of aggregates!). More often than not it simply means that no revision has taken place. Since no error is stated by the makers of the statistics in the first place, nothing is being said about any likely changes in the error either. The reader, of course, has no way of determining these changes for himself.

Figure 9 shows what paths of description of change in na-

by doubtful price indexes!) Cf. Arnold Zellner, "A Statistical Analysis of Provisional Estimates of Gross National Product and its Components, of Selected National Income Components, and of Personal Saving," *Journal of the American Statistical Association,* 53 (March 1958), pp. 54–65.

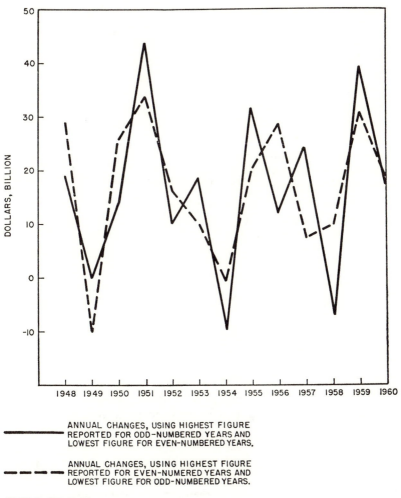

ANNUAL CHANGES, USING HIGHEST FIGURE
REPORTED FOR ODD−NUMBERED YEARS AND
LOWEST FIGURE FOR EVEN-NUMBERED YEARS.

ANNUAL CHANGES, USING HIGHEST FIGURE
REPORTED FOR EVEN-NUMERED YEARS AND
LOWEST FIGURE FOR ODD-NUMBERED YEARS.

SOURCE: TABLE 23

Figure 9. Uncertainty Imposed by Revision in Changes in
U.S. National Income 1947–1960

tional income could have been chosen, assuming that each of
the different values given for a certain year is equally likely
and would actually have been reported instead of the whole set
of figures given for each year. This chart expresses clearly some
of the uncertainties prevailing in this field, though—again—

nothing is shown about the far bigger uncertainty residing in the basic error of each number. If that were expressed it would demonstrate that the path, leading from year to year, can vary enormously, and that only the very broad tendency of an increase of national income over longer periods of time can be asserted with confidence. These observations, incidentally, should be viewed as casting serious doubts on the usefulness of national income figures for business cycle analysis. The idea that quarterly, let alone *monthly*, figures of gross national product, national income, etc., could be obtained, even with the most modern recording devices, without appreciable error, is nothing short of grotesque. And when we do have error and try to determine growth rates, we are by necessity exposed to the consequences described by the computations in the subsequent chapter on Growth Rates.

Similar statements apply to British data (cf. section 8 below). If these experiences are at all characteristic for the making of national income statistics, then one can form an idea of what ups and downs the revisions of other, perhaps less advanced, countries show or should show, and how uncertain it is to attribute to any one year a "true" figure, where "true" means merely conforming to the existing method with its known limitations and its unknown error.

Figure 10 shows the implications of ± 10 percent errors in the seasonally-adjusted quarterly national income figures. Between the shaded areas lies the zone of uncertainty surrounding the data. No single quarter-to-quarter change is significant within this band. Changes persisting for several quarters are seldom significant. By and large the national income figures contribute little confirmation of the post-war business cycle, its turning points shown by the small arrows, as the different possible profiles of national income shown by the dotted line bring out, its turning points marked by stars. This alternative path is not in any sense "correct"; but the point is that we do not know where in the region the statistics should lie.

In Table 26, the various revisions are shown as related to the principal component series; there is, clearly, an interest in observing which categories of economic activities contributed most or least to the revisions.

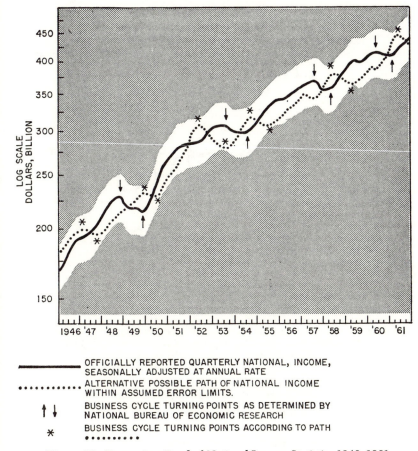

OFFICIALLY REPORTED QUARTERLY NATIONAL, INCOME, SEASONALLY ADJUSTED AT ANNUAL RATE

ALTERNATIVE POSSIBLE PATH OF NATIONAL INCOME WITHIN ASSUMED ERROR LIMITS.

↑ ↓ BUSINESS CYCLE TURNING POINTS AS DETERMINED BY NATIONAL BUREAU OF ECONOMIC RESEARCH

✱ BUSINESS CYCLE TURNING POINTS ACCORDING TO PATH

Figure 10. Uncertainty Band of National Income Statistics 1946–1961

Preliminary estimates for most series of the quarterly national income series are made available in the *Survey of Current Business* in the issue of two months after the end of the quarter; for corporate profits and national income, the lag is an additional two months. Subsequently, however, there are still sizeable revisions in the published series. The quarterly statistics are based generally on more limited information than the annual series. First revisions are made three months after first publication, and in the July issue of the *Survey of Current Busi-*

TABLE 26

SELECTED NATIONAL INCOME SERIES, 1947–1958:
Summary Measures of Quarter-to-Quarter Percent Movement

National Income Series	Average revision as a % of average movement of revised estimate of change	% of time direc- tion of move- ment missed	Average bias in first esti- mates of quarter-to- quarter movement
Compensation of employees	26%	6%	−.17%
National income	26	4	−.18
Personal income	28	6	−.15
Personal consumption expenditures	34	2	−.31
Gross national product	38	11	−.22
Corporate profits before tax	40	19	.53
Gross private domestic investment	61	19	.01
Proprietors' and rental income	96	28	.05

SOURCE: "Revisions of First Estimates of Quarter-to-Quarter Movement in Selected National Income Series, 1947–1958 (Seasonally Adjusted Data)," *Statistical Evaluation Reports, Report No. 2,* Office of Statistical Standards, Bureau of the Budget, February 1960, p. 23.

ness the data may be revised for the last two or three years. The three-year period allowed for possible revision permits the incorporation of data accumulated by such annual undertakings as the Statistics of Income of the Internal Revenue Service, various biannual censuses, etc.

The magnitude of the revisions may give some measure of the "firmness" of the particular component series of national income. A series with smaller quarter-to-quarter revisions does not necessarily indicate greater accuracy. It may mean simply that no better data have become available, and that the original data, however weak they may be, remain the best available. On the other hand, a series with large revisions certainly indicates that the original estimates were weak. As a practical matter, series which are usually considered among the better series have the least relative revision.[24] In this sense, national income, compensation of employees, and personal income are "good" series, whereas proprietors' and rental income and even corporate profits are relatively weak series. Observe, however, that corporate profits are based on (audited!) balance sheets (with all their limitations as discussed in Part I), and income tax returns, while for personal income not even the number of persons receiving income is reliably known (see reference in footnote 1, page 219).

In Table 26, the selected national income series have been grouped, using as criteria the relative revision of the first available estimates of change, the percent of times the first estimates missed the direction of movement, and, to a lesser extent, the average bias, which is generally insignificant in these series.

For most series the bias is small and therefore not significant, with the possible exception of corporate profits where initial estimates have averaged high. This series, so widely used, especially by security analysts, trying to determine the prospects of individual stocks, is one of the most difficult to measure with assurance. One of the principal difficulties is associated with making proper allowances for depreciation, which affect the magnitude of profits and are taken directly from income tax returns, no matter what method is used. In addition, this series has been revised on the basis of new data and by improvements in the processing of data.

The average revision is a measure of the dispersion of the original estimates of quarter-to-quarter percent change about the corresponding revised estimates. For the relatively "firm" series such as compensation of employees and national income, the average swing from quarter to quarter is about two percent and the average revision is about .5 percent, or about one-fourth of the quarter-to-quarter movement. For "weaker" series such as rental and proprietors' income, the *average* revision actually is about as large as the swing itself. In this case, then,

---

[24] The discussion in these paragraphs is based for the most part on "Revisions of First Estimates . . . ," (Source of Table 26). (Note that a "seasonal adjustment" of data of this kind is a most questionable operation, mechanically applied but devoid of meaning.)

the measure of change is not particularly meaningful. Since there is no bias, the direction of the revision is completely random; therefore, it is just as likely as not that the observed change will be completely washed out when new revised data are published. The point is, of course, very significant for the user of these data: "In current business analysis, it is of great importance that the 'truth' be as closely approximated within the current period as possible. Revision a year later, while significant for historical purposes, comes too late for the analyst in his diagnosis and prognosis of current trends."[25]

Thus, in series where the average revision is large relative to the quarter-to-quarter movements, the first estimates may often fail to give the "correct," i.e., ultimately asserted, direction of movement. For example, in the period 1947–58, proprietors' and rental income failed to detect the *direction* of movement 28 percent of the time and corporate profits 19 percent of the time. This may be compared with national income, which missed only 4 percent of the time, and compensation of employees, which was off course 6 percent of the time.

In summary, we conclude that while most United States national income series are relatively free from bias, there are large differences in the firmness of these series. When reliable estimates of the direction in which the economy is moving are needed and when such estimates are to be obtained from national income series, the firmer series should prove to be the better indicators. On the other hand the firm series are not always very important for more specialized purposes, since some of them, such as national income, are highly inclusive and so global in character that they can only figure in very aggregative economic models of low power of resolution. Corporate profits and gross private domestic investment on the other hand would be very interesting for estimating, say, future activity on the stock market, but they are definitely weak series and therefore of little use when needed.

[25] M. Cohen and M. R. Gainsbrugh, "The Income Side: A Business User's Viewpoint," in *A Critique of the United States Income and Product Accounts, op. cit.,* pp. 191–192.

8. British National Income Statistics and Revisions

The high level of British statistics and the pioneering work in the field of national income associated with such names as A. L. Bowley, Lord Stamp, and R. Stone, to mention only a few, does not remove the fact that British data are also of uneven quality and subject to important revisions with the associated uncertainties. The Central Statistical Office has frequently warned of the inherent unreliability of their estimates of national income.

In 1956, a system of reliability gradings was worked out[26] for the different components that appear in the various tables and accounts. There are three gradings: A grading of *A* indicates (with 90% confidence) that the reported figures are correct subject to a margin of error of less than 3% in either direction; *B* indicates an error of 3% to 10% in either direction, and *C* indicates that the error is greater than 10%. (This classification should be compared to the direct estimates by Kuznets, page 254, above.)

The items receiving the better ratings correspond in some ways to those which in the United States were subject to the least violent revisions (cf. Table 26). For example, consumers' expenditures, gross national product, wages and salaries received, received a grade of A, while profits, rent, income for self-employed received a grade of B. Note, however, that, as stated before, a lack of revision is precisely that and does not necessarily reflect reliability or trustworthiness of the estimate!

The nature and consequences of the British classification and the implications of the revisions of British national income figures were analyzed in an excellent study by Harry Burton.[27] This author has clearly and forcefully shown the magnitude of the errors of measurement when yearly revisions are considered, even for items that have an A rating. It is noteworthy that neither Burton's paper nor the original Blue Book has found the

---

[26] *National Income Statistics: Sources and Methods* (H. M. Stationery Office, 1956).

[27] Harry Burton, "The Reliability of National Income Statistics," *Accounting Research* (July 1957), pp. 246–261.

kind of reaction among economists and the public that they deserve. Instead, in Great Britain as in the United States and elsewhere, national income statistics are still being taken at their face value and interpreted as if their accuracy compared favorably with that of the measurement of the speed of light.

Table 27 summarizes the size of changes in estimates (in million £) for selected items for 1954 and 1955 when their corresponding errors are considered. There are two grade A items and one each for grades B and C. The official change is given in column 3. The changes in column 4 assume that the estimate for 1954 was too high by 1½% for grade A items, 6½% for grade B and 15% for grade C (there was a negative error for 1954) and that the estimate for 1955 was too low by corresponding amounts (a positive error for 1955). Column 6 gives the changes assuming the same magnitude of errors for grade A, B and C items, but this time assuming they are opposite in sign, i.e., that the 1954 figure is an underestimate and the 1955 figure an overestimate. Columns 5 and 7 correspond to 4 and 6 respectively, except that here the errors are assumed to be larger (2½% for grade A, 10% for B, and 25% for C).

Brief study of the table will indicate the tremendous uncertainties involved. Even for grade A items with low gradings error, the estimate of year-to-year change is very poor indeed—for consumers' expenditures a reported change of 788 might just as easily be as low as 417 or as high as 1159. For a high gradings error, the range is 169 to 1407! Clearly, we can say very little indeed for forecasting purposes.

For grade B and C items the situation becomes worse. Gross domestic capital formation (grade B), an extremely important item for business cycle analysts, was reported as increasing by £541 million from 1954 to 1955. Assuming a high gradings error, this figure could have been as low as −£37 million[28] and as high as £1119 million. In other words, from the figures alone

[28] A negative *gross* investment figure is of course conceptually impossible and is only the result of arithmetic illustration. Zero gross investment would imply that there were no expenditures on capital formation and that the capital stock was decreasing at a rate equal to depreciation estimates. Clearly this is the extreme and is not even characteristic of a major depression.

TABLE 27

CHANGES IN SELECTED ITEMS: 1956 BLUE BOOK (U.K.) 1954–1955
LOW AND HIGH GRADINGS ERROR[*]

(£ millions)

		Blue Book estimates		Change 1954 to 1955	CHANGE: 1954–1955 WITH			
					1954 negative 1955 positive		*1954 positive 1955 negative*	
		1954	1955		Low error	Higher error	Low error	Higher error
	Grade	col. 1	2	3	4	5	6	7
Consumers' expenditures	A	11,995	12,783	788	1,159	1,407	417	169
GNP (at market prices)	A	17,964	19,058	1,094	1,649	2,019	539	169
Gross domestic capital formation	B	2,624	3,165	541	918	1,119	164	-37
Investment income due abroad	C	604	591	-13	167	286	-193	-312

* Low gradings error: A ± 1½% B ± 6½% C ± 15%.
High gradings error: A ± 2½% B ± 10% C ± 25%.
Low negative bias for item in group A therefore means error of −1½%.
SOURCE: Burton, *ibid.*

the economy could have been in a major depression or in a superboom!

British national income statistics are subject to frequent and wide revisions, as are those of the United States (cf. Table 23). Table 28 gives the figures for selected items for 1952 as reported in 1953, 1954, 1955, and 1956. While the revisions for grade A are minor and generally go in the same direction, the opposite is the case for grades B and C, where increases of the original estimate are followed alternatingly by increases and decreases. The net income from abroad, a very important item of the British balance of payments, underwent the most drastic revisions, a situation which leaves the user of these statistics with a great deal of uncertainty.

9. INTERNATIONAL COMPARISONS OF NATIONAL INCOMES

If the great difficulties in making reliable national income statistics for the United States and the United Kingdom are a good indication of the problems any country runs into, then we can infer a great deal about the value, or rather the lack of

TABLE 28

REVISIONS OF BRITISH NATIONAL INCOME STATISTICS
FOR THE YEAR 1952
(£ millions)

| | Grade | As reported in: | | | |
		1953	1954	1955	1956
Consumer expenditures	A	10478	10440	10570	10582
GNP (factor cost)	A	13653	13738	13861	13928
Gross capital formation	B	1931	2116	2089	2158
Net income from abroad	C	128	139	114	93

| | | Percent and direction of revision from original (1953) report | | |
		1954	1955	1956
Consumer expenditures	A	−0.37	+0.87	+0.99
GNP (factor cost)	A	+0.62	+1.52	+2.01
Gross capital formation	B	+9.58	+8.18	+11.75
Net income from abroad	C	+8.59	−10.94	−27.35

SOURCE: Burton, *op. cit.*

value, of international comparisons in this area. Such comparisons are freely made and far-reaching consequences are drawn, for example, when the different degrees of welfare, economic development, etc., are being evaluated. Many uses are strictly of a political character. Although attention has been paid,[29] especially to the conceptual difficulties in making comparisons, there apparently exists no thorough exploration of the enormous obstacles in the way to meaningful results. We can only add a few remarks at this occasion.

There are two principal questions involved: the first is one referring to the comparability and applicability of concepts (essentially developed in advanced industrial countries), and second is one referring to the quality of the component data (our principal concern) whatever might be the answer to the first question. The main fact, as far as concepts are concerned, is that the organization and development of nations differ so widely that, to some extent, conceptually different situations arise for each class or category of countries. Concepts have been well analyzed in western industrial nations, but they have not been settled as the many revisions of data due to conceptual changes prove. They are less understood for more agricultural countries and for those which have incomplete monetary organizations, lack large markets, and have no all-pervading price system, and thus perhaps are oriented less towards pecuniary pursuits. There are many points in common (some of which have been discussed above), such as the difficulty of accounting for work done at home without pay and for the same work performed against money payment. What is negligible in one kind of country can be important in another. This applies in particular to home-consumed agricultural produce, which is an enormous part of the total in underdeveloped agricultural countries and practically irrelevant in the United States. Clearly, this is far more difficult to measure in the former than in the latter; yet U.S. agricultural statistics are far from

---

[29] Cf. especially, I. B. Kravis, "The Scope of Economic Activity in International Income Comparisons," in *Problems in the International Comparison of Economic Accounts*, Studies in Income and Wealth, Vol. xx (1957), p. 349 ff., as well as the discussion by E. E. Hagen and J. Viner. Cf. further P. Studenski, *op. cit.*

satisfactory. How, then, could the agricultural income of, say, Ceylon, the Congo, China, Bolivia, or Tibet be known at least as accurately? How can they be made comparable, e.g., on a per capita basis, when even the number of inhabitants in these countries is in far greater doubt than that of the United States?

Similar to hidden unemployment (that plague of meaningful unemployment statistics) there is *hidden income* which is probably the greater (on a percentage basis) the less developed the country is and the warmer is its climate.[30] Therefore, the numerical (money) expressions of income are in grave doubt as far as comparability is concerned. This is quite apart from the difficulty of converting different monetary units into a standard reference unit, especially when at the same moment of time some countries are undergoing inflation, others deflation, some have multiple exchange rates, others have virtually no foreign transactions, etc. The trouble of having to correct for changing money values exists, as we know, even for comparisons over time within the *same* country. Then it becomes important to realize that the deflation of national income figures is dependent upon the fact of whether it is done for aggregates or for components separately, when all have different degrees of reliability.

International comparisons are constantly being made. No doubt some information can be had from existing figures, and whether they are useful depends, as we shall not tire of repeating, on the purposes of the comparisons. To ascertain in a rather general manner the fact of gross differences of the income of different nations, to show that they differ by large factors,[31] and to see whether these differences have changed

---

[30] Sometimes in a "negative" sense, i.e., in warm climates, certain efforts are not required and therefore no corresponding income is generated. For example, even with a U.S. per capita income, one would not heat a house in the tropics (though one may want to cool it) or wear fur coats. Therefore, the financial inability to provide heat and furs is irrelevant in determining the meaning of tropical income levels. This is partly a conceptual matter; clearly it is a different matter regarding the ability to provide food and education.

[31] But probably not by as large factors as is suggested by the official statistics. As Kuznets has observed, if the frequently stated low figures were correct the inhabitants of the poorest countries would all have starved a long time ago.

over the years, etc., is one thing, but to believe that we can state this and much more reliably to two, three, or even four "significant" digits is an entirely different matter. On the basis of the discussion of the figures of the United States and the United Kingdom, we could not accomplish the latter even for these two advanced and "similar" countries. Yet we need only to look at numerous United Nations publications to see that this is being done for the whole world without any further excuse. The most startling use (or rather abuse) is for determining allegedly comparable growth rates for different countries, on the basis of which far-reaching policy decisions are made. (Cf., the chapter on Growth.)

The Office of Statistical Standards of the U.S. Bureau of the Budget has published a "Memorandum on International Statistics,"[32] rating countries in four groups (for 1956): I = Very Good, II = Good, III = Fair, and IV = Weak as indicated in Table 29.

Only 17, about one-fourth, qualify as "very good." The reader will remember that the best is probably the United States and that here the average error is probably in the order of ten percent. One wonders what it might in fact be for the 20 countries where the statistics are "weak." (Note: These have not been called "poor," or "bad"! Note also that an identification of the various countries was carefully avoided. This delicacy was perhaps dictated by the desire to avoid international incidents.)

TABLE 29

ACCURACY OF STATISTICS: VARIOUS REGIONS

Number	All	I	II	III	IV
	64	17	9	18	20
Continent					
Africa	9		1	2	6
America, North	11	2	1	5	3
America, South	8		2	4	2
Asia	15		2	5	8
Europe and Oceania	21	15	3	2	1

SOURCE: *loc. cit.*

[32] U.S. Congress, Joint Economic Committee, 85th Congress, 2nd Session, 1958.

The difficulties in this area of comparison are truly stupendous, and the many authors who have contributed so much to analyze and overcome them deserve praise and encouragement. There is no doubt that a gradual clarification of issues is taking place. Ingenious systems of national accounting have been worked out and are being widely used. There is a learning process under way that can bring beneficial results to those who participate in it.[33] But this is a slow process. And no matter how much the schemes and models improve, at the root of all trouble is the question of the basic statistics which are being put into a gigantic agglomeration. In a sense, we see here something similar to the process of increasing the gap between the "have" and "have not" nations: The statistics of those countries which produce the better figures still continue to improve, while those of the poor countries improve at a much slower rate, in spite of assistance given to them by the United Nations and other agencies. These can only help with methods and concepts, but not with the collection of the basic data, where the root of the trouble lies.

A special problem is offered by the Soviet Union. The statistics of that country are exceedingly difficult to assess, but it is generally known that they are seldom what they purport to be. This is in part due to the highly centralized administration of the country, a very different conceptual structure in the thinking about economics, the absence of a true price system, the immensity of the country (that is split into many semiautonomous republics), etc. There has been a great deal of deliberate doctoring of statistics at many levels, for example, in order to make production results appear better than they were or to receive assignments of raw materials that would not otherwise be allocated, etc. Even Khrushchev has repeatedly referred to falsified accounts of various activities, especially in farming, and there is no reason not to assume that practices were different in the time of Stalin. A particular trouble in measuring aggregates is (as in all other countries) the double counting, or rather the multiple counting. This becomes the more serious the more complicated the final products are, which is un-

[33] Vol. xx of *Studies in Income and Wealth*, quoted above, bears eloquent testimony to this fact.

doubtedly the case everywhere under the impact of the present industrial-scientific revolution. Double counting has apparently been a most serious defect of Soviet statistics, with the necessary result that accounts of national income have been exaggerated and increasingly so in more recent times (for the reasons just given). This is the upshot of criticism by S. G. Strumilin, a well-known Soviet economist.[34] For example, in 1945, industrial output was, according to him, more than 30 percent below 1940, rather than only 8 percent, as the official statistics show. Similarly, again according to Strumilin, industrial production rose from 1945 to 1956 only three-fold, rather than four-fold, as officially asserted. (This may, of course, still be an exaggeration, and is subject to our observations on growth rates, cf. below.) Though industrial production is not identical with national income, it is a substantial component; its difficulties are illustrative for the larger aggregate and show how limited the value is of any "growth factor" based on such data.

We do not propose to discuss the Soviet national income statistics any further here. They are analyzed by Studenski, where the international literature on this subject is mentioned.[35] It is clear that the arbitrariness in valuation, partly due to the attempted use of the obsolete Marxist labor value theory, is greater than in any country possessing a functioning price system. The difficulties exceed those in underdeveloped countries which also have a small market sector only; but there the market performs its true function of determining the allocation of resources, though it may not reach far into the economy. There can be no statistic of national income without measuring or postulating money streams, since there must be a common denominator and no one has as yet found a substitute for the money measure. That is why the Soviet national income is also

[34] *Ocherki Sotsialisticheskoi Ekonomiki SSSR* [Essays on the Socialist Economy of the USSR] (Moscow, 1960).

[35] The most important and authoritative work on Soviet national income is the recent book by A. Bergson, *The Real Income of Soviet Russia Since 1928* (Cambridge, Mass., 1961). This work takes up especially the above-mentioned difficulties regarding valuation, as well as many others, and attacks them with great ingenuity and competence. But the basic difficulties of the data remain, and our results concerning the lack of validity of commonly computed growth rates and their international comparability apply fully (cf. the following chapter).

given in terms of rubles, though what a ruble means is obscure: there is no free market and no free exchange rate at which to make comparisons. Apart from the assignment of monetary expressions on the basis of assumed, imputed values, there is still the underlying problem of the accuracy with which the physical phenomena can be recorded, whose values are to be expressed in monetary units. To count cows, to weigh the harvest, to enumerate machines, etc., is the same problem in all countries. Some solve it better than others. Most works dealing with Soviet national income pay little attention to these data problems, but more to the valuation question. Yet, in Russia, the former encounter even greater difficulties than in the United States or the United Kingdom.

Summarizing, we can state that statistics giving international comparisons of national incomes are among the most uncertain and unreliable statistics with which the public is being confronted. The area is full of complicated and unsolved problems, and in spite of the great efforts to overcome them, the progress is slow. This is a field where politics reigns supreme and where lack of critical appraisal is particularly detrimental.

❧ CHAPTER XV ❧

GROWTH STATISTICS AND
GROWTH RATES

1. Introduction

In recent years, there has been much concern among economists, politicians, and the general public about the rate of economic growth of the United States and other countries. In addition to the goals of maintaining a high level of employment and providing for general stability in the price level, a third goal, that of maintaining a satisfactory rate of economic growth, has been added to the responsibilities of fiscal and monetary authorities.

The increased emphasis on economic growth has two reasons: first, the desire to provide a higher standard of living for our citizens; second, to determine how effectively the Western world competes in the cold war with the Soviet Union.

In general, we have made it the rule in this book to concern ourselves chiefly with primary data and to stay away as far as possible from indexes, uses of data, and further conceptual issues. It became clear that this is not always possible, because the greater the inevitable aggregates are, the more important become concepts. Similarly, no index construction is trivial, and especially those indexes involving the notion of "costs of living" and their comparisons over time and among nations require a descent into considerable depths of economic theory and mathematics. And when classifications are the issue, concepts again assume great significance. In discussing national income, even such elusive notions as "community welfare" had to be touched upon. All these reappear by necessity when growth rates are mentioned, and therefore have to be given proper, though brief, consideration in what follows.

In these pages, we will therefore comment on the meaning of economic growth, the problem of the accuracy of growth statistics, and the difficulties confronting the user of such information. Finally we shall discuss the problems of comparison of growth rates for different periods and for different countries during the same period.

2. The Concept of Economic Growth

Economic growth is generally considered to be the increase in the "real" output of the economy over time. There is controversy about the best index of economic growth, which is not surprising since "growth" is a very complex phenomenon, wherever it is encountered. Many models of the economy have been suggested, showing growth of different kinds, and business cycle theory has been concerned with the "expansion" phase of a business cycle as distinguished from the "expansion" due to long term growth. These ideas will not be discussed here. But reference should be made to the work of biologists and others who have studied growth of organisms[1] where it is shown that growing and dying processes are closely related within the same individual, a fact that corresponds somewhat to the frequent changes in technology used in economic activities. This often takes the form that one activity declines (e.g., railroads) while others expand (e.g., motor cars). The question immediately arises whether these two tendencies compensate or whether one outweighs the other, so that while there are some declines and some expansions, one could nevertheless discern a clear overall tendency. Since conflicting tendencies develop in many areas simultaneously, the difficulties of assigning weights are compounded. It is clear, at any rate, that a complicated process of valuation is involved even when only the simple, current method for determining growth rates is used. This method is to take the movement of gross national product, adjusted for changes in the price level, as a satisfactory indicator. This rather crude procedure could be refined, for example, by

---

[1] Sir d'Arcy Wentworth Thompson, *On Form and Growth* (Cambridge University Press, 1948). Galileo has already shown in his *Discourses* that certain types of mechanisms, among them the bone structure of the human body, cannot be linearly extended at will. The idea of "broken economic trends" and the need for developing a theory of trend change (i.e., the interrelation of simultaneously rising and falling trends) is advanced in O. Morgenstern, *Wirtschaftsprognose, Eine Untersuchung Ihrer Voraussetzungen und Möglichkeiten* (Vienna, Julius Springer, 1928).

taking national income or personal income. The more we refine the measure, the greater are the conceptual problems and the more difficult the decisions. In view of the important purposes of the determination of growth, the best possible measurements are barely good enough and any evasion of the underlying issues is inadmissible. Yet here we are only concerned with one single aspect, the reliability of the figures expressing the currently used measures, whatever their conceptual justification.

Gross national product, national income, etc., are not the only possible representatives for a simple notion of growth. For example, a production index could be used. Whatever indices are used, however, would have to be corrected for price changes, a particularly important adjustment since "growth" implies necessarily long periods and there have been none in which there were no substantial price changes. A volume production index would have to be corrected for quality changes. Similarly, population growth has to be taken into account. Omission of this correction would be particularly serious since in some countries population has a tendency to outstrip the increase in production. Consider an extreme case where real gross national product increases by 10 percent per annum over a 3-year period, but population increases by 15 percent. Then the gross national product per capita would actually have decreased by about 5 percent per annum. This is a real possibility in populous underdeveloped countries, where it is notoriously difficult to obtain reliable data for production as well as for population. The possibility arises in particular with respect to Communist China, where no one can say with confidence what the population is and how production has developed. From all we know, the likelihood of a net decrease in income per capita cannot be ruled out. Note that the question of optimal or just *distribution of the national product* is usually evaded in these discussions. The matter is obviously controversial and cannot be settled before a true theory of social benefit with a method of its measurement has been established.[2] Similarly, the age distribution of the population should not be neglected in evaluating size, change, and meaning in real national product.

[2] This was already commented upon in the preceding section. We are, of course, far from this state.

We are here only concerned with the increases of real gross national product, i.e., the original gross national product series published by the Department of Commerce and deflated by various price indexes calculated by the National Income Division. These deflators are especially constructed price indexes for the various components of gross national product.

3. The Accuracy of Growth Rates

Obviously, the value of a growth rate depends on both the accuracy of the figures for gross national product and of the prices going into the construction of the deflator-indexes. The former are subject to the considerable uncertainties discussed in the preceding section, the latter depend on the precision with which actual prices, as distinguished from posted prices, list prices, etc., can be determined and applied to the correct sectors of gross national product. We know that this is far more difficult than generally assumed, but we shall discuss neither basic price data nor price indexes any further. The two factors do, however, combine in producing very serious doubts about the reliability and usefulness (in the current sense) of growth rates.

The reader who concurs in the preceding evaluation of national income statistics will have no difficulty in seeing that a reliable growth rate of two significant digits is impossible to establish. But even the first digit is in grave doubt. This will be clearly shown below. Yet the emphasis of the public discussion is on the second digit, usually the first decimal, and it is carried on in all seriousness as if a distinction of, say, 3.2 and 3.3 percent were really possible, and as if the transition, within a short time, from the former to the latter constituted progress of the country, offered assurance of progress in the international competition, and so on. Such contentions are entirely unwarranted. It is difficult to see how even a shade of proof can be offered by the proponents of these practices. A growth rate simply cannot be computed with the stated or demanded degree of refinement and reliability. This applies to the existing national income data of *any* country in the world.

Yet we *know* that countries have grown and that, at periods, some have grown faster than others. But such observations and statements can be made with confidence only qualitatively and for *longer* periods. They are impossible to make for one year (or less!), where a nation's growth is as imperceptible as the growth of a person's teeth in a month. These general statements are based on a host of qualitative and quantitative indications, of which the imperfectly measured change in gross national product or national income is only one. Many are essentially qualitative in nature for which, as yet, no measurements have been devised, such as the development of institutions of business, markets, law, enterprise, etc. By denying the alleged accuracy of precisely stated growth rates we apply a standard that has been used throughout this investigation. In addition, we express great doubt that as complex a phenomenon as "growth" can be stated adequately by as simple and almost trivial a measure as a percentage change in either gross national product or national income, even if reduced to real terms. This doubt, I am sure, must be shared in their hearts by numerous theorists who have tried to explore in depth the intricate phenomenon of economic development, growth, and expansion. Their work has led to some non-trivial models which for empirical application would require statistical measurements that differ by a wide margin from the simple percentage figures of a deflated gross national product.

Concerning the rates themselves, we observe the following: Table 30 shows growth rates as commonly computed, but for 1, 3, and 5 percent plus or minus variations of the underlying figures. We recall that the assumption of a ±5 percent accuracy of the non-deflated gross national product is conservative. The results of this simple computation should shake the confidence of anyone who thinks that the difference between, say, 3.2 and 3.3 percent is significant.

The computation is for a (hypothetical) change in United States gross national product from $550 billion in Period I to $560 billion in Period II. The first column lists the values of gross national product assuming the reported figure for Period I, i.e., $550 billion, to be subjected to the above-mentioned error of ±1%, ±3%, and ±5%. The top row carries the same assumption through for the Period II figures. The body of the table contains the growth rates obtained for all combinations

TABLE 30

APPARENT RATE OF GROWTH FOR ±1, ±3, ±5 PERCENT ERRORS

A. Assuming Reported Gross National Product Figures
550 and 560 in Two Successive Periods

Period I GNP 550 ± Error	Period II GNP 560 ± Error	532.0	543.2	554.4	560.0	565.6	576.8	588.0
	% Error	−5	−3	−1	0	+1	+3	+5
522.5	−5	1.8	4.0	6.1	7.2	8.2	10.4	12.5
533.5	−3	−.3	1.8	3.9	5.0	6.0	8.1	10.2
544.5	−1	−2.3	−.2	1.8	2.9	3.9	5.9	8.0
550.0	0	−3.3	−1.2	.8	1.8	2.9	4.9	7.0
555.5	+1	−4.2	−2.2	−.2	.8	1.8	3.8	5.9
566.5	+3	−6.1	−4.1	−2.1	−1.2	−.2	1.8	3.8
577.5	+5	−7.9	−5.9	−4.0	−3.0	−2.1	−.1	1.8

Computed rate of growth assuming the reported figures to be correct is $\dfrac{560\text{-}500}{550} = 1.8\%$.

B. Assuming Reported Gross National Product Figures
550 and 566.5 in Two Successive Periods

Period I GNP 550 ± Error	Period II GNP 566.5 ± Error	538.2	549.5	560.8	566.5	572.2	583.5	594.8
	% Error	−5	−3	−1	0	+1	+3	+5
522.5	−5	3.0	5.2	7.3	8.4	9.5	11.7	13.8
533.5	−3	.9	3.0	5.1	6.2	7.3	9.4	11.5
544.5	−1	−1.2	.9	3.0	4.1	5.1	7.2	9.2
550.0	0	−2.2	−.1	2.0	3.0	4.1	6.1	8.2
555.5	+1	−3.1	−1.1	1.0	2.0	3.0	5.0	7.1
566.5	+3	−5.0	−3.0	−1.0	0.0	1.0	3.0	5.0
577.5	+5	−6.8	−4.8	−2.9	−1.9	−.9	1.0	3.0

Computed rate of growth assuming the reported figures to be correct is $\dfrac{560\text{-}550}{550} = 1.8\%$.

of the assumed possible errors. When there is no error assumed or when an error of a given magnitude is exactly compensated by an error of the same magnitude and with the same sign, the growth rate is 1.8%. This rate would, according to current practices, be reported (and analyzed!) as *the* rate. It is, of course, impossible that there be no errors at all, and most improbable that they always exactly compensate for each other. The table now shows clearly what happens when even the modest 1% or 3% errors are introduced. Magnitudes and even signs are affected. If we assume that the reported figure of 550 for Period I is 5% too low and the figure for Period II 5% too high, we arrive, instead of at 1.8%, at 12.5% as the growth rate. If we reverse the signs, the growth rate is −7.9%. Suppose gross national product for the second year is only +1% off and gross national product for the preceding one is −1% off (a total error of only 2%), then the growth rate is 3.9%, but if the signs of the errors are reversed, the growth rate is −0.2%! It is in the essence of an error estimate that the occurrence of a positive and negative deviation has to be admitted. Surely, the assumption of only a 1% error for each period is a very mild one. (Recall that the *best* British estimate is up to ±3% and the *best* average Kuznets estimate is 7.5%!) The reader should contemplate what this trifling difference in our assumption entails. If our basic figures of 550 and 560 are more than 1.8% apart, say 3%, the results of a corresponding table are necessarily worse. For example, a −1% error in the first period and a +1% error in the second then give a growth rate of 5.1%, and if the signs are reversed a growth rate of 1.0%. With ±3% the corresponding figures are 9.4% and −3.0% respectively.

It is easily shown that the computations of Table 30 are independent of the absolute amount of the assumed *level* of gross national product, and that the rates depend solely on the *percentage* change of gross national product from Period I to Period II and the errors. Moreover, the computations obviously apply to any situation where rates of change are involved and where the data are subject to error. In other words they apply to all economic data.

This simple arithmetical exercise combined with the indisputable fact that our final gross national product or national income data cannot possibly be free of error[3] raises the question whether the computation of growth rates has any value whatsoever.

Table 31, which follows, shows the results of estimating the *compound annual rate of growth*, r, on the basis of two observa-

---

[3] Nor can it be assumed without further proof that the errors remain constant over time, that they change uniformly over time, and that the signs of the errors never reverse themselves.

TABLE 31

APPARENT COMPOUND RATE OF GROWTH IN PERCENTAGE

	A. Where $n = 5$ ($r = 1.8$)						
$E_F =$	−5%	−3%	−1%	0%	+1%	+3%	+5%
$E_I = -5\%$	1.8	2.2	2.7	2.9	3.1	3.5	3.9
−3%	1.4	1.8	2.2	2.4	2.6	3.0	3.4
−1%	1.0	1.4	1.8	2.0	2.2	2.6	3.0
0%	.8	1.2	1.6	1.8	2.0	2.4	2.8
+1%	.6	1.0	1.4	1.6	1.8	2.2	2.6
+3%	.2	.6	1.0	1.2	1.4	1.8	2.2
+5%	−.2	.2	.6	.8	1.0	1.4	1.8

	B. Where $n = 10$ ($r = 1.8$)						
$E_F =$	−5%	−3%	−1%	0%	+1%	+3%	+5%
$E_I = -5\%$	1.8	2.0	2.2	2.3	2.4	2.6	2.8
−3%	1.6	1.8	2.0	2.1	2.2	2.4	2.6
−1%	1.4	1.6	1.8	1.9	2.0	2.2	2.4
0%	1.3	1.5	1.7	1.8	1.9	2.1	2.3
+1%	1.2	1.4	1.6	1.7	1.8	2.0	2.2
+3%	1.0	1.2	1.4	1.5	1.6	1.8	2.0
+5%	.8	1.0	1.2	1.3	1.4	1.6	1.8

	C. Where $n = 5$ ($r = 3.0$)						
$E_F =$	−5%	−3%	−1%	0%	+1%	+3%	+5%
$E_I = -5\%$	3.0	3.4	3.9	4.1	4.3	4.7	5.1
−3%	2.6	3.0	3.4	3.6	3.8	4.2	4.7
−1%	2.2	2.6	3.0	3.2	3.4	3.8	4.2
0%	2.0	2.4	2.8	3.0	3.2	3.6	4.0
+1%	1.8	2.2	2.6	2.8	3.0	3.4	3.8
+3%	1.4	1.8	2.2	2.4	2.6	3.0	3.4
+5%	1.0	1.4	1.8	2.0	2.2	2.6	3.0

	D. Where $n = 10$ ($r = 3.0$)						
$E_F =$	−5%	−3%	−1%	0%	+1%	+3%	+5%
$E_I = -5\%$	3.0	3.2	3.4	3.5	3.6	3.8	4.0
−3%	2.8	3.0	3.2	3.3	3.4	3.6	3.8
−1%	2.6	2.8	3.0	3.1	3.2	3.4	3.6
0%	2.5	2.7	2.9	3.0	3.1	3.3	3.5
+1%	2.4	2.6	2.8	2.9	3.0	3.2	3.4
+3%	2.2	2.4	2.6	2.7	2.8	3.0	3.2
+5%	2.0	2.2	2.4	2.5	2.6	2.8	3.0

tions, I_0 (the initial observation) and F_0 (the final observation) after n years, with percentage errors of E_I and E_F, respectively, where

$$I_0 = (1 + \frac{E_I}{100}) \times (\text{actual figure initially given}),$$

$$I_F = (1 + \frac{E_F}{100}) \times (\text{actual figure after n years}).$$

We may use as the estimated rate of growth:

$$r_E = 100 \left[\sqrt[n]{\frac{(1 + \frac{E_F}{100}) (1 + \frac{r}{100})^n}{(1 + \frac{E_I}{100})}} - 1 \right]$$

which may be approximated by

$$r_E \cong r + \frac{E_F - E_I}{n}$$

It should be noted that the estimate r_E becomes closer to r as n gets larger but loses its realistic significance simultaneously. Also, for fixed errors E_F, E_I the part of r_E contributed by these errors gets smaller proportionately, as r gets large.

The apparent annual rate of growth is given for $r = 1.8$, $r = 3.0$, and for the various values of E_F and E_I, in the cases $n = 5$ and $n = 10$.

These effects of errors when growth computations are made over one, five, and ten years are summarized in Figure 11 where the apparent rate of growth is plotted against the difference in percentage errors in the final and base periods. This particular figure assumes the true rate of growth is 1.8 percent per annum. The steep slope of the line for measurement over a period of only one year shows how very much the computed rate of growth depends on the relative sizes of the two errors. The decline in slope as the period is extended brings out the way in which the effect of error declines as the period is lengthened. However, even for periods of ten years, the line still has a marked slope, so that errors nevertheless have an important influence on the computation.

It is clear from the above that the usefulness of growth rates is not increased when compound rates are considered. We

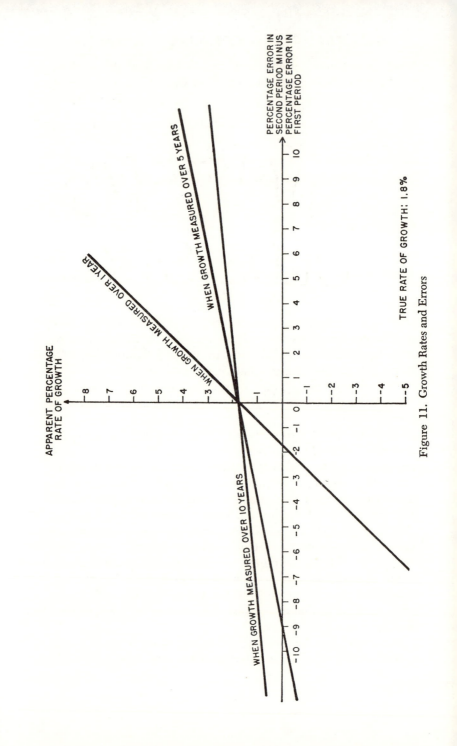

Figure 11. Growth Rates and Errors

continue, however, by looking back at Table 23, which showed the revisions throughout the years of initially given estimates of national income. Here the question of the growth rate is raised with respect to the particular moment in *time* when it is computed. Table 32 shows the results. If the rate is determined for the change from 1947 to 1948 in February 1949, when the first figures became available, it was 10.8%. In July 1950, using officially corrected figures, it became 12.5%; in July 1956 it fell to 11.8%, only to rise again in July 1958 to the highest of all values, 12.8%—a full percentage point! All this for the growth from 1947 to 1948! Similar observations apply to the other years for which this computation has been made. There is no consistency in the changes. In stating what the growth rate of the country is, much depends, therefore, on the moment of time when a growth rate is computed. Though not surprising in the light of our previous investigations, this result is nevertheless noteworthy. And all this applies to figures where we have *abstracted* from the fact that they are necessarily afflicted with errors which, when low, must be at least 5%. If we make the necessary and inevitable allowance for errors, however slight, the confusion mounts.

To round off this picture we refer to Table 33, where the growth rates from year to year are computed by taking alternatingly (from Table 23) the lowest and highest estimate of national income for one year and determining the growth rate to the highest and lowest estimate of the following year. Such differences exist and are sometimes appreciable, running in absolute terms up to about $9 billion for one year. Clearly the lowest to highest ratio will be the largest of all four rates for the same pair of years, as the highest to lowest will give the smallest rates, with the others in between. The differences are enormous (for the same pair of years), sometimes even the sign is switched! There is an apparent decrease of the difference for the last two years (1959 to 1960 and 1960 to 1961). But we do not know, at this time of writing, what surprises the revisions of these figures will bring during the next 8–10 years, if the experience of the past years, as seen from Table 23, is a guide for our expectations. Again, it has to be mentioned that this computation does *not* take into consideration errors; if that

TABLE 32

UNITED STATES GROWTH RATES

(based on consecutive corrections of original estimates of national income)

	1947–1948	1948–1949	1949–1950	1950–1951	1951–1952	1952–1953	1953–1954	1954–1955	1955–1956	1956–1957	1957–1958	1958–1959	1959–1960
Feb. 1949	10.8												
July '50	*12.5	-3.0											
July '51	12.5	-3.0	10.3										
July '52	12.5	*-3.2	*10.6	16.0									
July '53	12.5	-3.2	*11.2	*15.7	4.7								
July '56	*11.8	*-2.4	*11.0	*15.4	*4.8	4.1	-1.3	8.6					
July '57	11.8	-2.4	11.0	15.4	4.8	4.1	*-1.0	*8.4	6.0				
July '58	*12.8	*-2.6	*11.1	*15.5	*4.6	*4.6	*-1.2	*9.4	*5.8	4.2			
July '59	12.8	-2.6	11.1	15.5	4.6	4.6	-1.2	9.4	*6.2	*4.5	-0.1		
July '60	12.8	-2.6	11.1	15.5	4.6	4.6	-1.2	9.4	6.2	*4.6	*0.2	*8.7	
July '61	12.8	-2.6	11.1	15.5	4.6	4.6	-1.2	9.4	6.2	4.6	*0.1	*8.8	4.4

NOTE: Asterisk indicates change from previous value.
SOURCE: Table 23.

TABLE 33

UNITED STATES GROWTH RATES

Computational Effect of Utilizing High/Low Year-to-Year Estimates

	1947–1948	1948–1949	1949–1950	1950–1951	1951–1952	1952–1953	1953–1954	1954–1955	1955–1956	1956–1957	1957–1958	1958–1959	1959–1960	1960–1961
Lowest to Lowest	12.4	-2.4	9.0	17.1	5.0	4.4	-1.3	3.6	5.7	4.6	0.7	10.5	4.7	3.1
Highest to Highest	11.6	-2.1	9.2	15.5	4.6	5.3	-1.9	9.4	6.2	4.6	0.2	8.7	4.4	3.1
Highest to Lowest	9.4	-4.4	6.4	14.0	3.7	3.4	-2.6	7.4	3.7	2.1	-1.7	8.4	4.4	3.1
Lowest to Highest	14.7	0.0*	11.9	18.5	5.9	6.3	-0.1	10.7	8.3	7.2	2.7	10.8	4.7	3.1

* Not significant.

were done, as it should be, the "growth rates" would jump around even more wildly.

The computations of Table 30 should be applied, *mutatis mutandis*, to all other countries. Identical considerations are therefore valid regarding the growth rates of other nations, where the presumed average error will often exceed 5% by a wide margin. This was true even of Great Britain. One can well imagine what the value of growth rates of statistically less developed countries must be like.

4. THE CHOICE OF THE BASE YEAR

In addition to all these difficulties, there is the ambiguity in choosing the *base year*. The need for a base year arises from the desire to compare long periods by means of the compound rate. Such periods will often comprise a series of business cycles and therefore several decades. If a year with a *high* (*low*) gross national product is chosen as base year, this will *depress* (*raise*) the growth rate of subsequent years. Since there is no such thing as a "normal" year, the investigator has a great amount of freedom in determining a base year. An unscrupulous or politically oriented writer will choose that base year which produces the sequence of (alleged) growth rates best suited to his aims and programs. An advocate of government spending and inflation will pick a year with a high gross national product as base year in order to show a low rate of growth and thereby to strengthen his argument in favor of inflation, government deficits, and the like. An opponent of such policies will choose a relatively poor gross national product as base year, thus obtaining a series of growth rates carrying the comforting message that the development of the country is progressing well. These are, of course, standard tricks, used, undoubtedly, ever since index numbers were invented.

Consider Table 34. (In interpreting this table we make, for the sake of argument, the assumption that the growth rates are significant even to two digits; it was shown above that this need not be so.) Suppose a 3.5% growth is considered desirable: then only 1949 chosen as a base year shows that the goal has been reached; if others are chosen, a failure has to be recorded. 1949 and 1954 were recession years, in 1950 occurred the outbreak of

TABLE 34

UNITED STATES GROWTH RATES COMPOUNDED FROM
DIFFERENT BASE YEARS
(gross national product in 1954 dollars)

Growth from	Rate (%)
1949 to 1960	3.7 per annum
1950 " "	3.3 " "
1954 " "	3.2 " "
1955 " "	2.3 " "

the Korean War, and 1955 was a year of high business activity. We dispense with any more elaborate illustrations.

We have limited ourselves to growth rates based on gross national product, etc., but our remarks apply also to any of the many other widely used rates. To name only a few, there is investment as a percentage of national income, the value added by manufacturing as a percentage of total value added, exports plus imports as a percentage of national income, and so forth. There are countless others. In fact, the above considerations apply no matter what the substratum of computed rates of change. They may be data on production, foreign trade, prices, turnovers, etc., in short anything the economist has to deal with. All are based on empirical data and all have *some* error component. If the rates and the changes in the rates could be obtained in a reliable manner, economic analysis and economic policy would benefit immeasurably. They are, unfortunately, being computed freely[4] and are used indiscriminately as if no problem existed regarding their accuracy and therefore their value.

In addition to these indiscriminate uses, as expected, almost any argument can be supported by inobtrusive manipulation. The literature is full of examples, and although the matter is trivial, these abuses will continue as long as there are unscrupulous investigators and gullible readers.

5. INTERNATIONAL AND INTER-PERIOD COMPARISONS OF GROWTH RATES

The difficulties discussed in section 9 of the preceding chapter, relating to comparisons of national incomes for different

[4] Cf. *Yearbook of National Account Statistics,* United Nations.

countries and different periods of time even for a single country, reappear when growth rates are considered. Essentially, there are two observations, one pertaining to the data, the other to the concepts.

First, it is clear, and now requires no further comment, that in view of the high degree of unreliability of basic national income data the growth rates even for the United States are at best very shaky. From their *relatively* better quality we have to go over to the lesser and lesser quality of the national income statistics of other countries—even the United Kingdom would rank lower —until the 38 "fair and weak" countries of Table 29 are reached. The computation, and hence the comparison, of international growth rates under these conditions is a most dubious undertaking. Even gross differences do not reliably point to the true character of the underlying processes. Perhaps when very gross differences persist between two countries, say one showing about 10 percent growth and the other 2 percent, and if the general level of statistical reporting for both is approximately at the same high level, can one say that the former's gross national product has risen faster than the latter's, but when the reported rates are very close to each other, hardly any conclusions can be supported as scientifically acceptable.

It will always be necessary to supplement the rates by qualitative information as indicated above. We emphasize again that there can be no doubt that countries develop at different speeds and that this fact is noticeable over longer periods of time, particularly when the initial level of economic activity is low and the state of technology is primitive. When big gaps exist, a comparison of change can be made with some confidence provided a sufficiently long time interval is admitted. When countries are very similar in their structure, such comparisons become immeasurably more difficult and unreliable. It is ironical that the differences among highly developed and similar countries are harder to ascertain than for less advanced nations, especially when the latter's growth is compared to that of the former.

Second, the last remark points up the conceptual difficulties in comparing growth rates—assuming that they could be computed in the current manner from gross national product. It is doubtful that the same ratio computed for very different *kinds* of countries is equally meaningful. If there is any value at all in the notion that countries grow in characteristic patterns, depending on their history, technological age, geographic position, size, etc., then it is unlikely that a single simple number can state adequately (or at least not in a misleading sense) how they evolve relatively to each other. In this respect, the problems of finding a proper solution for describing the gross national product or the national income or developing an even more suitable concept for a given moment in time are compounded many times. It is well known that, thus far, the problem of finding a social benefit or welfare function is unsolved. Hence the hope that we could make meaningful international comparisons over time is vain when attempted in terms of such simple and unreliable percentages.

A particular fallacy in using growth rates for comparing different countries needs to be explained: the growth rates are frequently used as measures for determining the variations in strength or power of different countries in world affairs or in respect to the cold war situation. There is a conceptual problem involved that would have to be taken care of even if the statistics were in good shape. It is clearly possible to have two countries with the *same* growth rate, but where country A expands by adding to its output of automobiles, refrigerators, swimming pools, etc., while country B increases its output of machine tools, power plants, mines, etc. The second of these countries is laying the foundation for further output increase while the first is not. Similar considerations apply when weapons and other tools for war are involved. The ordinary growth rate, computed for the big gross national product aggregate, covers up these profoundly different developments and would easily give entirely erroneous and misleading information about the relative development of these countries. Yet this is the figure commonly used to assess past progress and future tendencies. The answer would be to compute instead "power indexes" (of growth) which would have to be based on the information given by special aggregates made up of better related components.[5]

[5] Cf. O. Morgenstern, *The Question of National Defense,* 1959, Second Revised Edition (Vintage Books V–192, New York, 1961), pp. 202 ff.

To summarize: There is no possibility of making concessions as far as the scientific use of growth rates is concerned. As available today, they are worthless in view of the exacting uses to which they are being put. The data are limited and untrustworthy, and the method of computation is at best based on the tremendous oversimplification that there are no errors in gross national product.

To put this differently: *Precise uses of "growth rates" are entirely inadmissible, whether for comparing different countries or short periods of the same country.* Their computation is largely arbitrary. The concept itself is vague and unreliable. Anyone using growth rates in the current manner will have to show that the above arguments are all taken into consideration and the corresponding objections have been overcome.

A recent example of the extravagant uses of growth rates is found in the *Proceedings of the American Economic Association* (Vol. LII, May 1962) reporting on the session on "The Lagging U.S. Growth Rate."[6] There no reference whatsoever is made to the accuracy of the underlying data and to the reliability of the various growth rates discussed. The chief speaker's assignment, given him by the President of the Association, was "to devise a package of proposals that can raise the growth rate over the next twenty years by one percentage point" (p. 67). He then assumes a rate of 3 1/3% to be raised to 4 1/3%. This leads to a search of components for a 13-part program in which the contribution of *each* proposal "will be stated

---

[6] E. F. Denison, "How to Raise the High-Employment Growth Rate by One Percentage Point," *loc. cit.*, pp. 67–75. The author is with the Committee for Economic Development, a generally valuable policy oriented group, supposedly concerned with the realities of the American Economy. In his discussion, G. Colm states (p. 87) that Denison's paper is "statistically well supported." Clearly, this is in complete contradiction to our findings. In another publication, Mr. Denison does recognize several of the problems connected with growth rates raised in this chapter, such as the effect of the choice of period over which the rate is computed, the large effects of even small errors in the basic data, and the consequent meaninglessness of discussing fairly small changes in the rate of growth, especially over periods which are not long. Cf. Edward F. Denison, *The Sources of Economic Growth in the United States and the Alternatives Before Us*, Supplementary Paper No. 13, Committee for Economic Development, Washington, 1962, pp. 16–19.

in *hundreds* [!] of a percentage point" (p. 70). This is clearly impossible both as far as goals and means are concerned. These authors obviously have in their minds a picture of the American (or any other) economy given with a precision and detail that has only a remote resemblance to the true picture we are capable of drawing and to that which is revealed by even a moderately critical examination of the data.

We conclude that growth rates as commonly computed from gross national product and national income data whose errors are known to be large, though they are not stated numerically by their makers, are completely worthless as far as international comparisons are concerned. International comparisons of the relative growth and development of different countries demand, in addition to qualitative, historical, sociological description, more specific indexes, carefully constructed from those activities that are relevant to these countries in regard to their location, climate, technology, policies, etc. Such indexes would, of course, also exhibit some of the faults described above, but they could perhaps be brought under some measure of control.

It would, indeed, be most peculiar if the economic "growth" of nations could be described with virtually no effort by merely comparing consecutive numbers, these being their gross national product or something similarly comprehensive. Should economics ever reach the pleasant state where "growth" can be measured reliably by a *single* (!) number, this condition will only be achieved after developments which now cannot be foreseen have taken place in this science.

It remains to point to the relation of the above results to the various theoretical models of economic growth. Their value lies, of course, in their conceptual construction. But they have all been devised with an expectation of application. They all contain rates of one kind or another and all make statements about stability, equilibria, and the like. Whatever their merits otherwise, it will be a long way before they can be applied, should the data they require exhibit characteristics of the kind described in these pages.

ORIENTATION OF FURTHER RESEARCH

IN DESCRIBING economic data from various fields, there was no intention to make a chamber of horrors, nor to belittle the efforts of the many good workers to whom our data are due. Some readers may have been dismayed by the faults that have been described, and in some cases were newly uncovered; but they should be aware that there are other data which are much better, such as interest rates, stock market prices, and volume transactions on the security exchanges. Thus there is a great mixture of quality, though the poor data clearly outweigh the good. And there are many areas where we have only a vague idea of how good our information is, since numbers are lacking altogether. Yet this happens in important cases such as expectations of the future.

The remaining task in this study is to comment on the proper attitude to be taken in this situation.

The first remark is that nothing in our study should give comfort to those who would prefer to insist on an *a priori* character of economic theory, who believe that this science is independent of the facts as observed, that it is somehow capable of deriving theorems of practical significance by pure thought. There is no way of making statements about the economic (or any other) world without some observation of reality, or what we take it to be, no matter how coarse and rudimentary our observations. This remark applies to those few who take a very doctrinaire stand that economics is a non-empirical science. Though few, there are always some; hence the need for this comment.

The second class of arguments to be heard in cases when it has been shown that information wanting in quality, shot through with error, sometimes consisting of wild guesses hidden behind sharply given numbers, is characterized by the following: "True, the statistics are not as good as we would want them to be, but what would we do without them?" This is, indeed, a dilemma. The answers, of course, are manifold. The primary consideration is to make the data better—easier said than done and at any rate involving costs and time delays, both of which may not be permissible. Many statistics are needed precisely because decisions have to be made at the moment when the first estimates become available, frequently even earlier! The next point is to distinguish in what sense the data are unsatisfactory: Is it due to inherent difficulties of measurement and observation which otherwise have been carried out scrupulously? Or is it due to deliberate obstruction, lies, falsifications, etc.?

In the second case there is but one answer: discard the data if the element of lying affects a significant part of the information or is suspected of doing so (e.g., data about gold holdings of central banks in times of dictatorship, or even in bad times as in the Great Depression). Or else, develop a statistical theory (with experimental applications) which would allow us to recognize the direction and extent of wilful distortion of information and to eliminate their influence. Such theory, unfortunately, does not exist. How could intelligent action or valid scientific argument be based successfully on falsified data except by accident? What is a better way of achieving success in battle or games than to mislead the opponent if he is stupid enough to allow himself to be misled?

In the first case, it is a matter of incomplete information, of inherent difficulties of measurement as they occur in varying nature in all sciences. It is difficult to give another answer, except to say: modify the theory into which the poor data are to be fitted. Here the truth is that much of economic theory merely appears to be highly accurate and precise. It can maintain this appearance, like any theory, by virtue of being an abstraction. The problems arise therefore in the act of application; it is here where the difficulties have to be faced. There is no objection against formulating highly abstract and rigorous theories. But there is objection against their extravagant and exaggerated use.

Economics is not nearly as much of a science as the free use of allegedly accurate figures would seem to indicate. On the other hand, there is no reason to conclude that there cannot be or is no theory at all. The belief, that we have to get more and more data, make more and more descriptions before we can formulate valid theories is entirely mistaken. A theory means a commitment and in scientific life that is exactly what is wanted. When new facts come to light and new interpretations are needed, a new situation can arise. This may then call for abandoning the old views and for making a new decision.

The process of improving data is an unending one. To be successful it will require a far closer cooperation between those who make and use theories and those who collect and prepare the data. The urgently needed greater cooperative interaction cannot be planned and organized. It has to come about gradually, by itself, from a better understanding of the mutual interests these two groups have in common. The theorists in particular will realize more clearly that efforts spent in improving measurements and designing new measurements where they now seem impossible, will reduce the difficulties of dealing with the data theoretically. Such closer contact will also have a great educational value: every theorist ought to be in intimate touch with the "facts," "get his hands dirty," in order to appreciate the very great difficulties encountered even with routine measurements. The difficulties vary from case to case as the above examples have shown. Therefore this contact ought to be a continuing one, since no hard and fast rules can be made how to deal with the perpetually renewing task.

There is, however, one area where definite action is possible, though it will take time before desirable results will become visible. That is to stop important government agencies, such as the President's Council of Economic Advisors, the various government departments, the Federal Reserve Board and other agencies, public and private, from presenting to the public economic statistics as if these were free from fault. Statements concerning month-to-month changes in the growth rate of the nation are nothing but absurd and even year-to-year comparisons are not much better. The same applies to variations in price levels, costs of living and many other items. It is for the economists to reject and criticize such statements which are devoid of all scientific value, but it is even more important for them not to participate in their fabrication.

Perhaps the greatest step forward that can be taken, even at short notice, is to insist that economic statistics be only published together with an estimate of their error. Even if only roughly estimated this would produce a wholesome effect. Makers and users of economic statistics must both refrain from making claims and demands that cannot be supported scientifically. The publication of error estimates would have a profound influence upon the whole situation.

A valuable, though still ineffective, means is the appointment of special commissions to examine particular fields of economic data. They may be created by presidential appointment, as in the case of unemployment statistics, or they may be due to pressure from statistical, learned societies, as in the case of price indexes. These means ought to be further exploited; at present the possibilities for the services such groups can render have barely been uncovered.

However, no amount of organization can replace the work of the economist in teaching and research. Students have to be brought up in an atmosphere of healthy distrust of the "facts" put before them.[1] They must also learn how terribly hard it is to get good data and to find out what really is "a fact."

The research economist, I hope, after having read this book will not simply turn around—though with a sigh, perhaps—and proceed as if the economic data and "observations" were as trustworthy as their appearance seems to warrant. It is, of course, a hard decision to reject information, to discard, to wait patiently for the slow accumulation of better designed data and to limit the hoped-for precision of one's findings. It is difficult to realize that the economy moves in a deeper penumbra than thought possible, that economic decisions, by business and government alike, are made largely in the dark. No wonder then, that the description of their outcome cannot have the precision and clarity which we long for.

Eventually a new generation of economists will have learned to live with data of widely differing quality and how to improve their observations. In that they will emulate the physicists who

---

[1] As a rule they have a lamentable lack of knowledge even of the most elementary data of the United States and world economy. This fact was commented on by M. R. Gainsbrugh in "Statistics We Live By," *Journal Am. Statist. Assoc.*, 1962. But, in addition, the students will have to acquire the right spirit in which to study and use the data.

have created a magnificent and terrifying theory though their data range in accuracy from better than 10^{-8} to only 50%—that is, when they can measure at all. In appreciating the true condition of the data, economists cannot fail but to develop economic theory in conformity with the high scientific standards set in the physical sciences.

THE following list of publications is intended to help readers who are interested in more specialized or detailed aspects of the matters treated in the text. No effort is made to give a complete listing of sources, nor are all titles repeated which have been referred to in the text.

CHAPTER I

Brunt, David, *The Combination of Observations* (Cambridge, 1917).

Churchman, C. W. and Ratoosh, P., *Measurement, Definitions and Theories,* (New York, 1959).

Commission on Organization of the Executive Branch of the Government (by F. C. Mills and C. D. Long): *Task Force Report on Statistical Agencies* (Appendix D), (Washington, D.C., January, 1949).

Committee of Statistical Experts of the League of Nations, Publications of: *Studies and Reports on Statistical Methods,* no. 1–9 (Geneva and Lake Success).

Deming, W. Edwards, "On Errors in Surveys," *American Sociological Review*, IX: 359–369, 1944.

Devons, E., "Planning by Economic Survey," *Economica,* August, 1952.

Festinger, L. and Katz, D., *Research Methods in the Behavioral Sciences* (New York, 1953).

Gainsbrugh, M. R., "Statistics We Live By," Presidential Address before American Statistical Association, 1961.

Haavelmo, Trygve, "The Probability Approach in Econometrics," *Econometrica,* XII (Supplement), 1944.

Hatanaka, M., *The Workability of Input-Output Analysis* (Ludwigshafen am Rhein, 1960).

Huff, D., *How to Lie With Statistics* (New York, 1954).

Leontief, W. W., "Computational Problems Arising in Connection with Economic Analysis of Inter-Industrial Relationships," *Proceedings of a Symposium on Large Scale Digital Calculating Machinery,* (Cambridge, 1948).

Mitchell, H. F., Jr., "The Inversion of a Matrix of Order 38," *Mathematical Tables and Other Aids to Computation,* III: 161–166, July, 1948.

Morgenstern, Oskar, "Remarks," Session on Input-Output Analysis and Its Uses in Peace and War Economics, *Proceedings of the American Economic Association,* May, 1949.

Parrat, L. G., *Probability and Experimental Errors in Science: An Elementary Survey* (New York, 1961).

Tukey, John W., "Memorandum on Statistics in the Federal Government," Part I, Chapters I–IV, *The American Statistician,* 1949.

Tukey, John W., "The Future of Data Analysis," *The Annals of Mathematical Statistics,* March, 1962.

U.S. Congress, Joint Economic Committee, "A Federal Statistics Program for the 1960's," Washington, 1962.

Whitehead, T. N., *The Design and Use of Instruments and Accurate Measurement,* (New York, 1934).

Whittaker, E. T. and Robinson, George, *The Calculus of Observations,* 4th edition (London, 1946).

Wong, Y. K., "Inequalities for Minkowski-Leontief Matrices," and "Some Mathematical Concepts for Linear Economic Models," in O. Morgenstern, Ed., *Economic Activity Analysis* (New York, 1954).

Wong, Y. K. and Morgenstern, O., "A Study of Linear Economic Systems," *Weltwirtschaftliches Archiv,* Band 79, Heft 2, 1957.

CHAPTER II

Coale, A. J. and Stephan, F. F., "The Case of the Indians and Teen-Age Widows," *Journal of the American Statistical Association,* Volume 57, pp. 338–347, (June, 1962).

Ferguson, T. S., "Rules for Rejection of Outliers," *Revue de l'Institut International de Statistique,* Volume 29 (1961).

Social Science Research Council Committee, *Report on Analysis of Pre-Election Polls and Forecasts,* (1949).

Stephan, F. F., "Sampling Opinions, Attitudes, and Wants," *Proceedings of the American Philosophical Society,* Volume 92 (February, 1948).

Stephan, F. F. and McCarthy, P. J., *Sampling Opinions,* An Analysis of Survey Procedure, (New York, 1958).

von Neumann, J. and Morgenstern, O., *Theory of Games and Economic Behavior* (Princeton, 1944; 3rd edition, 1953).

CHAPTER IV

Bray, F. S., "The Nature of Income and Capital," *Accounting Research* I: 27–49, (November, 1948).

Edwards, E. O. and Bell, P. W., *The Theory and Measurement of Business Income,* (Berkeley, 1961).

Moonitz, M. and Nelson, C. L., "Recent Developments in Accounting Theory," *Accounting Review,* Volume 35, (1960).

Norris, H., "Profit: Accounting Theory and Economics," *Economica,* (New Series), XII: 125–133, (1945).

Paton, W. A. and Dixon, R. L., *Essentials of Accounting,* (New York, 1958). (An introductory accounting text).

Paton, W. A. and Littleton, A. C., *Introduction to Corporate Accounting Standards*, Monograph 3 (American Accounting Association, 1940).

Vatter, W. J., "Limitation of Overhead and Allocation," *The Accounting Review,* XX: 163–176, (April, 1945).

CHAPTER V

Cowles Commission Research Staff Members (William C. Hood and Tjalling C. Koopmans, eds.), *Studies in Econometric Methods,* (New York, 1953).

Cowles Commission Research Staff Members and Guests (Tjalling C. Koopmans, ed.), *Statistical Inference in Dynamic Economic Models,* (New York, 1950).

Haavelmo, T., "The Probability Approach in Econometrics," *Econometrica,* Volume 12, Supplement, (1944).

Klein, Lawrence R., *A Textbook of Econometrics,* (Evanston, Ill., 1953).

Morgenstern, O., "Experiment and Large Scale Computation in Economics," in O. Morgenstern, ed., *Economic Activity Analysis,* (New York, 1954).

Theil, H., *Economic Forecasts and Policy,* (Amsterdam, 1961).

Weyl, H., *Philosophy of Mathematics and Natural Science,* (Princeton, 1949).

CHAPTER VI

Babbar, M. M., "Distributions of Solutions of a Set of Linear Equations (with an Application to Linear Programming)," *Journal of the American Statistical Association*, September, 1955.

Hotelling, Harold, "Some New Methods in Matrix Calculations," *Annals of Mathematical Statistics*, 14, (1942), pp. 1–33.

Lonseth, A. T., "Systems of Linear Equations with Coefficients Subject to Error," *Annals of Mathematical Statistics*, 13, (1942), pp. 332–7.

Turing, A. M., "Rounding Off Errors in Matrice Processes," *Quarterly Journal of Mechanics and Applied Mathematics*, 1, (1947), pp. 287–308.

von Neumann, J. and Goldstine, H. H., "Numerical Inverting of Matrices of High Order," *Bulletin of The American Mathematical Society*, 53, pp. 1071–1099, Part II, *Proceedings of the American Mathematical Society*, Volume 2, (1951), pp. 188–202.

CHAPTER VII

Copeland, M. A., *Fact and Theory In Economics, The Testament of an Institutionalist*, (Ithaca, 1958).

Morgenstern, O., "When is a Problem of Economic Policy Solvable?" in *Wirtschaftstheorie und Wirtschaftspolitik*, V. F. Wagner and F. Marbach, ed., (Berne, 1953).

CHAPTER IX

Allen, R. G., *International Trade Statistics*, (New York, 1953).

Ely, J. E., "Variations Between U.S. and its Trading Partner Import and Export Statistics," *The American Statistician*, Volume 15, No. 2 (April, 1961), pp. 23–26.

Ferraris, C. F., *Articles in Bulletin de l'Institut International de Statistique*, Volumes 11, 12, (1899–1900).

Ferraris, C. F., *La Statistica del Movimento dei Metalli Preziosi fra l'Italia e l'Estero*, (Rome, 1885).

Giffen, R., "The Use of Import and Export Statistics," *Journal of Royal Statistical Society*, Volume XLV, (June, 1882).

Graham, Frank D., *Protective Tariffs* (Princeton, 1942).

International Monetary Fund, *International Financial Statistics*, (a monthly source book of statistics in international trade and finance).

League of Nations, *Network of World Trade,* (Geneva, 1942).

Morgenstern, O., *International Financial Transactions and Business Cycles,* (Princeton, 1959).

Morgenstern, O., *The Validity of International Gold Movement Statistics,* Special Papers in International Economics, No. 2, International Finance Section, (Princeton, November, 1955).

Schelling, Thomas C., *International Economics,* (Boston, 1958). (A basic text in international economics.)

Standard International Trade Classification Revised, Statistical Papers, Series M, No. 34, United Nations, (New York, 1961).

United Nations, *Monthly Bulletin of Statistics.*

U.S. Department of Commerce, "Monthly Value Discrepancies Between the Official French and United States Statistics on Shipments from France to the United States During January–March, 1948," *Foreign Trade Statistics Notes,* (October, 1948).

Zuckermann, S., *Statistischer Atlas zum Welthandel,* (Berlin, 1920).

CHAPTER X

Cox, Reavis, "Non Price Competition and the Measurement of Prices," *Journal of Marketing*, X: 370–383, (April, 1946).

Granger, C. W. J. and Morgenstern, O., "Spectral Analysis of New York Stock Market Prices," *Kyklos,* (January, 1963).

Hamilton, Earl J., "Use and Misuse of Price History," *Tasks of Economic History,* Supplement IV to the *Journal of Economic History,* pp. 47–60, (1941).

Kruskal, W. H. and Teker, L. G., "Food Prices and the Bureau of Labor Statistics," *The Journal of Business of the University of Chicago,* XXXIII, pp. 259–79, (July, 1960).

Mills, F. C., *Price-Quantity Interactions in Business Cycles,* (New York: National Bureau of Economic Research, 1946).

Mills, F. C., *The Behavior of Prices,* (New York: National Bureau of Economic Research, 1927).

Morgenstern, O., "Free and Fixed Prices in the Depression," *Harvard Business Review*, X: 62–68, (October, 1931).

U.S. Congress, Joint Economic Committee, *Employment Growth and Price Levels*, (Staff Report, Hearings and various Study papers) (Washington, Government Printing Office, 1959).

U.S. Congress, Joint Economic Committee, *Government Price Statistics*, Hearings, 87th Congress, 1st Session, January 24, 1961.

CHAPTER XI

American Statistical Association, *Statistical Operations of the Bureau of Mines*, (Washington, July 1952).

Barger, H. and Schurr, S., *The Mining Industries, 1899–1939* (New York: National Bureau of Economic Research, 1944).

National Bureau of Economic Research, *Output, Input and Productivity Measurement*, Studies in Income and Wealth, vol. 25 (Princeton, 1961).

U.S. Bureau of the Census, *U.S. Census of Mineral Industries: 1958*, General Summary Report M1C58 (1)–1, Preliminary, U.S. Government Printing Office, (Washington, 1961).

U.S. Department of the Interior, Bureau of Mines, *Minerals Yearbook*, (Washington, annual).

CHAPTER XII

Barger, H. and Landsberg, H., *American Agriculture, 1899–1939*, (New York: National Bureau of Economic Research, 1942).

Bennet, M. K. and Wyman, A. F., "Official and Unofficial Statistics of International Trade in Wheat and Flour," *Wheat Studies*, VII: 267–294, (March, 1931).

Davis, Joseph S., "Some Observations in Federal Agricultural Statistics," *Journal of the American Statistical Association, Proceedings*, (1928).

Federal Statistics Users' Conference, "A Long Range Program for the Improvement of Federal Statistics," (Washington, 1961).

Moore, G., "Accuracy of Government Statistics," *Harvard Business Review*, XXV, (Spring, 1947).

Sarle, Charles F., "Reliability and Adequacy of Farm Price Data," *U.S. Department of Agriculture Bulletin*, #1480, (March, 1927).

Sarle, Charles F., "Adequacy and Reliability of Crop-Yield Estimates," *U.S. Department of Agriculture Technical Bulletin*, no. 311, (June, 1932).

Swerling, Boris C., *Agriculture and Recent Economic Conditions: Experience and Perspective*, Federal Reserve Bank of San Francisco, (August, 1959).

Taylor, A., "A Disposition of American Wheat Supplies—A Critical Appraisal of Statistical Procedure," *Wheat Studies*, I: 289 ff., (August, 1924).

U.S. Bureau of the Census, *U.S. Census of Agriculture: 1959*, (Washington, D.C., 1961).

U.S. Department of Agriculture, *The Agricultural Estimating and Reporting Services of the United States Department of Agriculture*, miscellaneous publication no. 703, (December, 1949).

Working, Holbrook, "Wheat Acreage and Production in the United States since 1866: A Revision of Official Estimates," *Wheat Studies*, II: 237–264, (June 1926).

CHAPTER XIII

Bancroft, Gertrude and Welch, Emmett H., "Recent Experience with Problems of Labor Force Measurement," *Journal of the American Statistical Association*, 41: 303–312, (September 1946).

Bureau of Labor Statistics, *Monthly Report of the Labor Force*, (Washington, monthly).

Hogg, Margaret H., "Sources of Incomparability and Error in Employment-Unemployment Surveys," *Journal of the American Statistical Association*, 25: 284–294, (September, 1930).

League of Nations, "Statistics of the Gainfully Occupied Population," (Geneva, 1938).

Meeker, Royal, "The Dependability and Meaning of Unemployment and Employment Statistics in the United States," *Harvard Business Review*, VII: 385–400, (July, 1930).

National Bureau of Economic Research, *The Measurement and Behavior of Unemployment*, (Princeton, 1957).

Nixon, Russell A. and Samuelson, Paul A., "Estimates of Unemployment in the United States," *Review of Economic Statistics*, XXII: 101–111, (August, 1940).

President's Committee to Appraise Employment and Unemployment Statistics, *Measuring Employment and Unemployment*, (Washington, 1962).

Roberts, David R., "Measures of Employment," *Survey of Current Business*, 27: 18–22, (October 1947).

Stolnitz, G. J., "Evaluation of the Accuracy of United States Employment and Unemployment Statistics," Econometric Research Program, (Princeton University, 1962).

U.S. Bureau of Labor Statistics, "Labor Force, Employment and Unemployment, 1929–1939, Estimating Methods," *Monthly Labor Review*, 67: 50–53, (July, 1948).

U.S. Bureau of the Census, *Current Population Reports*, series P-23, no. 5, (May, 1958).

CHAPTERS XIV and *XV*

Bergson, A., *The Real Income of Soviet Russia since 1928*, (Cambridge, 1961).

Kuznets, Simon, "Discussion of the New Department of Commerce Income Series, National Income: A New Version," *Review of Economics and Statistics*, XXX: 151–179, (August, 1948).

Kuznets, Simon, *National Income and Its Composition*, 1919–1938, 2 volumes, (New York: National Bureau of Economic Research, 1941).

National Bureau of Economic Research, *Problems in the International Comparison of Economic Accounts*, Studies in Income and Wealth, XX, (Princeton, 1957).

Ruggles, R. and Ruggles, N., *National Income Accounts and Income Analysis*, 2nd edition, (New York, 1956).

Stone, Richard, "The Measurement of National Income and Expenditure: A Review of the Official Estimates of Five Countries," *Economic Journal*, LVII: 272–298, (September, 1947).

Studenski, Paul, *The Income of Nations: Theory, Measurement and Analysis: Past and Present*, (New York, 1958).

Tukey, J., "The Future of Data Analysis," *The Annals of Mathematical Statistics,* (March, 1962).

U.S. Department of Commerce, Office of Business Economics, *National Income,* a supplement to the Survey of Current Business, (Washington, 1954).

U.S. Department of Commerce, Office of Business Economics, *U.S. Income and Output,* a supplement to the Survey of Current Business, (Washington, 1958).